WORDS OF WAR

WORDS OF WAR

ANTHONY RICHARDS

CONTENTS

INTRODUCTION

by James Holland

The Second World War was the most cataclysmic conflict ever experienced in world history and was truly global. From the Southern Ocean to the Arctic, across deserts and mountains, through jungles to major European cities, and from tiny atolls in the South Pacific to the Russian steppes, it seemed the fighting was everywhere. At its end, more than sixty million people had died, an astonishingly grim number, and equivalent to almost the entire population of the United Kingdom today.

Britain's part in the conflict was considerable, as is all too obvious reading this fascinating book and its wide-ranging collection of letters and documents, which Anthony Richards has drawn from the archives of the Imperial War Museums (IWM). What is so extraordinary about the war was the totality of the effort. In Britain, for example, it affected every man, woman and child in a way that no other conflict has before or since. Ordinary men and women, who in normal circumstances would never have imagined wearing a military uniform, suddenly found themselves on the front line. Even those beyond fighting age had to confront dramatic privations and curbs to normal freedoms, as well as the prospect of coming under enemy attack from the air.

While the far-reaching effects of the Second World War are still being felt to this day, for most people, it is the immense human drama of the conflict that makes it such an enduringly fascinating subject. It's the idea of ordinary men and women suddenly confronted with extraordinary circumstances and having to do extraordinary things. It is hard not to wonder how one would have dealt with such circumstances had one been of an age to fight in the war. Had I been twenty-one in, say, 1940, what would I have done? Joined the RAF? Or would I have volunteered for the Navy? How would I have coped with being away from home for, perhaps, four years? And with very limited means of communication? The best I would have been able to hope for was a curt telegram or a letter that might take months to reach my family and vice versa. I recently read a contemporary account of a young twenty-year-old tank commander whose parents had lived in Hong Kong. By 1944, when he was serving in Normandy, he had not seen his parents since 1938, and had not heard anything from either his mother or father since late 1941, on the eve of the Japanese invasion. Later, in August 1944, a letter from his father finally reached him that had been written and posted from a Japanese prisoner of war camp back in May 1942. Or what about Sam Bradshaw? He left Liverpool for North Africa in 1940, served all the way through that campaign, and was severely wounded in the process. He recovered and went on to fight in Italy, where he was badly wounded again. When he eventually got home at the end of 1944, he barely recognised the place he had left all those years before. His mother's hair had turned white, the little girl who had been his younger sister was grown up, and much of the city he had known had been ravaged by the Luftwaffe. It all depressed him so much he rejoined and was posted to north-west Europe. The privations experienced by so many during the war are sometimes hard to comprehend.

Yet Britain suffered less than most of the other major combatant nations in terms of destruction at home and of war dead. This was because Britain, at the start of the war, had enormous global reach and wealth, not to mention the world's largest navy and merchant navy, and access to around eighty per cent of the world's merchant shipping. Britain's war leaders were determined there should be no slaughter of a generation of young men, as had happened in the First World War, and so followed a policy of 'steel not flesh'. Broadly speaking, this meant using Britain's vast access to the world's resources, along with mechanisation, modern science and industrialisation, to ensure machines, not men, did as much of the hard yards as possible. It meant a growing army that was entirely mechanised and dependent on machines and a long logistical tail; it meant enormous bomber fleets and combat aircraft; it meant ever more artillery and firepower; and it meant even larger naval forces. By 1944, infantry accounted for just fourteen per cent of the British Army in north-west Europe, those in tanks eight per cent, artillery twenty-two per cent and service troops forty-three per cent. If you were unfortunate enough to be in a tank or in the infantry, the chances of getting through unscathed were worse than they had been in 1914–1918; the difference, though, was that those at the coal-face of war were a far smaller proportion – and number – than had been true a generation earlier.

Casualties were still extreme, however, and the suffering immense, as this book makes all too clear. IWM has a justified reputation internationally as one of the finest museums of its kind anywhere in the world. Yet, while the displays are fabulous, what can be seen in public galleries is very much the tip of the iceberg. The museum is home to an enormous and very important archive that contains astonishing objects and artefacts, but also paintings, film, photographs, extensive sound archives of interviews with tens of thousands of veterans of multiple conflicts, and also personal papers, including diaries, letters, documents and unpublished memoirs. Anthony Richards is IWM's Head of Documents and Sound, and is ideally placed to pick out a range of such testimonies from the Second World War to show the extent of the conflict. The result is an incredibly rich and, frankly, awe-inspiring set of accounts covering the entire breadth of the conflict. Unsurprisingly, the majority of entries are British, but by no means all; IWM houses papers and collections of people from all around the world.

One such is a letter written by Vittorio Caressa, an Italian officer serving in the Italian Expeditionary Corps on the Eastern Front. Caressa was among those Italians who joined the Germans for Operation 'Barbarossa', the German invasion of the Soviet Union in June 1941. Despite sweeping early victories, by the autumn the wheels had literally begun to fall off 'Barbarossa' and the Germans – and their Italian allies – were consigned to a long, bitter winter of dramatically increasing losses in conditions for which they had not been prepared. Vittorio Caressa survived this winter, but as he made clear in a letter to his sister, he and his fellows had suffered terribly. He was angry and afraid. 'I don't think you have any idea of what winter has done here,' he wrote. 'Don't think that I just have a runny nose at night. When I'm told of certain things it makes me shiver and my white hair shall grow visibly.' He told his sister of men losing feet and even noses to frostbite. Survival, he wrote, was 'just a matter of luck'. There are German accounts, too: a soldier stuck at Stalingrad, for example, and a letter from a German Jew, Max Bock, who had somehow managed to stay alive in Berlin and was still there in April 1945 as the Soviet Red Army closed in. He described in vivid detail the din of battle, the fizz of bullets, the boom of guns. He mourned the death of the last elephant at Berlin Zoo, another victim of the war. 'At lunch time I saw them bury a soldier in the grass verge outside my house,' he wrote. 'A simple mound and a few shrubs is all that remains – an unknown soldier who has given his life for a lost cause.' Later, he saw another dead soldier in the entrance hall of his apartment – the man had apparently bled to death. 'The devastation in the street is constantly increasing – rubble lying around, buildings in ruins everywhere.'

Most letters are from ordinary men and women, although some names do spring out. IWM holds the Roger Bushell papers, and one of his letters is included. Bushell, a fighter pilot and squadron leader of 92 Squadron, was shot down over Dunkirk in May 1940 and sent to Stalag Luft III prisoner of war camp, where he later orchestrated what became known as the Great Escape. He was subsequently executed on Hitler's orders, so to see such a cheery letter from him to his family after being recaptured following one of his earlier escape attempts is very moving. So, too, is the reproduced note from Violet Szabo, a British secret agent with the SOE, who parachuted into France in 1943. 'I hereby appoint Miss Vera Maidment and her mother Mrs Alice Maidment the legal guardian of my child Tania Damaris Desiree Szabo in the event of my death,' she wrote. Szabo was caught, tortured and killed at Ravensbrück.

Elsewhere in this rich, wide-ranging and stunningly illustrated book, there are testimonies of those serving in North Africa, in the Far East, in north-west Europe, out at sea, in the air and also on the Home Front. There is a note from an ARP warden, accounts of the Blitz, stories of strange events in the Home Guard, a letter from a Land Girl working on a farm in Yorkshire, and one from a student conscientious objector. There are also accounts of what was left after the fighting was over. Flight Lieutenant Geoffrey Dawson had been a bomb aimer with RAF Bomber Command, but a couple of weeks after VE Day, he flew in daylight – rather than at night on combat missions – and saw the remains of Germany. 'Mannheim used to be a city, a thriving city,' he wrote in a letter dated 25 May 1945. 'Mannheim is nothing more than a grey smudge on the bank of the Rhine. Mannheim is a total loss. There is not a building left intact.'

It is impossible not to be profoundly moved by this letter, and by so many others in this book. It is a remarkable treasure trove, beautifully assembled, and a snapshot testimony to the incredible breadth and extent over which the war was fought and experienced first-hand.

AUTHOR'S INTRODUCTION

When I was asked to compile one hundred examples of personal testimony from the Second World War to feature in this book, I knew it would provide an excellent opportunity to showcase the archives preserved by Imperial War Museums (IWM). The original letters, diary entries, first-hand accounts and transcripts of audio recordings reproduced here all originate from the IWM collection, which remains one of the biggest and most important personal-experience archives in the world. As a source of eloquent and informed first-hand accounts of warfare, it truly remains second to none.

One of the biggest strengths of the IWM collection lies in its broad diversity: it covers the experiences of people from all walks of life, regardless of their gender, class, age or background. This multiplicity of voices combines to provide an invaluable gathering of testimony, which reveals, in an immediate and empathetic way, what it was really like to live through the events of the Second World War.

I am, of course, potentially biased in saying this, since I happen to work at IWM as the Head of the Documents and Sound collections. For over twenty-five years now, I have had the immense privilege of helping to develop the collections through the acquisition of insightful new stories, and the cataloguing of older material to reveal new and valuable information. The significance of such archival work is frequently misunderstood and overlooked, but to appreciate the importance of preserving the past, one need only look at the wealth of publications, films and documentaries that use first-hand testimony to engage audiences.

I have chosen one hundred different extracts from personal testimonies, each illustrating a particular subject, event or theme. While featured in a roughly chronological order, each extract might be usefully seen as a stand-alone 'snapshot' taken during a particular moment of the conflict. When read together, I hope they will provide an engaging narrative of what the Second World War meant for so many people. I have chosen to edit only when absolutely necessary for length. Spelling mistakes may sometimes have been corrected, but remain when contextually important.

For those readers interested in learning more about the experiences of the particular writers featured, or indeed for anybody wishing to explore the accounts in the museum's care in more detail, I would encourage a visit to the website iwm.org.uk. A searchable catalogue is available, alongside articles, blogs and videos that reveal more about the many, many stories from the Second World War preserved by IWM.

CHAPTER ONE
PHONEY WAR

Clockwise: Prime Minister Neville Chamberlain is greeted by Adolf Hitler at the Hotel Dreesen in Bad Godesberg, 22 September 1938. •An injured passenger, wrapped in a blanket, is helped on shore after being brought into Galway Harbour following the sinking of SS Athenia. •Workers fill sandbags to protect a Gothic cathedral in France against air-raid damage. • Men of the Non-Combatant Corps undergo training at a camp on the east coast of Britain.

German SS troops enter Kufstein in Austria during the Anschluss, *March 1938.*

THE *ANSCHLUSS*

The beginning of the war in Europe was inextricably linked to the rise of fascism within Germany. Adolf Hitler was appointed German Chancellor in 1933, and the following few years would see the rapid establishment of his totalitarian National Socialist regime. A central tenet of Nazi racial policy was to incorporate as many 'ethnic Germans' as possible into a greater state or *Reich*, and therefore the potential annexation of neighbouring territory, such as Czechoslovakia and Austria, became an increasingly popular idea among Hitler's most ardent followers. While significant resistance to annexation (or *Anschluss*) remained within Austria, pro-Nazi Austrians attempted a coup in 1934 that led to the assassination of the Austrian Chancellor, Engelbert Dollfuss. His successor, Kurt Schuschnigg, sought to hold a referendum to settle the matter once and for all, but, under pressure from Hitler, was forced to resign before this could take place.

The German Army marched unopposed into Austria on 12 March 1938. Charlotte Leahy received the following letter a few weeks later, written by a school friend who had witnessed the annexation.

"Hôtel Atlantic + de Malte"
  Menton.
      Alpes Maritimes.
          France.

10·IV '38.

Darling Petrol,

Thanks so much for your nice letter I was so glad to get. Mummy appreciates you thinking of sending her such nice stamps. You do seem to be enjoying yourself, having a regular holiday. The climate seems to be extreme?! But are you considered as a pupil, or like Marie-Louise was? As you see we are now on the lovely french Riviera. Since 3 weeks. We had to fly away from Austria with only 2 days notice!! Its wonderful here! It has been real summer weather, we have all been wearing summer clothes. Crowds of smart english people everywhere, with lovely cars + private yachts. But mostly elderly! There has been no rain for 5 months, its so dry, there was an enormous fire on the mountains behind the town, which raged for 15 hours + it got jolly near the town too, it was awful!!

10.iv.38

Darling Petrol

... Yes, there are thousands and thousands of Jews in Austria and they are all being imprisoned now, they were all directors of firms and shops! Of course I must tell you all about Austria! But I don't know how much I have already told you?!

Did I tell you about the beginning when there was a procession of 'true Austrians'? Nazis lined the roads silently and 'we' (a handful of English females) from a hotel window shouted 'Schuschnigg', they all answered 'Heil' and smiled up at us, we didn't stop shouting for the 2 hrs. Which the torchlight procession followed!! We had started them off, next day there was an article in the paper of the enthusiasm of the English!! All the Nazis were furious!!

If there had been voting, Schuschnigg would have won, only 'the trades people' are for Hitler. All peasants and aristocrats are for Schuschnigg. Hitler did use violence, main force too, and when I get back to England I shall tell the truth of all the horrors we have seen!

At midnight we saw the German troops enter! Thousands and thousands of them. Horses, guns, tanks, mules all ready to fight us sometime soon... The 'creepiness', we didn't sleep at all for the last 3 nights, everyone was so scared! All the church bells tolled, aeroplanes buzzed *incessantly* overhead dropping advertisements and propaganda! Messengers teared backwards and forwards to the frontier, soldiers everywhere!!! They took possession of hotels, schools, even pulling down all crucifixes!! I dread what will happen to religion now, the last Sunday we *dared* to go to church, but it was nearly empty!! Priests and nuns were about trying to hide. We were greeted 'Heil Hitler' in the streets. I *never* answered them, they were so unpleasant! The horrid 'swastika' was stuck up everywhere – men, women, children went about with these flags yelling and screaming, the noise was terrible, deafening!! They forced their way into the town hall, imprisoned the Archbishop, and governor of the town after having insulted him. Many I know have been imprisoned and FLOGGED!! Marie-Louis's father was taken! The count was in danger when I left. All Nazis will now have the good positions, aristocrats already and poor will get third rate ones!! Houses were raided to find anti Nazi papers, my poor family spent nights burning all photos of the Kaiser and Schuschnigg who was their personal friend!

No more Austria! Of course I shall never go back, where Hitler rules... They were cowards not to resist more though. They were all too frightened, they all *pretend* they want Hitler. Poor Mummy was scared stiff alone in her hotel, only one other lady was staying there, it was filled with officers! If Hitler had come he would have slept at the hotel!

We were both in a terrible state of nerves when we arrived here, after a week of terror and anxiety; we had trouble about having too much money at Innsbruck, as we of course rushed to the bank and took our deposit out. But happily the English consul helped us out. I have been having awful nightmares, but now I try to forget about it all, but I have so many friends left there! They cannot write the truth, all letters are opened...

Now France is in a terrible state too. It's a pity, Hitler will spring on us all unprepared!! The English were too good, to even think of trusting a German.

All best love

Betty[1]

Hitler receives an ovation from the Reichstag after the successful annexation of Austria.

APPEASEMENT

Following the annexation of Austria, Hitler's attention moved to Czechoslovakia, where further 'ethnic Germans' were resident. Aware of the likelihood of an imminent annexation, as well as their own shortcomings in reacting to the earlier *Anschluss*, the governments of Britain, France and Czechoslovakia sought to avoid a war at all costs. Following a conference in Munich, hastily convened by Italian leader Benito Mussolini, the major European powers agreed to appease Hitler's demands by allowing his occupation of the Sudetenland border region on 1 October 1938. Yet Nazi Germany would only be appeased for so long, with their desire to annex the rest of Czechoslovakia finally being carried out in March 1939.

Having flown to Munich in September 1938 in order to discuss the Sudetenland problem with Hitler, British Prime Minister Neville Chamberlain took the opportunity to draw up a so-called Anglo-German Accord, which both leaders signed. It was intended to avoid any future war between the two powers, although history would show that Hitler did not keep to his promises.

Neville Chamberlain reads out the text of the Anglo-German Accord to onlookers at Heston Airport on his return from Munich.

We, the German Führer and Chancellor and the
British Prime Minister, have had a further
meeting today and are agreed in recognising that
the question of Anglo-German relations is of the
first importance for the two countries and for
Europe.

We regard the agreement signed last night
and the Anglo-German Naval Agreement as symbolic
of the desire of our two peoples never to go to
war with one another again.

We are resolved that the method of
consultation shall be the method adopted to deal
with any other questions that may concern our two
countries, and we are determined to continue our
efforts to remove possible sources of difference
and thus to contribute to assure the peace of
Europe.

[signature] A Hitler

[signature] Neville Chamberlain

September 30, 1938.

We, the German Führer and Chancellor and the British Prime Minister, have had a further meeting today and are agreed in recognising that the question of Anglo-German relations is of the first importance for the two countries and for Europe.

We regard the agreement signed last night and the Anglo-German Naval Agreement as symbolic of the desire of our two peoples never to go to war with one another again.

We are resolved that the method of consultation shall be the method adopted to deal with any other questions that may concern our two countries, and we are determined to continue our efforts to remove possible sources of difference and thus to contribute to assure the peace of Europe.

[signed] A Hitler
[signed] Neville Chamberlain

September 30, 1938[2]

THE RISE OF THE NAZIS

Central to Hitler's Nazi regime was the concept of *Volksgemeinschaft*, a 'national community' made up of racially pure citizens who would work together in order to strengthen and benefit the state. A compulsory Reich Labour Service was therefore introduced in Germany in 1935, which led to a significant fall in unemployment and a boost to German industry, yet was based upon mass indoctrination. Individual rights were removed through the militarisation of German society and a strict adherence to Nazi ideology.

In 1938, twenty-six-year-old Briton Marjorie Elkins began a pen-friend correspondence with a sixteen-year-old German girl, Christa Beyer. This letter, describing Christa's compulsory work for a Reich Labour Service camp in Thuringia, was one of the last letters they exchanged before war was declared between Britain and Germany. Fortunately, the two friends were able to resume contact in 1946 and continued to correspond for more than fifty years afterwards.

The VDA (National League for German People and Culture Abroad) requests 'Your contribution to the struggle of the German people, to the people's political work, to the greatness of the people and Reich.'

Christa Beyer, in a photograph taken in September 1938.

Christa

Hanaü, den 30.5.39.

Dear Marjorie,

I thank you very much for your letter and the two illustrated-books. Just, I am at home in Hanaü. But at 10 o'clock, my train goes to Gräfendorf. My leave is over. I believe, I forget the english language in the labour-service. Please, don't be bad if I write to you no big letters and if I (write) do not write immediately. In the labour-service, the time is very scanty.

We all in Germany are glad if we have peace. The German will not go to war against any nation; he only wishes the peace.

The labour-service has the aim: we shall discharge the woman on the country (the farmer-woman).

I will explain you what we do the day: At 4⁵⁰ o'clock in the morning we get up.

Will you be so kind and give the letter to Jack F.

Hanau, 31.5.39

Dear Marjorie

I thank you very much for your letter and the two illustrated books. Just, I am at home in Hanau. But at 10 o'clock my train goes to Grafendorf. My leave is over. I believe I forget the English language in the labour-service. Please, don't be bad if I write to you no big letters and if I (write) do not write immediately. In the labour-service the time is very scanty.

We all in Germany are glad if we have peace. The German will not go to war against any nation; he only wishes for peace.

The labour-service has the aim: We shall discharge the woman on the country (the farmer-woman).

I will explain you what we do the day. At 4.50 o'clock in the morning we get up. Then, we make till 5.15 o'clock sport. At 5.45 o'clock we must have made our beds, we must clean the shoes and must wash us. At 5.45 we go to the flag, which is hoisted. From 6 – half 7 we have singing. There, we learn new songs. From half 7 – 7 is breakfast. From 7 – 14 o'clock we go to the farmers and help there. At 14 o'clock we must be back. From ¾ 3 – ¾ 4 we sleep. From 4 – 6 o'clock we practise gymnastics or we have lessons. At half 7 we eat to evening and in the evening, we either read or make games or we make needlework or have free. At half 9 o'clock we fetch the flag back and go to bed. Then we are always very, very tired. But we are all so glad, and it is very beautiful. I shall stay in the labour-service ½ year. In September I come back, now I have no time.

I must away to the train.

Many, many greetings

Your Christa[3]

EXPECTATIONS OF WAR

Nazi Germany's thirst for new territory, coupled with the increasing militarisation of their society and political aggression towards other European nations, made the prospect of war increasingly likely. Britain began to prepare for the worst by introducing civil defence measures across the country. Aerial bombing raids were particularly feared, with gas shells expected to be a serious threat, while vulnerable groups were moved away from the larger towns and cities.

This letter was written to Joyce Pavey by her friend Adeline on the very morning that war was about to be declared, and appears to have been posted mere minutes before the Prime Minister's official announcement. As Adeline describes, London was gearing up for war.

Government campaigns prepared the country for civilian evacuation well before war was declared.

Sept 3, 1939

Dear Joyce

... It is Sunday morning. All here are tuned to concert pitch awaiting events. I still wonder if we mean literally to help Poland how our troops etc. can reach the Baltic? Everybody here who has a uniform or tin hat or armlet is arrayed in such. Trenches are open, First Aid and Warden's post are arising, all our balloons were up yesterday (but are all down this morn – probably the heavy storm we had early this morning has something to do with it).

Evacuation has gone well (one kid in next street cried so for its mother that it is home again!!). The LCC [London County Council] took over so our WVS [Women's Voluntary Service] was only required to lend and drive motors for hospital work. Green Line busses took off hospital cases: it was a sad sight. As far as the children were concerned, one would think they were off for a school treat, the row they made, although one could see the mothers quietly crying. Poor souls.

London is a dark city at night – in fact it is dangerous for one to cross roads – plenty of white lines about, but not a great help. No lights, or only tiny ones on traffic. All soldiers are in khaki with tin hats and police have tin hats, gas masks and first aid kit, I believe. All hooters have ceased and the only sirens we shall hear will be Warnings. Sand bags and adhesive paper on windows can be seen everywhere and people who have flats in industrial dwellings are filling their own sandbags and digging, etc.

My black curtain is a success. Mr Pallent has 'blued' windows and fanlights and put on adhesive paper, so as a landlord he is doing what he can.

I hear the Duke and Duchess of Windsor are coming back – he is being given a post in National Defence.

Library has closed – it is now a SHELTER for the public. Oh! The offices and banks that have moved their headquarters – there won't be any work in London if it continues.

(Mrs Pallent has just been up to tell the house we may be at War at 11am).
Well RIGHT is RIGHT and we must defend it.

... So here ends my last 1939 PEACE letter to you. There may be some
restrictions as to your letter writing as a Govt official, so if you don't say
much in your letters in future, I shall quite understand.

Cheerio, chin chin, Love from

Adeline[4]

14, Cornwall Street.
S.W.1
Sept. 3. 1939

Dear Joyce,
Very many thanks for your monetary gift: a kindly thought.

You are a Government Official, so naturally you will be kept employed with arduous tasks. I do hope your fingers are better – you evidently had to do by hand what a machine should do. Never mind, you are very noble.

It is Sunday morning. All here are tuned to concert pitch awaiting events. I still wonder if we mean literally to help Poland how are troops etc. can reach the Baltic? Everybody here who has a uniform or tin hat or armlet is arrayed in such. Trenchs are open, First Aid & Wardens post are arising, all our balloons were up yesterday (but are all down this morn – probably the heavy storm we had early this morning has something to do with it)

THE OUTBREAK OF WAR

Hitler's territorial demands continued as the rest of Czechoslovakia was annexed in March 1939. In an attempt to limit further expansion by Nazi Germany, Britain and France pledged to support the independence of Poland, Romania and Greece. In turn, Germany formed its own alliances with Italy and the Soviet Union. August 1939 saw German troops begin to mobilise at the Polish border and, after negotiations broke down, an invasion began on 1 September. For Britain and her allies, it seemed that war with Germany was now inevitable.

At 11.15am on Sunday, 3 September 1939, Neville Chamberlain made the following BBC Home Service radio broadcast to the nation. Life would never be the same again.

A crowd gathers in Downing Street after Chamberlain's broadcast to the nation announcing that Great Britain is at war with Germany.

I am speaking to you from the Cabinet Room of 10 Downing Street.

This morning the British Ambassador in Berlin handed the German government a final note, stating that unless we heard from them – by 11 o'clock – that they were prepared at once to withdraw their troops from Poland, a state of war would exist between us.

I have to tell you now that no such undertaking has been received and that, consequently, this country is at war with Germany.[5]

Prime Minister Neville Chamberlain raises his hat to the crowd as he leaves 10 Downing Street on the day that Britain declared war, 3 September 1939.

THE SINKING OF *ATHENIA*

The very day that war was declared between Britain and Germany, the first fatalities occurred.

Since Britain was an island nation dependent on imported goods, Germany immediately instituted a naval blockade to stop ships delivering supplies. The so-called Battle of the Atlantic would last for the entirety of the war, with *Kriegsmarine* U-boats hunting and sinking merchant vessels in a deadly game of 'cat and mouse'. While transport ships were their main objective, not all U-boat captains demonstrated care when deciding upon their targets.

The passenger liner SS *Athenia* had left Liverpool on 2 September 1939, bound for Canada. She was tracked by the German submarine *U-30*, which misidentified her as a troopship or armed cruiser, and at 7.40pm the following day she was torpedoed. *Athenia* was the first British ship to be sunk by Germany during the Second World War, and the incident resulted in the deaths of 117 passengers and crew.

Among the survivors were the American couple Jack and Bella Coullie, who were travelling home to North America. Jack wrote this letter to relatives after their safe return.

An elderly woman is hoisted aboard the American freighter SS City of Flint *after spending the night in a lifeboat, having been rescued from the torpedoed SS* Athenia.

There were no lifeboats being lowered... so we went down to the next deck and soon a boat came alongside. I yelled to them to take us off. A fire hose was over the side and a man in the lifeboat got hold of the end of it and told us to slide down. I asked Bell if she thought she could make it. She said she could, I helped her over the rail and watched her slide down. She was just at the lifeboat when a wave washed the boat away, the hose was jerked from the man's hands and Bella fell into the water between the lifeboat and the ship. I thought she would be crushed to bits. I yelled to her to hold on and climbed on to the rail and jumped far out to clear the lifeboat. In a minute I was at Bella's side and got her to hold on to the rope that is round the lifeboats. I tried and tried to boost her into the boat but oil was pouring from a burst fuel tank and everything was so slippery that quickly realised I had to do something else. I got one leg over the side of the lifeboat and a man held on to me as I reached down and got hold of Bella's foot another man came as I yelled for help and he reached down and got hold of Bella's lifebelt strap and we got her into the boat. We were both soaked through to the skin with oil, dirty black stuff.

I got an oar and we had a hard time getting clear; we would get away a little bit and then were washed back again. At one time we were right under another lifeboat that was being lowered but they held it in midair until we got clear. After a hard struggle we got clear away. There were only five men in the boat, all the rest women and children. We got the boat moving and tried to keep it head on to the waves. Several times we got broadside on and we shipped a lot of water and also got soaked. Some of the women got sick then Bella got sick and then sometime later I was sick. We had swallowed so much oil and the taste was awful, then it got cold and we were utterly miserable. We saw some lights go on, on the *Athenia* they had got an auxiliary dynamo working and were sending an SOS. We saw a faint gleam on the horizon and thought it was a ship but it was the moon. This helped to make things clearer and we could see the other lifeboats. Many were burning flares...

... We of course lost everything, all Bella had was her two rings and wrist watch. I had my shoes, ring and wrist watch. All our beautiful things are gone and everything you gave us, but we are safe now and gradually

to see my way down stairs people were
jambed tight on the stair and my match
lit up the place and let them get clear
our cabin was near the ~~bottom~~ foot of the
stairs and I got to our cabin I lit
another match and got our lifebelts
women were pulling my coat and
asking for a lifebelt, we had three
in our cabin so I gave one to a woman
then I lit another match and got
Bella's red coat and her sweater,
then I lit the last one to see my
way upstairs again, the top of the
stairs was badly smashed but I
got over all right and soon was
back beside Bella. I put on her
sweater, her coat and lifebelt then
I put on my own lifebelt still no
sign of a lifeboat, I went to the
other side of the ship and saw the
submarine come up about as near
as I could judge a quarter of a mile

getting over the shock. We both have sore throats and head colds and a few bruises but getting better every day. The folks here have been very good to us. Bella has received a lot of underclothes and I have gotten a lot of things too, even gifts of money from our friends... We are so glad we had no broken bones as so many have, we think we came out very well considering all we went through.

With warmest love from us all, yours very affectionately

Jack[6]

Mr and Mrs Coullie featured in press accounts of the sinking, such as this example from a Chicago newspaper of 16 September 1939.

PHONEY WAR

Despite the declaration of war, the next eight months or so would see little significant military campaigning in western Europe. Germany still hoped to persuade Britain to accept peace terms, while the only real action was undertaken by the French, who launched a limited and unsuccessful offensive to test the German defences around Saarbruecken.

Yet tensions remained high. The Soviet Union invaded Finland on 30 November 1939, and Germany maintained its aerial and naval attacks on Allied shipping. It was surely only a matter of time before the next big step was taken to make the war a more 'real' threat to those in Britain, and civil defence preparations on the Home Front continued in earnest.

Margaret Noble lived in Hawkchurch in Devon, and was among those in her village who welcomed evacuated families into their homes. Writing to her younger sister in Sarawak, modern-day Indonesia, Margaret described how normal life was slowly changing due to the war.

This London police box has been shielded behind a thick brick blast wall to protect it from air raids. The black and white stripes on the lower part of the wall were to make it clearly visible to pedestrians in the blackout.

CASTLE HOUSE,
HAWKCHURCH, DEVON.
TEL. HAWKCHURCH 237.

5th October 1939.

My Darling Blessed,

It is a queer feeling to sit down to write to a sister on the other side of the world having no idea when she will get the letter – how long it will be delayed in the Censor's office or how long at their best mails take to reach you in these days we know not – or what you will most want to hear. Family news will be the most welcome, I expect, for of world news you are probably much better informed than we are, and I know you must be worrying about all of us. Not that there has been anything so far of an alarming nature; the feeling everywhere is queer and tense and in a way the most difficult thing to bear is the absence of events. It's really almost impossible so far to realize that there is anything more going on than an intensification of the suspense that we have endured for the last year – Of course black-outs and evacuees brought it home a bit, but even these things were nothing new – we had been hearing about them for so long. When they did come it was not strange, only unendurably pathetic. I was on the village committee for receiving and housing our lot. It was a pouring wet day and they all arrived tired and wet and hungry and frightened, mothers with small children. Jill and I did short work, taking them round in batches to their new homes in his car. We got five in our hiring house – a woman with three little children and a small sister. They were of the very poor from the Waterloo Road district; they were grubby from the journey but otherwise scrupulously clean. We were lucky in ours because

5th October 1939

My Darling Blessed

It is a queer feeling to sit down to write to a sister on the other side of the world having no idea when she will get the letter – how long it will be delayed in the Censor's office or how long at their best mails take to reach you in these days...

Not that there has been anything so far of an alarming nature; the feeling everywhere is queer and tense and in a way the most difficult thing to bear is the absence of events. It's really almost impossible so far to realise that there is anything more going on than an intensification of the suspense that we have endured for the last year. Of course black-outs and evacuees brought it home a bit, but even those things were nothing new. We had been hearing about them for so long. When they did come it was not strange, only unendurably pathetic. I was on the village committee for receiving and housing our lot.

It was a pouring wet day and they all arrived tired and wet and hungry and frightened, mothers with small children. Jill did stout work, taking them round in batches to their new homes in the car. We got five in our tiny house – a woman with three little children and a small sister. They were of the very poor from the Waterloo Road district. They were grubby from the journey but otherwise scrupulously clean. We were lucky in ours because Mrs Branch was a very nice woman, quite young and a devoted mother, and the little sister, Ethel aged eleven, was a tower of strength and wisdom. The children were five, two and six months.

I went up to London about three weeks ago to have a look round... It was weirder and eerier than anything you can imagine. It seemed at once muffled and echoing. There wasn't any moon at that time, so I didn't get the benefit of the much advertised beauties of the black-out. None of the solaces that we have come to rely on so habitually were available – galleries all shut and empty, cathedrals sandbagged out of all recognition, parks all trenches and notices... I was glad to get back to the country and sanity again...

Margaret[7]

TENSIONS CONTINUE

Despite the absence of any significant military campaigning until the following year, the European powers continued to mobilise their armies and stood in readiness. The last few months of 1939 were marked by a small German force manning the fortified Siegfried Line along the border with France. As tension between the Allies and Axis powers continued to fester, French and Belgian troops stood in readiness along their borders, accompanied by a small British Expeditionary Force. Minor, localised skirmishes occurred regularly, while aerial dogfights and bombing were also fairly common.

Alexandre-Jacques Louis, a soldier serving in a radio company of the French Army, wrote regularly to his English pen-friend.

Le 31 Octobre 1939

My dear Tinckle

... For my side, many changes since I have written to you. We were during a fortnight sent to a battery of 75 to join them with others with one wireless. At the beginning we were quite safe and quiet but at the end we have been seen by German planes and we have had many bombardments to experience, especially one night that we were obliged to spend in an awful muddy trench. After a full month spent in first line, we went back to take our rest, and we needed it very much. For a month I could not take my clothes off – and we were so covered with mud (it has been raining nearly all the time) that it was impossible to see the cloth of our trousers and vests. During this time I had the pleasure to shoot down a German plane. He had just shot down a French one. They were three and after that fight they were machine-gunning us. I was frightfully upset for the airman had just come down near us and two friends of me and myself, we fight with the planes instead of going in the trenches. As soon as one of the German planes came down, the others flew away. German airmen were dead, and I am proposed for the Military Cross.

Le 31 Octobre 1939.

Monsieur Alexandre - Jacques Louis.
Compagnie radio.
Secteur postal 94.

—————

My dear Tuckle;

I have just received your two letters
... and the day before. You have no excuse
to give me for not having written before, for I did
not do it myself. Your letters were greatly
welcome and cheered me up a lot.

I have begun this letter and obliged
to let it for a duty I have not been able to
take it again before to-day 5th of November.
A lot of things have faned since. I will
tell you of them after. First I want to
thank you for your parcel. They were twice
greated, coming from you first, and secondly

What I am the most fearing are the swines, but now we are at nearly
50 miles from the front. After a month's rest we are just been leaving
our rest and from Nancy we went to Montreuil quite near Le Touquet.
I don't know what they are expecting of this side; certainly a big attack
through Belgium, because our division is a flying one which is sent where
reinforcement is needed.

... With blessings and love, Yours very affectionately

Jacques[8]

TOTAL WAR

Even more so than the Great War of just over twenty years before, the current conflict would prove to be an example of Total War – a conflict in which *everybody* was involved to some degree, regardless of their age, gender or background. The distinction between combatant and non-combatant was no longer clear. There would be ways in which anybody could make an important contribution to their nation's war effort, and expectations of mass involvement meant that the first few months of the conflict saw much consideration about how best to use one's talents.

Artist and sculptor Henry Moore was forty-one years old at the outbreak of war and too old for conscription, yet undertook valuable work later on in the conflict for the War Artists Advisory Committee. He and his wife would be forced out of London in September 1940 when their Hampstead home was bombed.

Henry Moore in 1949.

Sunday 8th Oct/39

Dear Arthur Sale

... When war broke out I was in full swing with work, trying to get a satisfactory lot done for the sculpture exhibition I had fixed at the Leicester Galleries this November. Lately I've been making ideas and figures for metal and in the last five or six weeks I've modelled in wax and then cast into lead, some eight or nine things. So the war doesn't so far seem to have interfered with work. But of course the war atmosphere might get closer and more intense, it's sure to, and for how long it will be possible then to concentrate well enough for proper work, who can tell.

... At present I'm a couple of months over the military service age. But if the war goes on for any length of time, the limit won't stay for long at 41. I was in the trenches in the last war, and so all the more don't want to shoot or be shot at, again. And like every other sane person I hate war and all it stands for. But I can't say with complete certainty that there aren't some things I might find myself ready to fight for, and so I can't call myself a wholly consistent conscientious objector. I'd be glad if I could, for I respect greatly the real pacifist point of view, and I'm glad to know that you are a C.O., and will have the courage to remain so. I think this war need not have come – if we'd had a better government and a different attitude to Russia. Now it's here, I think it's more or less the same set up as in 1914, that is it's largely an Imperialist war again, but with this difference that in place of the Kaiser and the old German militarists there is the more reactionary and barbaric regime of Hitler and the Nazi party. And now the war's started, if Fascist Germany wins then I think most of the civil liberties in Europe would go: there'd be less freedom of expression and a poor chance for the existence of the kind of painting, sculpture, literature, music, architecture, that I believe in. Although no one can say there's democracy in England in the real sense of the word, and although British Imperialism has a pretty bloody record, I hate Fascism and Nazism and all its aims and ideology so intensely, that I don't think I could refuse to help in trying to prevent it from being victorious.

However when the time comes that I'm asked, or have got to do something in this war, I hope it will be something less destructive than taking part in the actual fighting and killing. There ought to be ways of being used even as a sculptor, in making of splints etc, or jobs connected with plastic surgery, though the most likely thing I suppose is camouflage work. But until I'm prevented from doing so, my idea is to go on working just as I am, for as long as it's possible, or our finances last out.

With all best wishes

Yours, Henry Moore[9]

Sunday 8th Oct/39

'Burcroft'
Kingston
Nr Canterbury — Kent

Dear Arthur Sale,

I was very glad to hear from you, telling us how you both are + your reactions to this dreadful business, and have meant to write in reply long before this. I hadn't realised until looking at your letter again today that it's so long since I received it. But one effect this war seems to have had on me, is to upset all proper ideas of the passage of time.

Yes my teaching job at Chelsea has finished, + there'll be few or no exhibitions to send to, + so small chance of selling any work. Therefore we're giving up the Hampstead studio, + settling here at our cottage to live as economically as possible. In this way we hope to last out on our present small savings for some few months. I'm going on working just as usual, — that seems the most sensible thing to do, besides being what I want to do. When war broke out I was in full swing with work, trying to get a satisfactory lot done for the Sculpture exhibition I had fixed at the Leicester Galleries for this November. Lately I've been making ideas of figures for metal.

OVERSEAS EVACUATION

Fear of enemy bombing led to the British government's decision to move civilian groups, particularly children, from larger cities to safer areas in the countryside. Beginning on 1 September 1939, some 1.5 million people were evacuated in this way. Further officially organised schemes were carried out the following year, in response to the Blitz on key cities and the increased likelihood of a German invasion.

As well as evacuation to rural areas, the Children's Overseas Reception Board arranged for 24,000 children to be sent overseas, mainly to Canada, but also to South Africa, Australia and New Zealand. But the official scheme would be terminated after the transport ship SS *City of Benares* was torpedoed by a German U-boat, resulting in the deaths of seventy-seven out of the ninety children aboard.

Among the victims was the nine-year-old Beryl Myatt, whose parents received the following letter two days after the sinking.

London was believed to face the biggest threat from enemy bombing, but many other large cities and industrial centres would see members of their civilian populations evacuated.

BERYL MYATT

Children's Overseas Reception Board, 45 Berkeley Street, London W1

19th September 1940

Dear Mr Myatt

I am very distressed to inform you that in spite of all the precautions taken the ship carrying your child to Canada was torpedoed on Tuesday night, September 17th. I am afraid your child was not among those reported as rescued, and I am informed that there is no chance of there being any further lists of survivors from the torpedoed vessel.

The Children's Overseas Reception Board wishes me to convey its very deep sympathy with you in your bereavement. Like so many other parents you were anxious to send your child overseas to one of the Dominions to enjoy a happier and safer life. You courageously took this decision in the interest of your child, believing that this course was better than leaving the child here in a vulnerable area subject to continuous air raids. Hitherto there have been no casualties among the thousands of children sent overseas; unhappily the course of the war has shown that neither by land nor sea can there be complete safety and all of us are subject to the risk whether we stay at home or proceed overseas.

As a parent I can realise the anguish that this letter must cause you and the great sadness which will be brought into your home. I should like to assure you how profoundly I, personally, sympathise with you and how deeply I share your grief.

Yours very truly

Geoffrey Shakespeare[10]

CHILDREN'S OVERSEAS RECEPTION BOARD
45, BERKELEY STREET
LONDON
W.1

Replies to this communication should be
addressed to the Director-General,
quoting

MAx. 5334. D.11.

Telephone : Mayfair 8400.
Telegrams : Avoncorb, London.

Your reference.............................

19th September, 1940.

Dear Mr. Myatt,

    I am very distressed to inform you that in spite of
all the precautions taken the ship carrying your child to
Canada as torpedoed on Tuesday night, September 17th.
I am afraid your child was not among those reported as
rescued, and I am informed that there is no chance of there
being any further lists of survivors from the torpedoed vessel.

    The Children's Overseas Reception Board wishes me to
convey its very deep sympathy with you in your bereavement.
Like so many other parents you were anxious to send your
child overseas to one of the Dominions to enjoy a happier
and safer life. You courageously took this decision in
the interest of your child, believing that this course was
better than leaving the child here in a vulnerable area
subject to continuous air raids. Hitherto there have been
no casualties among the thousands of children sent overseas;
Unhappily the course of the war has shown that neither by
land nor sea can there be complete safety and all of us are
subject to the risk whether we stay at home or proceed overseas.

    As a parent I can realise the anguish that this letter
must cause you and the great sadness which will be brought
into your home. I should like to assure you how profoundly

I/

PACIFISM

Once war was declared, it became a time of soul-searching for many pacifists. The horrors of the First World War had encouraged a rise in pacifism during the 1920s and 1930s, and one of the most prominent advocates during this period was *Winnie-the-Pooh* author A. A. Milne, who published his influential work *Peace With Honour* in 1934.

Yet Milne was one of many to change his mind in the face of Nazism, as illustrated by this letter written from his home in Hartfield, Sussex, in December 1939.

1.xii.39

Dear Sir

I am afraid I am not with you; for I believe that war is a lesser evil than Hitlerism. I believe that Hitlerism must be killed before War can be killed. I think that it is more important to abolish War than to avoid or stop one war.

I am a practical pacifist. In 1933 when I began *Peace With Honour* my only (infinitesimal) hope of ending war was to publish my views and hope that they would have time to spread before war broke out. They did not. One must try again. But since Hitler's victory will not abolish war; and since Peace now (which is the recognition of Hitlerism) will not abolish war; one must hope to be alive to try again after England's victory – and in the incentive to do all that one can to bring that about.

Yours faithfully

A. A. Milne[11]

COTCHFORD FARM,
HARTFIELD,
SUSSEX.

1. xii. 39

Dear Sir,

I am afraid I am not with you; for I believe that war is a lesser evil than Hitlerism. I believe that Hitlerism must be killed before war can be killed. I think that it is more important to abolish war than to avoid or stop one war. I am a practical pacifist. In 1933 when I began Peace with Honour my only (infinitesimal) hope of ending war was to publish my views and hope that they would have time to spread before war broke out. They did not. One must try again. But since Hitler's victory will not abolish war; and since Peace now (which is the recognition of Hitlerism) will not abolish war; one must hope to be alive to try again after England's victory — and in the meantime to do all that one can to bring that about.

Yours faithfully,
A. A. Milne

CHAPTER TWO

BLITZKRIEG

Clockwise: British soldiers wade out to a waiting destroyer off Dunkirk during Operation Dynamo. • Firemen at work in Ludgate Hill near St Paul's, London. • Pilots of No. 32 Squadron RAF in front of a Hurricane Mk I. • Troops in Brest during the evacuation of British forces from France, June 1940. • The front of the Gaumont Palace Cinema in St Peter Port, Guernsey, during the German occupation.

THE FALL OF FRANCE

On 10 May 1940, the 'Phoney War' in western Europe well and truly ended, with German troops marching into the Low Countries of Belgium, Luxembourg and the Netherlands, and then into France. The invasion used Blitzkrieg attacks – quick and powerful offensives – to unbalance the defenders and allow the German armies to sweep through and consolidate their gains.

An unexpected German assault via the Ardennes region served to cut off those Allied units that had advanced into Belgium, and the result was that a large number of French and Belgian soldiers, together with much of the British Expeditionary Force, which had landed earlier to assist them, were forced to retreat towards the coast.

Among the BEF troops facing the constant Blitzkrieg was Sergeant John Atkinson of the 2/5th Battalion Sherwood Foresters.

French-African colonial troops, captured by the advancing German 56th Field Artillery Regiment, are marched to captivity in June 1940.

Saturday

Dear George

I was pleased to hear from you, and congratulations to you and Rene in your forthcoming happy event, even if I am a little premature, and tell Rene not to get too frightened if the Jerry bombers come, because if you keep below ground level, the same as in your shelter, its more than a thousand to one against you getting hurt. I expect they told you at home, but we experienced air raids practically every day while we were in France and Belgium.

When we marched out of Belgium towards Arras we came through a town called Tournai and they bombed it while we were coming through, that was about midnight. We slept the night in a Dutch barn just outside the town and next morning about 6 o'clock they came over in droves and the noise of the bombs and the AA batteries which were quite close to us nearly deafened us. Another place where we got bombed severely was Le Forres. There was a lovely big golf course surrounded on three sides by woods, we were in those woods for two days, and also there was a French ammo dump in them. We had eight raids on those two days, but by good providence they just didn't hit the part of the wood where we were or the ammo dump, they also dropped parachutes and although we went after them the French got there first and made short shrift of them.

Then the bombers used to come over in flights of about 20 accompanied by fighters, they first flew over and then turned round, dived and laid their eggs. We could always tell when they were going to bomb as their machine gunners went to open up on the Ack Ack batteries. Then you could hear the wind screaming in their wings as they dived. Still, we got so used to being bombed and shelled that they didn't seem half so bad as their trench mortars. We were blasted out of several positions by these deadly weapons and most of our casualties were caused by either them or by their sub machine guns, but we got so hungry and tired that we didn't care what happened. To look back at it, it seems rather like a bad dream... When we landed in England it seemed like heaven not to have the incessant pounding of artillery in your ears...

Cheerio and good luck

John[12]

4976854
Cpl Atkinson
C Coy
2/5 Sherwood Foresters
Knox School
Haddington
East Lothian
Scotland
Saturday

Dear George,
I'm starting this letter while I have a
bit of time, I should get it finished to day through.
I was pleased to hear from you, and congratulations
to you & Rene on your forthcoming happy event, Even
if I am a little premature, and tell Rene not to
get too frightened if the Jerry bombers come, because
if you keep below ground level, the same as
in your shelter it's more than a thousand to one
against you getting hurt. I expect they told you
at home, that we experienced Air raids practically
every day while we were in France and Belgium.
When we marched out of Belgium towards Arras
we came through a town called Tournai and
they bombed it while we were coming through
that was about midnight, we slept the night in a
Dutch barn just outside the town and next morning

DUNKIRK

In the face of the German invasion of the Low Countries, some 400,000 outflanked Allied soldiers retreated to the coastal area of France around the port of Dunkirk. A lucky pause in the German advance allowed the British and French to fortify their defences, providing enough time for a mass evacuation from the beaches.

Between 26 May and 4 June, Operation 'Dynamo' saw over 338,000 Allied soldiers successfully evacuated back to British shores via a hastily assembled fleet of over 800 different ships. Over the next couple of weeks, almost 192,000 more Allied troops were evacuated from ports further south along the French coast, before the Germans seized Paris on 14 June. France, Britain's largest ally at the time, surrendered eight days later.

Based at Dover, signalman Les Mallows served in the minesweeper HMS *Princess Elizabeth,* which was among the large flotilla of rescue ships sent to Dunkirk.

British troops during the evacuation from Dunkirk, 1940.

Now for us, the first unforgettable sight. Six miles of beaches leading westward up to the distant port of Dunkirk, and this long stretch of light sand appears spotted and blotched with small groups and larger formations of soldiers. The lorries, trucks and Bren-carriers which have got them there are standing abandoned around the dunes that lie along the top of the beaches, except where the smart white hotels of La Panne intrude on the scene.

Along this seafront there are something like forty ships, anchored as close inshore as their draught will allow; 'pusser-built' naval vessels such as destroyers and fleet-minesweepers are mixed up with small merchant-ships, trawlers and drifters, smart motor-yachts and a goodly number of paddlers. All their small boats are plying to and from the beaches, and as some ships move away with crowded decks, others like ourselves are constantly moving in to 'join the club'.

To make this panorama even more spectacular, the last daylight air attack is in full swing. Some thirty or forty bombers are wheeling and darting over and around the rescue-fleet, who being at anchor are sitting ducks. But all ships' guns blaze away as an aircraft approaches within range, the bombers having split up to circle the area while they select their targets and the moment for a run-in. One of the most vivid memories is the battery of Bofors guns firing from somewhere just behind the elegant hotels of La Panne – so redolent of peacetime holidays, except that they have tracer shells streaming over their roofs. The clips of Bofors shells make a glorious rhythmic thumping sound, like a giant beating a huge brass drum; and the sinister black bombers jink and weave to avoid the line of the tracer.

It was quite dark when the first of our two boats, rowed by a mixed volunteer crew of seamen and stokers, grounded its bows close to the shore. Nobody seemed to be aware of their arrival and the Sub-Lieutenant in charge was surprised to find himself splashing ashore and groping along the beach for some time before he found a column of soldiers and led them back to the boat. The first arrivals disposed themselves in the bottom of the boat between the four pairs of oarsmen and soon afterwards they were being helped up on to the ship's port sponson – the entrances on the paddle-box. And so we welcomed aboard the first soldiers that the *Princess Elizabeth* was to bring home during that week.

Our passengers amused themselves by propping up against various parts of the upper deck and firing their rifles at any bombers that cruised even vaguely within range. The ship's own light armament consisted of one twin and one single Lewis-gun, and there was rather a peashooter feeling about it. Oh, for the Oerlikons and Pom-poms of two years later!

Our steaming away from the beaches and the ragged line of shipping brought a kind of disquieting silence. The Bofors guns ashore, plus whatever guns were sported by the assorted rescue-vessels, had formed a very spirited Ack-Ack club. Now we had left the club premises, so to speak, we felt very alone.[13]

Troops evacuated from Dunkirk take shelter in the minesweeper HMS Princess Elizabeth.

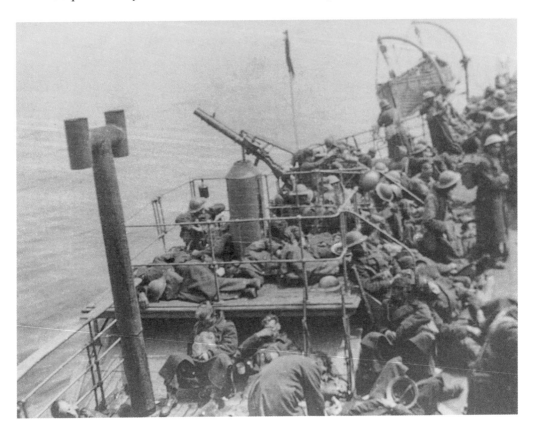

THE OCCUPATION OF THE CHANNEL ISLANDS

Jersey, Guernsey and the other Channel Islands located off the French coast of Normandy proved to be the only part of the British Isles to be invaded during the war. Preceded by aerial bombing, the first German troops landed on Guernsey on 30 June 1940 and quickly consolidated their hold of the islands. Fortifications were constructed, communications established with occupied France, and restrictions imposed on the civilian population.

Richard Foley and his wife were resident on Guernsey throughout the German occupation, which only ended on 9 May 1945. During that time they experienced a gradual deterioration in living conditions as food ran out, forced labour was introduced and mass deportations began to internment camps on the mainland. The following letter was written to their family following liberation.

A German military band march past Lloyds Bank in St Peter Port, Guernsey.

11-6-45

Dear Mum and family

We shall not of course easily forget the first landing of the German occupying troops, which was made by whole hosts of German Air Force men and our bewilderment at what was in store for us would just have to be imagined. However, it was all very orderly and the original Kommandants and High Officers were extremely charming men as they were not, as we understand, Military Kommandants but were here to take charge of all civilian matters. The unpleasant Nazi military officials came later and gradually put the screws on as the Channel Islands became more and more fortresses.

Almost everybody on the Island managed somehow or the other to get things apart from the basic rations, as on these alone, I do not see how any of us could possibly have survived. The principal method of obtaining extras was on the Black Market, conveniently provided by the damned Germans themselves. The Organisation Todt members started this racket first of all by thieving and depriving the thousands of slave workers in Guernsey of their already small rations allowed by the German High Command, and eventually in some extraordinary manner smuggling whole boatloads across. It was done on such a large scale that the German military and civil Kommandants must have known about it and were probably principals in the game themselves.

On the whole, we have not been personally very unhappy during the Occupation, and have always tried to make the best of each changing situation. When electricity, for example, finally ceased and everything had to be cooked on a few bits of very often wet wood in a fireplace that smoked us out, and when it became pitch dark at 5 o'clock in the evening, still we were fortunate in that I managed to get hold of a couple of gallons of diesel oil, obviously stolen from the Germans (if they had discovered it in the house, I would have got anything up to 10 years in Siberia or something, as anything like this was of course a very serious offence), and we had a little improvised lamp made.

There were quite a number of murders committed, the worst one was only a few months ago, when an elderly man and his wife were brutally murdered for the sake of their Red Cross parcels. The few days following our issue of

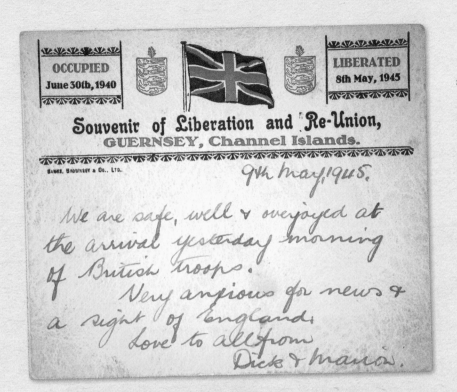

Handwritten on postcard:

OCCUPIED
June 30th, 1940

LIBERATED
8th May, 1945

Souvenir of Liberation and Re-Union,
GUERNSEY, Channel Islands.

BARNES, BROWNSEY & Co., LTD.

9th May, 1945.

We are safe, well & overjoyed at the arrival yesterday morning of British troops.

Very anxious for news & a sight of England.

Love to all from
Dick & Maria.

Red Cross parcels were always a very dangerous period, as a very large proportion of houses were broken into by German soldiers and a terrific number of robberies took place during these last six months. It began to get quite frightening, especially when the dinners were stolen off the fire whilst the women were upstairs cleaning the bedroom, for instance!

Sometimes when we were sneaking back across the fields late at night after having gone to listen to a secret radio, we came across marauding Germans and we were sometimes afraid of being shot at by sentries as suspected thieves. We were very thankful to have the opportunity of listening in from time to time as although I failed to give my set in when the order first came into force, it became increasingly dangerous as the penalties for discovery were greatly increased and when following raids on the houses by the Gestapo sets were discovered, the death penalty was being mentioned far too frequently for my liking, but nevertheless we still held on to it.

[But now] to have as much bread as we want, a pound of flour each week, a few raisins, a little bit of cheese, some tinned meat, some biscuits, even of poor quality, a cup of tea whenever we want it, English cigarettes, is all too luxurious for words.[14]

INVASION SCARES

Back in Britain, the fall of France and other countries to the Nazis, coupled with the massive battering inflicted on the nation's army after having been forced to evacuate from the continent, meant that an imminent German invasion was deemed very likely. Civil defence measures had already been widely introduced, yet suddenly a war on home turf seemed a very real possibility.

Noel Streatfeild, famous for her children's books, including *Ballet Shoes*, wrote the following letter to her sister-in-law, describing the 'militarisation' of Britain as witnessed from her flat in Piccadilly. Attitudes were changing as the war drew ever closer to the very doorsteps of people's homes.

Above: Posters such as this example prepared the civilian population for a potential enemy invasion.

Below: A pile of signposts removed as part of the anti-invasion precautions.

13th June 1940

Dear Binkie and Champion

... Here life is going on its rather sad and weary course, we've had unusually lovely weather, which has helped things a bit, in fact the country has never looked more beautiful. There seem to be large crops of the summer fruits and vegetables, thank goodness, which I suppose saves us bringing in a good many ship loads of stuff. We've become very war-like in appearance, the whole country bristles with barbed wire, and behind every hedge there seem to be soldiers with bayonets and guns, and the roads are heavily guarded.

Every able bodied man who can hold a gun is now a parashot. I don't think, as a matter of fact, that the able bodied with the guns are going to be the only people to attack the parachuters, if they should attempt a landing here, for the country people are waiting for them with scythes and clubs. Myself, serious as I know the parachute danger to be, can only find them funny. The thought of a German descending through the skies, disguised as a clergyman, even perhaps as a bishop, with his machine gun under one arm, and his bicycle under the other, is hard to take seriously. The wireless broadcast a description of how the parachuters will be dressed, and in spite of the fact that the country is grimly determined to exterminate the lot, everybody died with laughter. One of the comforts of war seems to be when a great deal of what is happening makes the public laugh.

I am still busy as an Air Raid Warden, though now I've confined that mostly to turning out in the night hours, whenever we get a preliminary warning of an air raid. As you will know from your papers and the wireless, there have been no real air raids on England yet, and none at all on London, but there has been a lot of standing by at unpleasant hours in the early dawn. I feel that the route from my flat to the Report Post will be worn away by my running feet, before this war is over.

... My love to you all three.

Noel[15]

11 BOLTON STREET,
PICCADILLY,
LONDON,
W. I.

GROS. : 2970.

13th June, 1940.

Dear Binkie and Champion,

I am writing this in the hope it will reach you some day, but there seems to be no Air Mail to send it to you by, so I suppose in the wildest dreams this can't get to you before September.

Here life is going on its rather sad and weary course, we've had unusually lovely weather, which has helped things a bit, in fact the country has never looked more beautiful. There seem to be large crops of the summer fruits and vegetables, thank goodness, which I suppose saves us bringing in a good many ship loads of stuff. We've become very war-like in appearance, the whole country bristles with barbed wire, and behind every hedge there seem to be soldiers with bayonets and guns, and the roads are heavily guarded. Every able bodied man who can hold a gun is now a parashot. I don't think, as a matter of fact, that the able bodied with the guns are going to be the only people to attack the parachuters, if they should attempt a landing here, for the country people are waiting for them with scythes and clubs. Myself, serious as I know the parachuter danger to be, can only find them funny. The thought of a German descending through the skies, disguised as a clergy-man, even perhaps as a bishop, with his machine gun under one arm, andhis bicycle under the other, is hard to take seriously. The wireless broadcast a description of how the parachuters will be dressed, and in spite of the fact that the country is grimly determined to exterminate the lot, everybody died with laughter. One of the comforts of war seems to be that when one horror piles on another there comes a point when a great deal of what is happening makes the public laugh.

I am still busy as an Air Raid Warden, though now I've confined that mostly to turning out in the night hours, whenever we get a preliminary warning of an air raid. As

Soldiers and police inspect a Messerschmitt Bf 109E-4 after it force-landed at East Langdon in Kent on 24 August 1940.

THE BATTLE OF BRITAIN: FROM THE GROUND

Hitler had continued to hope that Britain might be encouraged to accept peace terms with Germany, avoiding the need for a large-scale German invasion of mainland Britain. Yet by July 1940, with no sign of such negotiations succeeding, Germany began to plan for Operation 'Sea Lion': the invasion of Britain. Key to the plan's success would be German air superiority, which would mean incapacitating the RAF's Fighter Command defences.

The Luftwaffe attacked coastal targets and British shipping in the English Channel, and from 13 August 1940 their campaign extended to bombing raids on airfields and ground installations, as well as centres for aircraft production. The battle reached a critical phase at the beginning of September, when German bombing raids on civilian areas also began in a campaign which would become known as the Blitz.

The Battle of Britain was ultimately a test of strength between the Luftwaffe and the RAF. Although the Luftwaffe could boast the largest air force in the world at this point, the RAF held the advantage of what were arguably the best fighter aircraft – the Hawker Hurricane and Supermarine Spitfire. Britain also had an advanced air defence network involving radar and ground defences.

Gordon Clarke served in the local Home Guard near Canterbury, Kent, during the Battle of Britain. Like many others living in the south-east of England, he was able to witness the regular aerial battles that were conducted in the skies above.

15.8.40

Dear Mum and Dad

As you will have seen from the news, we are living in the middle of a battlefield here now, so thought I would drop you a line to say we are all OK in case you have been worrying about us. The fighting has been going on almost continuously for the past week, and the country around us is littered with German 'planes. Early on Tuesday morning we had about 30 'planes fighting right over the house. The noise of the machine-guns and the German cannon-guns is terrific – like 500 clog dancers performing on corrugated iron sheeting. There were three German planes crashed within a mile or so of the house.

One of the German planes machine-gunned a gang of navvies just as it crashed, and now all the road gangs in Kent seem to have sworn revenge. Wherever a German airman comes down, all the navvies in sight make a dash for him with their picks and shovels, whilst the military chase up on motorcycles to save his life. The hospital here is full of wounded German airmen.

As I am writing (11am) we have just had our third Air Raid Warning of the day. The sky to the south-east is full of little white puffs where the AA shells are bursting, but we cannot see any planes yet.

11.15 Three of our planes are now circling slowly round the city, waiting for something to turn up. It is a lovely day and a cloudless sky – just what the RAF pray for. There is heavy AA fire to the southeast still, but nothing nearer. The Germans have so far confined themselves strictly to military objectives. We were bombed on Monday evening about 6 o'clock and seven people killed, but the bombs were intended for the barracks.

11.40 Nine Spitfire have just gone over, flying very high.

11.50 All clear is sounded.

What we like to hear most is machine-gun fire starting, as that means the RAF have arrived. After that it is usually all over in about five minutes, and sometimes a Spitfire will come down low and do a loop to show that he's brought a plane down.[16]

(Letter from Gordon Blake)   15.8.40.
to Mr & Mrs L.S.   Bollikill.
Blake

Dear Mum + Dad,

As you will have seen from the news, we are living in the middle of a battlefield here now, so thought I would drop you a line to say we are all O.K., in case you have been worrying about us. The fighting has been going on almost continuously for the past week, and the country around is littered with German 'planes. Early on Tuesday morning we had about 30 'planes fighting right over the house. The noise of the machine-guns and the German cannon-guns is terrific – like 500 clog dancers performing on corrugated iron sheeting. There are 3 German planes crashed within a mile or so of the house. I enclose part of one of them, which we pinched off it.

One of the German planes machine-gunned a gang of navvies just as it crashed, and now all the road-gangs in Kent seem to have sworn revenge. Whenever a German airman comes down, all the navvies in sight make a dash for him with their picks + shovels, whilst the military chase up on motor-bykes to save his life.

The hospital here is full of wounded German airmen.

As I am writing (11 a.m.) we have just had our 3rd Air Raid Warning of the day. The sky to the south-east is full of little white puffs where the a.a. shells are bursting, but we cannot see any planes yet. 11.15 Three of our planes are now circling slowly round the city, waiting for something to turn up.

THE BATTLE OF BRITAIN: IN THE AIR

During the final week of August and the first week of September 1940, the Luftwaffe intensified their efforts to destroy the RAF. But while many airfields were significantly damaged, most remained operational. The Germans overestimated the damage they were inflicting, and their switch to attacking London proved to be a mistake, as it gave Britain's defences time to recover. The severe losses inflicted on the Luftwaffe were also becoming increasingly unsustainable for the Germans.

Although the Battle of Britain would continue for several more weeks until the end of October, it was clear that Germany had failed to secure the air superiority it needed for its proposed invasion of Britain.

Pilot Officer Ken Gundry was based at RAF Martlesham in Suffolk, flying Hurricanes. No. 257 Squadron were involved in protecting convoys over the North Sea and Thames Estuary, which were frequently pestered by the Luftwaffe.

Main image: Spitfires of No. 610 Squadron RAF, based at Biggin Hill, photographed on 24 July 1940.

Inset: Camera gun footage of a Ju 87 Stuka being shot down by an RAF fighter, 1940.

9.10am Tuesday, 27 Aug '40

My dear 'love bugs'

... I expect you heard of my first piece of luck down over the Isle of Wight,
and it really was luck as I was the only member of the section to return.
However, I did not mention a later schmoygle over the same spot a few days
later when old Jerry had his own back. We separated as a flight and found
ourselves sitting under about 80 Me 110 fighters milling around in a huge
circle; above them were about 50 or more Me 109s. Two of our five got split
away and by few stray Jerries buzzing around, and then the next thing I
knew was a ruddy great earthquake in my aircraft and my control column
was almost solid. On my left another Hurricane was floating about over a
complete network of smoke trails left by cannon shells and incendiary. We
had been attacked by another unseen bunch of Me 110s.

After shaking the bleeder off my tail I managed to get some fairly close but
ineffective deflection shots into him, but he used his extra speed and dropped
clean away down out of range, leaving me with plenty of others to contend
with. I joined up with another Hurricane, and Jerry seemed just to dissolve.
We couldn't find any at all. When I landed afterwards I found that my tail
was all shot to hell and that my flap spar was bust in two up near the wing
root, and my starboard aileron was split almost in two halves and jammed
against the wing. In my excitement of getting away I had wrenched the
broken part free. I haven't yet had a real chance of getting my own back.

One poor swine of a Ju 88 was spotted while going back from a raid in
Portsmouth or somewhere inland, and about seven of us whooped with joy
and dived on him from all directions. His rear gunner put up a marvellous
show and was replaced later by the observer, I guess, but he finally went
down in a complete inferno of red hot metal, and we could see the column of
smoke rising from where it crashed on the cliffs near Bognor Regis from our
'drome at Tangmere for several hours afterwards. We had about a week of
this 'blitz' at Tangmere during which we lost rather a frightening lot of
fellows, either down and out or just down...[17]

ROYAL AIR FORCE,
MARTLESHAM HEATH,
WOODBRIDGE,
SUFFOLK.
TELEPHONE, KESGRAVE 71.

P.S. Say! My crocus have disappeared, but here are
an assortment of old ones, they may be some use to you,
but I doubt it! Incidentally, What news of
my BSA. Sleighlddie ought to be woken up!
Have'nt seen Jim N. officially.

9.10 am. Tuesday. 27 Aug. '40.

My dear love bugs,

How's life going down your way? I was
hoping, but not expecting, to have heard from you by now,
but no doubt you are both busy writing your thank you
letters to New Zealand and elsewhere! — (I hope that sounds
like - nasty crack).

I got a letter from home last week and
have since had a telegram asking me if I received the
former. Unfortunately, it is almost impossible to get
through on the phone in the evenings now; I've tried for
over two hours, two nights running now without success.
All they say is 'indefinite delay'. However, I sent a
telegram and they should have received a letter of mine
written last Friday by now. We are miles away from
anywhere stuck in the centre of a large heath, and the
postman only comes twice, lunch time & tea, and as we are

THE BLITZ ON LONDON: 1940

As the Battle of Britain continued, 7 September 1940 saw the Luftwaffe move the primary focus of their attacks away from RAF targets and on to the capital city, London. What became known as the Blitz began, leaving 430 dead and 1,600 injured on that first night alone. London would be bombed for fifty-seven consecutive nights, and there were often additional bombings during daylight hours.

While London suffered from heavier and more regular bombing than anywhere else in Britain, very few areas of the country were left untouched by air raids. Respite only came in June 1941, when much of Germany's air capability was redirected to their fight against Russia and targets in the Mediterranean.

Michael Stoker was a junior doctor working at St Thomas' Hospital in central London. The following letter, written at the very beginning of the London Blitz, indicates how disruptive the bombing could be to civilian life in the capital.

At 8.02pm on 14 October 1940, a 1,400kg semi-armour piercing bomb was dropped on Balham Underground Station, causing the massive crater shown here. A number 88 bus, travelling in the blackout, drove straight into the crater. About 600 people were sheltering in the station when the bomb exploded; 68 people were killed.

St Thomas' Hospital

Sunday [8 September 1940]

Dear Missus

I hope you're having nice weather and no 'hot apples'... The Hun seems to have a personal grudge against Veronica and I. Yesterday he followed us all over London.

In the afternoon we went to bathe in a big open air place in Brixton. They turned us out when the sirens went and we went into a park. There they came over in waves of about a hundred right over our heads. They were pretty disorganised by the Spitfires and AA guns, there were dozens of dog-fights and we saw several come down. A lot got through though and before long it looked as though the whole of the east end was on fire. Eventually the all clear went and we got back and went to a restaurant. Then the warning went again and in a few moments there were five colossal explosions which knocked everything off the tables. Actually they fell about 100 yds up the road.

We picked ourselves up and finished our coffee, then made for the basement at 41 Penywern Road. At 10pm there was a lull in the proceedings so we decided to make for the hospital. The nearest we could get was by tube to Piccadilly and we started walking from there. Just as we got to Westminster there was a screech overhead so we flung ourselves flat on the pavement (Veronica backwards, me forwards). It weren't 'alf a whopper. It landed on the other side of the river luckily.

At this juncture we decided that it was rather hazardous to cross the bridge so we dived for a street shelter in Parliament Square and remained there until 5am this morning. Veronica went on duty at 6.0! It was only a brick contrivance above ground and every 'screamer' seemed like the last. When we emerged (pale but proud) there were fires all around. You could have read a newspaper in the street alright (if you wanted to!). The docks were the biggest blaze but they had them all under control by morning. The AFS [Auxiliary Fire Service] had a hell of a time because they were bombed and machine gunned continuously. They lost 43 men, most of them cut off on burning timber wharves and jetties.

A great many bombs fell in the Lambeth district and some big tenement buildings were destroyed. Luckily most of the people were in shelters. Thomas' suffered from a few incendiaries which fell in the road but nothing else. Damn – there go the sirens. Luckily we're both in the hospital. I can fix up a bed in the basement.

Pip pip. Love to all from us both

Michael[18]

EUROPEAN PRISONERS OF WAR

Those Allied soldiers remaining in occupied Europe after the Nazi invasions were by now in German hands as prisoners of war. Airmen who bailed out behind enemy lines or sailors retrieved from their sunken ships might similarly be captured and held in camps in Germany or the Reich's occupied territories. As the war progressed and campaigns opened up in North Africa and the Mediterranean, there would be even more opportunities for Allied servicemen to enter captivity, where many remained for the entirety of the conflict.

Conditions varied across different camps and locations, yet all prisoners of war shared a longing for home. Food and diet were a common concern, and most relied on the parcels supplied by the International Committee of the Red Cross to supplement their otherwise meagre rations.

Major George Matthews of the Royal Army Medical Corps was one of many captured at the Fall of France in April 1940, and by July that year was being held in Oflag VII-C at Laufen in Upper Bavaria.

Above: Red Cross parcels being handed out at Stalag VIII-B prisoner of war camp, Lamsdorf.

Right: British prisoners of war at work in a quarry at the town of Laband, the base for working parties from Stalag VIII-B.

Tues 23 July 40

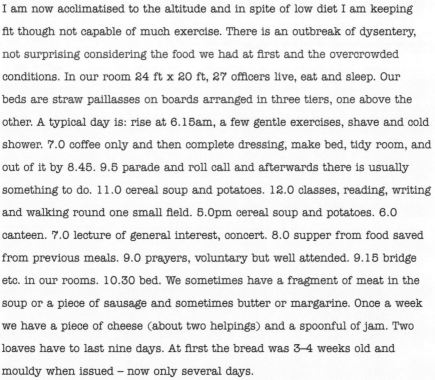

Dr George Matthews,
photographed with a colleague.

My darling wife

Yet another week and still no news of communication
with home. My last three letters (or cards) were on 3rd,
9th and 16th July. My love to mother, father, Gillian
and Adrienne. Tell them I often wonder how they are and
what they are doing. What are your plans for summer
holidays? The German news bulletin has given Christopher's
probably whereabouts. Send via Gwen my best wishes. You might usefully
write to Mrs Dunlop (Enid), The Vicarage, Funtington, Sussex and exchange
information. Borman and I have arranged a weekend there on our return.
Among the many things I have 'lost' are the photographs of you and the
children. Can you send small ones and also of mother and father?

I am now acclimatised to the altitude and in spite of low diet I am keeping
fit though not capable of much exercise. There is an outbreak of dysentery,
not surprising considering the food we had at first and the overcrowded
conditions. In our room 24 ft x 20 ft, 27 officers live, eat and sleep. Our
beds are straw paillasses on boards arranged in three tiers, one above the
other. A typical day is: rise at 6.15am, a few gentle exercises, shave and cold
shower. 7.0 coffee only and then complete dressing, make bed, tidy room, and
out of it by 8.45. 9.5 parade and roll call and afterwards there is usually
something to do. 11.0 cereal soup and potatoes. 12.0 classes, reading, writing
and walking round one small field. 5.0pm cereal soup and potatoes. 6.0
canteen. 7.0 lecture of general interest, concert. 8.0 supper from food saved
from previous meals. 9.0 prayers, voluntary but well attended. 9.15 bridge
etc. in our rooms. 10.30 bed. We sometimes have a fragment of meat in the
soup or a piece of sausage and sometimes butter or margarine. Once a week
we have a piece of cheese (about two helpings) and a spoonful of jam. Two
loaves have to last nine days. At first the bread was 3–4 weeks old and
mouldy when issued – now only several days.

Longing for your letters.

All my love, George[19]

TUES. 23 JULY 40. My darling Wife. Yet another week & still no news of communication with home. My last three letters (or cards) were on 2nd, 9th, & 16th July. My love to Mother, Father, Gillian & Adrienne. Tell them I often wonder how they are & what they are doing. What are your plans for summer holidays? The German news bulletin has given Christopher's probable whereabouts. Send via Gwen my best wishes. You might usefully write to Mrs Dunlop (snd), The Vicarage, Funtington, Sussex and exchange information. Norman and I have arranged a week-end there on our return. Among the many things I have 'lost' are the photographs of you & the children. Can you send small ones & also of Mother & Father? I am now acclimatized to the altitude and in spite of low diet I am keeping fit though not capable of much exercise. There is an outbreak of dysentery, not surprising, considering the food we had at first & the overcrowded conditions. In our room 24ft x 20ft, 27 officers live, eat & sleep. Our beds are straw paillasses on boards, arranged in 3 tiers, one above the other. A typical day is :- Rise at 6.15a.m., a few gentle exercises, shave, & cold shower. 7.0. Coffee only & then complete dressing. Make bed, tidy room, & out of it by 8.45. 9.5 Parade & roll call & afterwards there is usually something to do. 11.0. Cereal soup & potatoes. 12.0 Classes, reading, writing & walking round our small field. 5.0 p. Cereal soup & potatoes. 6.0 Canteen 7.0 Lecture of general interest, concert &c. 8.0. Supper from food saved from previous meals 9.0 Prayers, voluntary but well attended 9.15 Bridge &c. in our rooms 10.30 Bed. We sometimes have a fragment of meat in the soup or a piece of sausage and sometimes butter or margarine. Once a week we have a piece of cheese (about two helpings) and a spoonful of jam. Two loaves have to last 9 days. At first the bread was 3-4 weeks old and mouldy when issued — now only several days. Longing for your letters. All my love. George.

THE BATTLE OF CRETE

Italy declared war on Britain and France in June 1940, and in October launched an attack on Greece. To allow the Greeks to concentrate resources on defending their mainland, British troops helped to garrison the island of Crete, which remained strategically important as an Allied naval base in the eastern Mediterranean.

Where the Italian attack on mainland Greece floundered, a subsequent German invasion in April 1941 succeeded. The Luftwaffe was keen to seize Crete next through an audacious airborne invasion, perhaps intended as a means of regaining credibility after having been beaten by the RAF in the Battle of Britain. The attack began on the morning of 20 May, with German paratroopers meeting a strong defence. Once the Germans were able to land reinforcements, however, the island was quickly seized, along with over 12,000 Allied prisoners.

In a memoir written some years after the war, infantryman Tom Beel of the New Zealand Expeditionary Force described how the Allies sought to repel the German invasion, but at great cost. Although wounded, Beel eventually managed to be evacuated from Crete, along with 18,600 others.

A blazing German troop-carrier during the invasion of Crete, May 1941. Parachute troops and equipment are seen descending.

Pressing on with the attack over the flat terrain between road and coastline we met with fierce resistance with the reluctance of the Germans to give up their positions. Heavy concentrated machine gun fire from left and right – as well as in front of us – took heavy toll of our troops, but one by one we winkled them out of ditches and clumps of cane.

We were now coming under attack from the immediate front in the direction of the airfield, heavy mortar and machine guns were directed at us. A soldier beside me dropped his rifle with a cry of pain, he had been hit in the wrist by an explosive bullet, all but severing his hand. By now it was broad daylight, and as we feared our situation became desperate. With daylight the German fighters were everywhere making strafing runs at us, we had to take cover wherever we could, and there was very little of that.

Finally we fought our way to the perimeter of the airfield which was like a plateau in front of us, on slightly higher ground, we advanced to the edge of the 'drome shielded by the raised ground in front of us from fire from the airfield. Once we were in position we were told by our officer that this was to be the final assault on the 'drome.

At his command we rose as one man and stormed up the slope. I had just gained the higher ground in full view of the aerodrome and with Bren gun at hip, when I felt a tremendous blow to my left shoulder which flung me backwards down the slope I had just surmounted, at the same instant that I came to rest a mortar bomb exploded with a terrific blast several yards from me, and I felt another blow in my right arm, this blast momentarily stunned me and when I eventually clambered to my feet I felt a numbing sensation in my arm, and realised I had been hit by a splinter from the bomb. I had difficulty in carrying the heavy Bren gun but at this moment a soldier passed me and I exchanged the Bren for his much lighter rifle.

As I was making up my mind as to what I should do a medical officer approached me and asked if I was alright. Having told him of my wounds he set to work and applied field dressings, then tying a 'wounded' label on my battledress blouse he told me to make my way back to the first aid post – about a mile back. As he was telling me this a German fighter plane skimmed over us at tree-top level machine gunning, one soldier had been caught in the hail of bullets, he ran past me screaming holding his intestines in his hands, my last glimpse of him was the medical officer had thrown him to the ground and was doing what he could for the soldier.

At this point I was joined by three other 'walking wounded', all of us were carrying rifles over our shoulders, one man had been wounded in the leg, and was being supported by his comrades. We set off for the first aid post.[20]

German mountain troops of the 5th Gebirgs-Division before flying to Crete, 20 May 1941.

VICHY FRANCE

As the German armies swept through western Europe, many foreign nationals found themselves fleeing the advancing Blitzkrieg and likelihood of internment. For those in German-occupied France, a popular 'escape route' was through unoccupied Vichy France, an independent puppet state in the southern half of the country headed by Marshal Philippe Pétain.

Music student Edna Churchill had been living in Paris at the time of the German invasion in June 1940 and fled the city by car, making the long journey south to Marseilles. From there, she was able to find passage on a ship to England via Gibraltar, Spain and Portugal. The success of her difficult wartime journey was attributed to her famous surname, although she was in fact unrelated to the prime minister! On her safe return home to Sussex, she wrote the following letter to Winston's wife, Clementine Churchill.

Philippe Pétain, head of the French collaborationist government based at Vichy, shakes hands with Adolf Hitler in June 1940.

July 22nd [1941]

Dear Mrs Churchill

Having just arrived back from unoccupied France where I have been since the beginning of the war, I feel I must write and tell you how wonderfully I was treated everywhere by the French, not only because I was English, but because I had such a celebrated name.

As you must already know, the people are for us heart and soul, and I was able to make rather special contacts especially in my journey home, because of my name. Passport officers, policemen, customs men, workers in telegraph offices, one and all exclaimed and asked the same question: *nous ches parent de Churchill?* And although I had to admit that I was not, unless perhaps a far-off connection, they became most friendly and talkative and I was given a number of messages to bring over. They all say that although they are unable to act they are with us – they are willing to suffer from our blockade if it is really touching the enemy; they are ashamed of their government and they only believe the news that comes from London. It is difficult for them to listen in but they manage it. I think that our broadcasts cause them to suffer a great deal because their feelings are roused and they are unable to act. The little energy they have left is taken up in trying to find enough to eat. The food question is terrible and we in England seem immensely rich in comparison.

Before ending, I would just like to thank you for the wonderful way in which we were repatriated home. It has left us with a fine impression of our navy and aircraft and we could have no fear on the water under such an escort. Both in Spain and Portugal we were looked after well by our consulates.

Yours sincerely,

Edna Churchill[21]

Westering

Littlington

Polegate

Sussex

July 22nd.

Dear Mr Churchill.

Having just arrived back from unoccupied France where I have been since the beginning of the war, I feel I must write and tell you how wonderfully I was treated everywhere by the French not only because I was English, but because I had such a celebrated name.

As you must already know, the people are for us heart and soul, and I was able to make rather special contacts especially in my journey home, because of my name. Passport officers, policemen, customs men, workers in telegraph offices, one and all exclaimed and asked the same question; "vous êtes parent de Churchill?" and although I had to admit that I was not, unless perhaps a far off connection, they became most friendly and talkative and I was given a number of messages to bring over. They all say that although they are unable to act they are with us — they are willing to suffer from our blockade if it is really touching the enemy; they are

CHAPTER THREE
AIR AND SEA

Clockwise: Fire crews cover an Avro Lancaster of Bomber Command with foam in an effort to save it from burning, following the attack on a Belgian airfield by the Luftwaffe. • A Whitley crew preparing for a night sortie in November 1941. • HMS Suffolk • The SS Lancastria

THE BATTLE OF THE RIVER PLATE

Since the beginning of the war, the German heavy cruiser *Admiral Graf Spee* had been operating in the Indian Ocean and South Atlantic, targeting and sinking Allied merchant shipping. The British Admiralty sent several groups in pursuit of the troublesome ship, and on 13 December 1939 the South American Cruiser Squadron, under the command of Commodore Henry Harwood, sighted the *Graf Spee* off the estuary of the River Plate, between the coasts of Argentina and Uruguay.

In the ensuing battle, HMS *Exeter* was severely damaged and forced to retire, while HMS *Ajax* and HMS *Achilles* both suffered moderate damage. The *Admiral Graf Spee* received critical damage in the battle but remained afloat, her fuel system ruined. The British followed the German cruiser until she entered the port of Montevideo, the capital of neutral Uruguay, to seek urgent repairs. Apparently believing that the British had a larger force awaiting his departure, Hans Langsdorff, captain of the *Graf Spee*, ordered the ship to be scuttled. Three days later, he took his own life.

A month after these events, Kathleen Vesey received the following letter from her cousin Enid, who was a British resident of Montevideo at the time.

The German battleship Admiral Graf Spee *in flames after being scuttled.*

January 13th 1940

My dear cousin Kathleen

... There has been a great deal of wonder as to why the *Graf Spee* sought
refuge in Montevideo so soon, why she didn't want to fight longer, but the
general opinion soon was that she was more damaged than was apparent.
We could see though that she had large holes in her hull, that the aeroplane
had had its tail, wings and engine knocked off, etc... We saw her several times
in harbour there, the last time on the Sunday morning after church.

We were out on the Sunday evening when we heard she had put to sea, and
later we felt dreadful... in spite of her being an enemy ship... when we heard
on the wireless that she had been sunk, imagining that she had been sunk
by our cruisers. Anyhow we were relieved when we heard, before going to
bed, that she had sunk herself and no lives had been lost. We surmised at
once that Hitler had ordered... otherwise it was not at all compatible with
what we had heard of Capt Langsdorff. It barely fits in here, but it is said
that on arrival here the first thing he asked... was for ambulances to take his
wounded to hospital and that he said, 'These English are hard to beat!'

On the Tuesday night Evelyn and I went over to Buenos Aires... and we think
probably because we had diplomatic people on board, we went within 150 to
200 yards of the *Graf Spee*... and when nearest a searchlight was played on
to her from our bridge. It was a very gorgeous although a very sad sight, two
huge columns of flame rising from her deck, one a deeper yellow than the other
and the enormous volumes of smoke, in many places tinted red by the flames.

[On Wednesday] we heard the news of Capt Langsdorff's suicide... it had been
discovered early in the morning but even his men were not told, we heard,
until about the same time as it appeared in the papers, three o'clock in the
afternoon... and on the next day, the second of our two in Buenos Aires, we
went where we could see the funeral procession pass, again very sad. All
people, Argentine, Uruguayan, British, etc. have expressed their sympathy,
the general opinion being that if a new Germany is to be built up after the
war he was the type of man to do it and it is dreadful to think that such a
man should have been forced to do what he was. There were four lorries

covered in wreaths, a lovely scent as they went by, then the hearse, which for some reason stopped almost directly in front of us for a minute or two... The coffin was covered with the Nazi flag, of course, though it is said he shot himself enveloped in the old German flag... That night we came back and then went no nearer than two miles of the still burning ship. Smoke issued from her for nine days before the fire was quite burnt out.

Of course everyone is very thrilled at the British victory, but certain here it has been spoilt by the after-happenings... the sadness of them. Perhaps Hitler would be pleased to hear that, but both here and in the Argentine he has lost sympathy among people who before upheld him.[22]

A victim of the Graf Spee: *the SS* Doric Star *is sunk on 2 December 1939 by the German battleship.*

THE SINKING OF *LANCASTRIA*

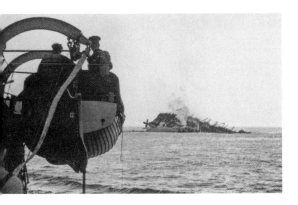

The SS Lancastria *sinks.*

Once the evacuation of troops from Dunkirk as part of Operation 'Dynamo' was completed, additional attempts were made to rescue soldiers and British nationals from other French ports further south. Operation 'Cycle' collected troops from Le Havre, while Operation 'Aerial' targeted other ports along the coast. One of the requisitioned ships sent to collect people from Sainte-Nazaire was the former passenger liner *Lancastria*.

Although *Lancastria*'s normal complement as a troopship was 2,180, including her crew, by the middle of the afternoon on 17 June 1940 she had collected from Sainte-Nazaire well in excess of this number, with estimates ranging from 5,500 to 7,200. During a German air attack, the ship was hit by a number of bombs and sank quickly, within twenty minutes. As many as 5,800 people may have been killed as a result of the sinking, which remains the largest loss of life from any single ship in maritime history.

The following letter was written by Gunner A. J. Ward of the 53rd Heavy Anti-Aircraft Regiment, Royal Artillery, who managed to escape the *Lancastria* after she sank.

30.7.40

Dear Trib

... Eventually I got on the boat and congratulated myself on a safe getaway. It was a fine day but cloudy and ideal for sailing (not the pitiless blue sky and blazing sun of the *Daily Express*). I was leaning over the rail of the boat when I saw a plane swoop out of the clouds and recognised it as a Heinkel. It let fly a load of shit and derision about 200 yards from us. Thenceforwards the raids were intermittent. We were ordered below each time they came over but we could tell that the bombs were not falling far away.

The final alarm came when I was queuing up for a beer at the bar in the next deck to the bottom of the boat. As there were steam pipes overhead I thought it best to hurry out into the mess room. Soon after I entered it I heard a bit of a crash (not loud) and a tinkling of broken glass. I said to the fellow I was with, 'That was a lucky break. It couldn't have burst far away'. However I was wrong as the boat suddenly lurched over steeply. Tables and chairs slid all over the place and complete panic broke out. Fortunately a sergeant stood up and called everyone 'a yellow-livered lot of bastards' and restored order. Then she took another and heavier list and it became obvious that she was going down fast. A crowd from the deck below charged up and rushed the stairs (from their condition I should imagine that there was water in their hold). The banisters bent outward under the weight of numbers, splintered and broke and a number of men fell over the sides. Again a man rose to the occasion and took charge of the stairs and allowed the men up one at a time. By this time I had given up hope and felt fairly resigned. I got caught in the panic but managed to make my way out and hung about until the stairs cleared. I do not blame the fellows who panicked – actually when someone took charge they were very good.

No sooner had I put my head on deck than I heard a burst of machine gun fire and I took cover thinking that they were gunning the decks. Now I think that it was probably a fighter engaging the Jerries. I stood up but I heard a couple of bloody great bangs and chucked myself down again. Someone said to me, 'Stand up you silly sod. That's your own Ac Ac gun firing'. It was the sergeant who took control in the mess room.

I then stripped off everything except my glasses and sat down, lit my pipe and had a smoke, hoping for something to turn up. However I couldn't see any life jackets and the lifeboats were full so it seemed that I would have to swim for it. As I was sitting there the deck suddenly shot up to an angle of about 80 degrees and stuff started breaking away. Something hit me between the shoulder blades and knocked me flying and I realised that it was time to go. However I didn't have to make up my mind as the water came up to me and I started swimming. I swam for about 100 yards in order to get clear of the boat and met an RAF chap. We searched for pieces of wreckage to try and make a raft and I saw something floating in a pool of oil. I swam over and found it to be an air cushion. I straddled it and started paddling over to a French trawler about a mile away. On the way I met one of our officers who was assisting a fellow who couldn't swim and he asked me to help him. We both grabbed the fellow and after something like an hour in the water we reached the trawler. Bombs were falling about and the water was covered in dead fish. Once on the boat we all joined in hauling up the fellows from the water. It was very difficult as everyone was covered thickly in oil and many were too weak to help themselves much. The decks were a shambles – dead, wounded and dying all over the place. I don't know how you felt during your raids but I found myself surprisingly unaffected. I should have thought that it would have made me feel sick.

… I thought it best not to tell Mother anything of this.[23]

THE GUINEA PIG CLUB

As the war continued, medical services had to keep pace with the increasing number of casualties requiring treatment. Fire could prove a particular danger, especially for those involved in aerial warfare, and aircrew frequently needed treatment for burns.

One medical advance that benefited directly from war was reconstructive surgery. Among the pioneers of this experimental work was Archibald McIndoe, based at East Grinstead in Sussex, whose patients formed

Thomas Pace photographed before the war.

'The Guinea Pig Club'. Membership was open to all serving airmen who had undergone at least two surgical operations. Equally important work was carried out by Harold Gillies, commonly considered the father of modern plastic surgery.

During a mission over France on 10 May 1940 with No. 85 Squadron RAF, Flight Lieutenant Thomas Pace's Hurricane fighter was severely damaged by fire from a German Heinkel bomber. He managed to crash-land his aircraft, but suffered serious injuries as a result, as this letter attests.

Undated [November 1940]

... then my 'chute caught on the seat and I hiked myself out and landed on my right shoulder on the port petrol tank which was burning beautifully. I picked myself up after rolling off the wing onto the ground, and how I did it I don't know, I walked half-a-mile and then came across an army motor-cycle and he got an ambulance. I climbed into it myself and very nearly fell out but I managed it and climbed out the other end. Then they put me to sleep and I woke up a fortnight later in the hospital. A lot of the time I was dreaming I was flying and kept wanting to get up, the sister told me about it afterwards, they had to hold me down.

Then after getting transferred to another hospital and trying to get aboard a hospital [ship] and the Germans having sunk it as we were getting on it and then machine-gunned us on the quay, we finally arrived at another hospital and got over to England. I was at Exeter Hospital for a bit and then came up here, arrived here on my 22nd birthday. Sir Harold Gillies the famous plastic surgeon is working on me. He has given me two new eyelids and put my nose straight, the broken cheek bone mended itself because they only found it out when I pointed out a

to get out halfway, then my 'chute caught on the seat & I hiked myself out & landed on my right shoulder in the port petrol tank which was burning beautifully. I picked myself up after rolling off the wing onto the ground, & how I did it I don't know. I walked half-a-mile & then came across an army motor-cycle & he got an ambulance. I climbed into it myself & very nearly went out but I managed it & climbed out the other end. Then they put me to sleep & I woke up a fortnight later in the hospital. A lot of the time I was dreaming I was flying & the heat wanting to get up, the sister told me about it afterwards, they had to hold me down.
Then after getting transferred to another hospital & trying to get aboard a hospital & the Germans having sunk it as we were getting on it & then machine-gunned us on the quay. We finally arrived at another hospital & got over to England. I was at Exeter Hospital for a bit & then came up here & arrived here on my 22nd birthday. Sir Harold Gillies the famous plastic surgeon is working on me. He has given me two new eyelids & put my nose straight, the broken cheek bone mended itself because they only found it out when I pointed out a little lump on my cheek that I could feel but couldn't

little lump on my cheek that I could feel but couldn't see. I've had four operations, shin graft, the first one failed but the place healed up on its own afterwards. They are trying to send me away on leave before my next operation but I want to be finished first, then I might take a week or so before I go back to my squadron. I had a medical board and they said I could go back to active service flying straight away after my last operation, which should be in another 2½ months. So I shall be here for say another three months.

I received a letter from your mother but couldn't answer it owing to the eyes. But I know you'll show this to her. The doctors at the hospital say that beer is good for burns so I drink beer now, but as soon as I've been discharged from hospital I am going back to orange juice.[24]

HUNTING *BISMARCK*

At the time of her commission in August 1940, the German navy's *Bismarck* was the largest battleship ever constructed. On 19 May 1941, accompanied by the heavy cruiser *Prinz Eugen*, *Bismarck* was ordered to proceed into the North Atlantic to engage and destroy Allied merchant shipping. The British Royal Navy were determined to locate and sink the German surface fleet, and assembled the largest naval force of the war so far to deal with the threat.

British ships spotted *Bismarck* and *Prinz Eugen* on the evening of 23 May, and HMS *Suffolk*'s radar allowed them to shadow the Germans throughout the night. Early the next day, further British ships engaged and battle commenced.

At first, it seemed that the Germans had the upper hand. *Bismarck* hit HMS *Hood* near her aft ammunition magazines, causing an explosion that sank her within three minutes, with the loss of all but three of her crew. HMS *Prince of Wales* continued to exchange fire with *Bismarck*, but suffered malfunctions that caused her to retire. The battle was considered a victory for the Germans, but not for long. Angered by the loss of HMS *Hood*, a large British force pursued *Bismarck*, which led to her sinking on 27 May.

Serving in the cruiser HMS *Suffolk*, Peter Proops sent a diary account home to his wife that recalled how his ship was involved in the hunting of the German battleship.

The German battleship Bismarck *underway in the North Sea.*

Friday 23rd May

Bismarck and cruiser sighted to north of Iceland about 7pm. Commenced shadowing and later *Norfolk* joined in, that is after *Suffolk* had sighted *Bismarck*. Both ships shadowed enemy all night.

Saturday 24th

Hood and *Prince of Wales* come up and engage *Bismarck* and *Prinz Eugen*. *Hood* lands with first broadside and puts one engine room of *Bismarck* out, and reduces enemy to 24 knots. The fifth broadside of *Bismarck* hits the after turrets of *Hood* and it is believed that the blast went down to its magazine and *Hood* blew up. *Bismarck* also inflicted damage on the after part of *Prince of Wales*, which temporarily retires but later joins up with us and *Norfolk* and all three continued to shadow the enemy.

At about 10pm the *Bismarck* laid a trap for *Suffolk* by going into a veil of mist and waits for us. Doubtless our persistence in shadowing her forced her to this action. Our Captain however senses the trap and veered to avoid her. Nevertheless when the *Bismarck* and *Suffolk* next saw each other, only ten miles separated them. The enemy opened fire and the broadside fell about fifty to a hundred yards astern of us. We returned his fire and at the same time laid a smoke screen and retired out of range. Whilst retiring we engaged the cruiser *Prinz Eugen* and it is thought that we may have registered on this. The mist prevented us from confirming this, but our broadsides certainly fell very close and some ratings on upper deck believe we straddled target. We continued to shadow the enemy in company with the *Prince of Wales* and the *Norfolk* as we know that the battle fleet is in the vicinity and we continually reported the enemy position to it. For twenty four hours now the *Suffolk* had been doing this and had managed to keep contact through a snowstorm. At about 12pm planes from the aircraft carrier *Victorious* (which had come up) were reported overhead. They attacked *Bismarck* and we later learned that a hit with an aerial torpedo was scored on the enemy, further reducing her speed by 4 knots. She could now only maintain 20 knots at full speed.

Sunday 25th May

After the planes had withdrawn (owing to darkness) the signal to attack was hoisted on the *Norfolk*. All three ships were making ready to attack when for reasons unknown the flag was pulled down and we reverted to shadowing tactics at ten to fifteen miles. However darkness fell (we had been travelling south for some time and had left the region of 24 hrs daylight) and under cover of darkness we lost touch with the enemy at about 3am.

Later the next day the aircraft located the *Bismarck* which led to the destruction of her.

... Your ever loving husband

Pete xxxxxxx[25]

Survivors from Bismarck *are pulled aboard HMS* Dorsetshire *on 27 May 1941.*

LAST LETTERS

It was common practice for servicemen in regular danger to write a 'last letter', intended to be opened only in the event of their death. These missives allowed the writer to provide comfort to their family and friends, while explaining their own justifications for putting themselves in potentially life-threatening danger. Such letters were particularly common among aircrew, who were regularly involved in operations over enemy territory and suffered a lower life expectancy as a result.

Flight Sergeant Jamie Dunlop wrote this 'last letter' to his parents while serving in the Royal Australian Air Force. Less than four months later, he was killed when his bomber aircraft crash-landed on its return from an operation.

12/6/41

Dear Mother and Father

I have no reason to believe or feel that this letter will ever be read since it will only be opened if and when I am killed, or at least listed among those who 'failed to return'. I have no feeling of impending fate so please do not feel that I knew what lay ahead of me when I wrote this. I know that my duty, not only to my country and humanity but to myself, lies ahead. I know that in carrying out my duty I must run great risks. Risks, I may add that leave me little chance of seeing you again. Yet, it is because of the risk, rather than any certainty that I write this letter.

Firstly, I want you to realise and try even to be proud, that you have given a man to the cause of human liberty. Please don't make the error of mourning me on account of my youth. That youthfulness is only apparent to you because you are considerably older than most parents with a son my age. Young as I am I have seen a great deal of this world and of the life of this world. I have lived in free countries among free peoples and have grown to manhood loving the liberty I have enjoyed. True, all has not been easy for me in life nor was freedom so widespread as it might have been for others. Still, progress was being made along the correct lines.

That progress must never be stopped by anyone or anything. All men must learn to live at peace with his fellow men and to grant to all, regardless of station or birth, creed or colour, the same rights and privileges which he himself deserves or enjoys.

Class distinction MUST be wiped out. Surely, if there is a God, he did not intend that his creatures should live amid hate and distrust here on earth as a preparation to entering his kingdom. If we are to live with God we must learn first to live like God or as he would have us live. In other words we must work out our own Salvation. Jesus was and is the 'formula',

it is up to us to follow the formula to reach the same answer. By this I do not intend to condone the organised bodies of men and women which dictate the rules, judge the participants and ostracise the sinners. Each man to his own life, his own belief or lack thereof and to his own morals or code of ethics.

Since my early childhood I have tried to steer my own life along the path that led to the achievement of my ambition – to be a brain surgeon. There is no hope of that now but, as I explained to you once, my death may make it possible for some other lad to do the work I envisioned for myself. I go in that belief, be it vain or otherwise. Dropping bombs seems like a far cry from medicine yet I found it was my duty for once to 'be cruel to be kind'. I hate killing and suffering with all my soul yet I have killed and caused suffering. If I am to be excused it must be on the grounds that I killed the few to save the many. Nazism has and would continue to destroy truth and independent thought without which we must inevitably suffer and die. Die deaths of the soul and mind as well as the body! If there isn't thought there is no freedom, no progress, no life.

If there is any message which the coming generation should have from mine let it be a message from us who have fought and died to make future generations of human beings possible. Let the message be this – we have cleared the site and laid the foundations – you build. This time let us hope they take the plans out of that hip pocket.

Well folks, I had better draw this to a close. This won't have been pleasant reading yet I want no tears on my behalf. I have done my duty, completed my life's work. If there be any honours or rewards due me let them be these two. One: That you regard me as worthy of being your son. And two, that there come to pass at last 'A Good Earth'.

Goodbye and God Bless You.

Your loving son, Jamie.[26]

Vickers Wellington Mk Is of No. 149 Squadron RAF Bomber Command, shown in flight in 1940.

THE SIEGE OF MALTA

The Mediterranean island of Malta was a significant base from which British ships, submarines and aircraft could launch attacks on Axis convoys to North Africa. Recognising its strategic importance, the Germans besieged the island in June 1940, aiming to bomb or starve Malta into submission. While the Allies were able to deliver enough supplies to ensure the islanders could continue to resist, Malta still lacked adequate fuel. Operation 'Pedestal' was therefore organised to deliver oil to the island, with a convoy of fifty ships leaving British shores on 3 August 1942.

The Germans fought hard to prevent the convoy reaching its destination and made regular attacks from both air and sea, resulting in more than five hundred Allied sailors and airmen being killed. Only five of the fourteen merchant ships finally reached Malta's Grand Harbour, yet despite the enormous cost in lives and resources, it proved a strategic victory. The aviation fuel carried by the American tanker *Ohio* in particular enabled the Allied air offensive against Axis shipping to continue. The siege of Malta was finally broken by the Allied successes in North Africa towards the end of 1942.

Commander Denys Barton sailed in the *Ohio* as its Royal Navy liaison officer.

Left: The Italian submarine Axum's *torpedo strikes the tanker* Ohio *on her port side, 12 August 1942. Right: The damaged tanker* Ohio, *literally supported by Royal Navy destroyers, approaches Malta after its epic voyage across the Mediterranean as part of Operation 'Pedestal'.*

September 1st [1942]

Dear Mum

...When I reported at the Admiralty on 30th July I was told to go to Greenock and join a tanker called *Ohio* in which I was to be Liaison Officer and advise the Master in any way necessary. We weren't told where we were going but when I got there and saw a loaded tanker – obviously a fast ship and with a lot of extra guns – it was pretty obvious to me where we were off to!

The escort was I think the biggest that has ever escorted a convoy – two battleships, three aircraft carriers, a large number of cruisers and a whole swarm of destroyers.

The first part of the trip, until we were one day east of Gib, was very peaceful but the fun started on 11th August as we got nearer to Sardinia and the first thing of course was the torpedoing of the *Eagle*, one of our three aircraft carriers. I saw that as I happened to be looking in that direction and it made one think a bit – four torpedoes and she sank in less than ten minutes. I thought they would only get about two hundred away but I heard later that over nine hundred were saved.

Shortly after this big attack the big ships and four of the destroyers and cruisers

Orchard Hotel
London.
September 1st.

Dear Mum,

Please excuse the pencil but I lost my pen in this last job – and you can't get one for love or money now – I've tried dozens of places!

Well to start at the end! I got back here and after seeing the Admiralty – they have given us a fortnight's leave – and then a very soft job for a week after that.

I wired to Betty when I arrived and got the reply that Penelope Ann was born on Aug. 9th and the Christening is next Saturday – so I'm going down there tomorrow to stay a few days and will come up to Shrigham on Monday 7th until the end of the week – I shall have to be in either Manchester or Liverpool by the 14th to start the next job. But still turned back towards Gib... We were having a bit of a lull and the convoy was steaming peacefully on when there was a big explosion in the cruiser flagship and she keeled right over and looked as if she was going to sink. She had been torpedoed and all the ships turned away to get away from the U-boat. Then the *Cairo* suddenly had an explosion which seemed to blow her stern off – I saw great bits flying about 400 yards. And then while we were still looking at *Cairo* there was a tremendous sheet of flame just abaft our bridge – and we too had been torpedoed. I ought to say that all these three explosions happened within a minute or so – although it seemed much longer. Well, our cargo caught fire and there was a pretty big blaze – it was kerosene in that particular part of the ship. We all started to get the boats lowered but the flames didn't seem to get any bigger so they thought they would try and put it out. The flames were about fifty feet high I should think and it seemed rather a forlorn hope. However by pouring all our chemical extinguisher on to it the fire very quickly went down and was out in about five minutes.

So we then started to take stock of the damage. There was a big hole in the side where the torpedo hit us and it had also torn up the deck nearly half way across the ship, the engines had stopped but otherwise there wasn't very much wrong so the engineers set about getting the engines going again. By this time of course the rest of the convoy were some way away and it was nearly dark. Then they were attacked by dive bombers and torpedo bombers and you could see masses of red and white tracer going up in every direction...

The ship finally got into the Grand Harbour at Malta at daylight on the 15th... almost every drop of the cargo except the kerosene which caught fire when we were torpedoed is safe. I doubt if the ship will sail again this war but the cargo was all they wanted.

And now I must go to bed, so goodnight everybody, goodnight.

With much love, Denys[27]

DEFENDING BRITAIN

Although the Battle of Britain had been won, the work of the RAF's Fighter Command continued, with regular defensive patrols across the skies of Britain. Small formations of German fighters flew 'hit and run' nuisance raids all along the southern and eastern coasts, while bombing also continued over the larger cities and ports. This life of tedious routine interspersed by sudden, intense action could prove immensely stressful for aircrew.

Squadron Leader Harry Bodien served as a pilot with No. 151 Squadron, RAF Fighter Command. Based at Bramcote in Warwickshire, he flew Defiant night fighters on patrols over the Midlands, and in this letter to his sister recalls the excitement of dogfights.

This photograph was taken from the nose-camera of a Bristol Beaufighter during an attack on two German Sperrbrechers *(magnetic-mine detonating vessels) moored off Royan, France.*

Undated [circa May 1943]

Dear Doff and Vina

… Last Tuesday week I shot a Dornier 17z down
at night. It was the second time I had ever used
a Defiant on an operational patrol. I had been
scratching around over Birmingham trying to make
contact when I got the vector for home, and was told
to orbit base at 4,000 ft and ask permission to land.

I'd been at 15,000 ft and was throttled back losing
height on the way home when at 10,000 ft the
stupid Hun nearly rammed me head on – I pulled
the kite round as tight as I could keeping my eyes

Harry Bodien (centre, in cap),
with members of his squadron.

on his exhaust flame. My gunner was a New Zealand chap of 19 – he had only
flown 18 hours – never fired Brownings before – never flown at night before
and never seen a Hun. I was worried in case he panicked and opened fire too
soon. Anyway he was good-oh and I got up in formation with the Jerry about
20 yards on his starboard side and about 5 yards below. My gunner opened
fire and the bullets tore in just in front of the main plane – it was a good burst
and as we were using explosive bullets I could see where all the shots were
going. The two rear firing gunners were killed with that burst and he broke
away upwards and to the left – I followed round turning outside him, so that
when he was straight and level again I was dead astern about 200 yrds behind.

We overhauled him much quicker than I anticipated and I had to throttle
right back and waggle my rudder to drop into tight formation with him just
below his wing. This time there was one gun firing at us but the bloke must
have been nervous because his shots were going about two feet above my
hood. We started firing again and this time the bullets sent into the starboard
engine – he did a gentle turn to the left and presented his belly into which
the bullets went just between the main planes. There were a few explosions
in there and small flames streaking out – bits were flying off so I slid out
a bit – his turn got steeper until it developed into a spiral on its back.
I followed it down and it exploded as it hit the deck.

I was very lucky because he crashed 10 miles from the 'drome. Next morning I went out there and had a look at what was left. There was a lot of meat strewn around and five people were in it because nine feet were found. I took a gun, a quick release from one of the parachutes and a few scraps from the wireless operator's log including a photo of the bloke in his identity card showing him to be 19 yrs old, and a photo of his girl – not bad either. Tho! I don't expect she would like me very much.

… Cheerio and all the best.

Harry[28]

Sgts Mess,
R.A.F. Wittering,
Northants.

Dear Diff and Vina,
I'll write to you both at once so as to save paper – my war effort – and time. Number one on the list is quite important and speed is rather essential. :—

Please don't tell a soul, and I mean that, – I've been recommended for a commission there's only one snag – I've passed the medical and have only to go to London to see the A.O.C. I can get passed him OK. but if I am to accept this commission I must have at least £60 to get my uniform – it will be refunded

THE BATTLE OF THE NORTH CAPE

Nazi Germany terminated the non-aggression pact it had held with the Soviet Union by launching Operation 'Barbarossa', their invasion of Russia, on 22 June 1941. Convoys of ships were sent from Britain and Iceland in August 1941 to assist their new Russian allies, providing essential war supplies to Archangel, Murmansk and other northern ports in the Soviet Union. These Arctic convoys suffered much hardship, being frequently attacked by German ships and aircraft while enduring sub-zero temperatures.

Britain's Royal Navy escorted the valuable shipping to protect it as far as possible, with the greatest danger to the convoys being German battleships, such as *Tirpitz* and *Scharnhorst*.

The Battle of the North Cape, fought off the coast of Norway on 26 December 1943, proved to be a decisive victory against the German fleet. In the final big-gun battle of its kind, *Scharnhorst* was sunk by ships including the battleship HMS *Duke of York*.

Royal Marine Bill Withers was present during the battle in the cruiser HMS *Belfast*, the flagship of the Home Fleet's 10th Cruiser Squadron.

British destroyers arrive at their anchorage after the Battle of the North Cape.

Dec 29th 1943

Dear Mother

Just a 'few lines' to let you know I'm well and safe after our scrap with the *Scharnhorst*. I suppose you heard all about it on the wireless last night.

Boxing Day we went to action stations at 0900 (seven o'clock your time) and we remained at the guns for about 13 hours, we 'relaxed' about 11 o'clock that night, we had one final contact with Jerry about 10.30 in the forenoon. When we found that Jerry was out we changed places with the convoy and so that put us in the place of the convoy and when the *Scharnhorst* came in to sink a few merchant packets, as she thought, she got a very big shock. As I've said, she first came in at 10.30 and found out her mistake when we three cruisers opened fire on her, as soon as we all fired she turned round and 'opped it at 28 knots, we left the convoy in charge of the destroyers and gave chase. The *Duke of York* was abaft of us, I don't know the exact distance but it must have been about 60 miles behind and when she got the signal Jerry was out she opened up and got between the *Scharnhorst* and her base.

Anyway we continued to chase her, and what a chase, we were ripping along like hell, I don't know how many knots we were doing but the admiral told us after the action she did more speed that day than she'd ever done in her life, it must have been round about 33 knots, and that's shifting some. Anyway we kept on her tail and when she found out that the battleship had got between her and her base she turned round on us cruisers again, she had one shock when she found three cruisers instead of a convoy and she had another when they saw a battleship as well. When she turned on us we opened fire and gave her a good bashing. It was then that the *Norfolk* 'got it' and a destroyer, after she'd took a parting off us she turned back towards the *Duke* and they started to hammer hell out of each other. Us cruisers and the destroyers lay off and left them to it for a bit, the *Scharnhorst* had got nine 11" guns and the *Duke* ten 14" with shells about a ton each so you can guess how peaceful it was round there with about 6 ton of shell in the air every few mins.

It was about 6.30 (our time) when the two battle wagons met and they kept swinging away at each other for about two hours, two hours is a long time

The
Scharnhorst

Mme. D. Within. X5128.
H.M.S. Belfast mess 44
C/o G.P.O. London.

Dec. 29th. 1943

Dear Mother,

Just a "few lines" to let you know I'm well and safe after our scrap with the Scharnhorst, I suppose you heard all about it on the wireless lastnight. Well they've told you the main points of the battle so there isn't a lot left for me to tell, except how lucky we were and we had no hits, for which we are thankful. We had about two injured on board us but it wasn't through enemy action, one chap had a cordite case drop on his head and he only saw a few stars, the other chap was me (trust me to be in it when there's trouble about) I caught my finger in the

but as they said in the news you don't get any daylight right inside the Arctic circle so it was mostly blind firing at each other. The *Scharnhorst* could out speed the *Duke* and there was a fear she might make a run for it so the destroyers were ordered to go in and torpedo her, this they did with great success and they reduced her speed to 26 knots. One destroyer went in at about 700 yds range and let go with everything and I think it was through her the *Scharnhorst* was slowed down, anyway Jerry had about three tin-fish in her and that slowed her down enough to let the *Duke* close in again.

It wasn't long after when Jerry caught fire and it was the beginning of the end, a lot of Jerrys were jumping off the *Scharnhorst* into the sea, it said in

Able Seaman Thomas B. Day stands against the ice-encrusted 'B' turret onboard HMS Belfast *during arctic convoy duty in November 1943.*

the news the cruiser *Jamaica* gave the coup-de-grace but there's a feeling on here that it was us because after the *Jamaica* had fired her torpedoes we went in and fired three and we wouldn't have fired if she'd gone down. If it was us or the *Jamaica* who finished her off I don't know and I ain't worrying much, we were all there and we did our bit and I came out of it with my life so I'm thankful. With things like this someone's got to go though and we had about twenty casualties in all, dead, and wounded, etc. After the *Scharnhorst* had sunk, she went down about quarter past ten, I came out of the turret to get my finger dressed, after the action, about 10.40 and I stood on the upper deck looking at the destroyers picking up survivors and it was sleeting down. I thought how lucky we were as it might have been us, we and the other ships played our searchlights on the water and I could see Jerry on rafts and some were swimming about, the water wasn't exactly what you'd call warm in that spot, the Arctic circle and at night, I was shivering with cold and I was dry. I've got to hand it to Jerry he went down fighting and her for'ard turret was still firing when she went down so the gunners must have been drowned, they were either damned good sailors or else they were locked in and couldn't get out.

The *Scharnhorst* was all she was boasted to be and she gave us all a run for our money and it took a lot to sink her and we had our hands full doing it even if we were a crowd, she took a hell of a battering.

Your loving son

Bill[29]

NOTIFICATIONS OF DEATH

It remained the sad duty of officers in every branch of the armed forces to write letters of condolence to the next of kin of those killed during active service. The pressures of war meant that such letters were, by necessity, largely brief and to the point, yet sometimes circumstances allowed an officer to compose a more personal and heartfelt message of sympathy concerning the comrade alongside whom he had been serving.

The following example was written by Flight Lieutenant William Reid, VC, and describes the circumstances of Air Gunner Albert Holt's death during a bombing mission over occupied France in July 1944. The letter was written to Holt's mother immediately after the end of the war in Europe, following Reid's repatriation from captivity, and he was therefore able to reveal details about their mission that would otherwise have had to remain secret.

By the time of this mission, Reid had already been awarded the Victoria Cross for having carried out a bombing mission over Dusseldorf despite sustaining serious wounds.

Short Stirling bombers and crews of No. 90 Squadron RAF lined up on the perimeter track at Ridgewell, Cambridgeshire, circa May 1943.

20th June '45

Dear Mrs Holt

Am sorry I have taken so long to write
you, but I've been in Aberdeen on holiday,
recuperating. At any rate I am now in a
better position to explain exactly what
happened to us, when we were reported
missing on 31st July '44.

We were flying in a daylight raid on V1
storage bomb depots (i.e. flying bombs
stored in a tunnel near Reims) that
evening, and just after we had dropped our
12,000 lb bomb I felt the plane being badly
hit. Told the crew to bail out and Bert
being my Mid-Upper gunner had to climb
down, get on his 'chute and bale out of the
rear door... It all happened so suddenly

William Reid vc

that I had just been given my 'chute from the Engineer, then he rushed
forward to get out of the escape hatch. All of those in the main cabin viz.
The Bomb Aimer, Navigator, Wireless Op, Engineer and myself go out of the
first hatch. Whereas the Mid-Upper and Rear Gunners go out the back door
when there is no time to get to the front. I found that the controls had been
knocked away by the hits and while the others piled into the front the plane
went into a steep dive and began spinning down. By this time I had my
'chute on and began to get out, being unable to do any more at the controls.
The control column was holding me down against my chest type 'chute pack.
I then tried to open the side window and get out that way but it wouldn't
open. Managed then to struggle out of the seat and tried to open the other
side window which wouldn't open either. Still spinning down I couldn't get
forward to the escape hatch; I then thought of the dinghy escape hatch above
my head and a little behind. Struggled to this and as I turned the handle felt
a lot of banging and scuffling. Next thing I knew, I was falling thru the air
pulled the rip cord of my 'chute and it opened.

A chap who was on the same raid that evening from our Squadron was up seeing me. He told me how he saw bombs falling from a plane above us, on top of us, hitting us in the wing and fuselage. This sort of thing rarely happens, but on a small target and with a fairly heavy force made it more likely.

After I was captured on landing the Germans took me to their headquarters about a mile away. On the way I saw part of my plane and asked them to let me look at it. Beside the plane they had my two gunners laid out and I looked to identify them. You've no idea what a great shock it was to me, to find Bert and my Rear Gunner to be killed. I don't know whether they were hit by the bombs or not, but I was certain I was the only one trapped in the plane when it was spinning down. It was only that the nose of the plane came off or I'd never have lived myself.

I do hope I haven't been too callous in describing everything as it happened, but I thought you'd want to know everything. I'm afraid that only the W/Op and myself are alive out of the crew and he too was thrown clear on the way down – I have no idea at all what happened to the others – whether their 'chutes didn't open or not I couldn't say.

I need hardly say what a fine fellow Bert was and I can assure you, you have the greatest sympathy from myself and all on the Squadron, in your sad bereavement. He was exceedingly well liked especially having completed almost two tours of operations. Please give my sympathy to his wife and if there is anything I can do at all for you, let me know and I will try my very best to do it.

Goodbye for now and I thank you for Bert, a fine lad and worthy member of my crew.

Yours very sincerely

William Reid[30]

20th June '45. F/Lt. Wm Reid VC.
                        Baillieston
                            Glasgow.

Dear Mrs Holt,

            Am sorry I have taken so
long to write you, but I've been in Aberdeen
on holiday, recuperating. At any rate I
am now in a better position to explain
exactly what happened to us, when we
were reported missing on 31st July '44.

            We were flying on a daylight raid
on V1. storage bomb depots, (ie. flying
bombs stored in a tunnel near Reims)
that evening, and just after we had
dropped our 12,000lb. bomb I felt the
plane being badly hit. Told the crew
to bale out and Bert being my Mid-
Upper gunner had to climb down get on

WHY WE FIGHT

Matthew Todd enjoyed a long career in the Royal Navy that began during the war. He trained at the Royal Naval College at Dartmouth before being posted to the 4th Submarine Flotilla, based in the Far East, in 1944. Confined in a claustrophobic submarine, with all the associated dangers of working underwater for extended stretches of time, Todd would invariably question his chances of survival.

Such thoughts were not unique to those serving inside submarines, of course, and almost every person involved in fighting the war would have considered at some point their personal justification for participating. For many, though, the chances of being wounded or killed were outweighed by the overall moral importance of what they were fighting for.

A display panel produced by the Ministry of Information for show all over Great Britain.

Lieutenant R. Bulkeley at the forward periscope of the submarine HMS Tribune *in 1942.*

Anybody setting out on such operations as we did would be an insensitive idiot not to think carefully about what we were about to do and the chances of our not coming back. Naturally, therefore, it always crossed my mind that we might not return from our forthcoming patrol: we were, after all, heading into enemy-controlled waters, steaming perhaps over seven thousand miles entirely unsupported, when a breakdown or defect could be fatal, and running out of water or fuel meant disaster. The possibility of being captured by the Japanese gave little comfort, because it was well known that captives such as airmen and submariners did not need to be accounted for and could be disposed of quite easily. Apart from this, there were the usual hazards of being attacked... and being mined or bombed, apart from going aground.

Our aircrews had similar problems, but they completed their operations within hours, while we spent weeks over ours: I always had deep respect for men who flew far into enemy territory in very vulnerable aircraft, but I envied them the ability to sit down to a good breakfast on the home airfield the next morning (if they got back).

To offset this fleeting unease in wartime, we were doing something very positive to finish the war by defeating the Japanese. They had wrongly occupied territory not their own by any argument, and had behaved appallingly while doing so. Facing a bit of danger to further their destruction seemed reasonable, and we all went to sea determined to do this. Luckily there was no Health and Safety Executive to attempt to unseat our resolve.[31]

CHAPTER FOUR

WORLD WAR

Clockwise: Indian soldiers fraternising with the local civilians during the Italian campaign of 1944.•
Shortages of men for essential jobs led to appeals for women to take over these vital roles.• American soldier
John J. Lawson collects some eggs from Mrs Annie Northover in Burton Bradstock, Dorset.

WOMEN'S SERVICES

In order to release men for front-line duty, women were provided with an unprecedented opportunity to undertake a variety of military roles. The largest of the women's services was the Auxiliary Territorial Service (ATS), with more than 250,000 members throughout the war. When it was formed in 1938, the only jobs available were as cooks, clerks, storekeepers or drivers, yet war brought over a hundred different roles, including manning anti-aircraft batteries.

By 1943 the Women's Auxiliary Air Force (WAAF) could boast 182,000 members, who worked on the maintenance of aircraft, weather reporting and intelligence. Women also volunteered for the Women's Royal Naval Service (WRNS), First Aid Nursing Yeomanry (FANY) or Women's Voluntary Service (WVS), while others served in Civil Defence, the National Fire Service, Air Transport Auxiliary (ATA) or as military nurses. Conscription was introduced for women in December 1941, when they were given the choice of either joining one of these auxiliary services or working in industry.

Sybella Stiles enlisted as a driver for the Mechanised Transport Corps, a voluntary civilian organisation recognised by the government. She wrote the following letter to her future husband in November 1940 to inform him of her arrival in far-off Pretoria.

Mrs Sherington of Number 3 Company standing by her Peugeot van.

Begun Nov 12th, finished Nov 17th [1940]

Dear Denis

I never thought I should be writing to you from Africa. Maybe your mother told you I had joined up to come to Kenya as an ambulance driver.

There seems so much to say since I last wrote that it is difficult to condense. But the circumstances all seemed to lead up to leaving Stone's of which I was beginning to feel fed up with and the ARP who did not seem to want part-timers and life in general so that when I saw an advertisement in the *Evening Standard* that women drivers were wanted for Kenya I jumped at it and went to enrol the next day. There were various preliminaries such as a driving test on car and ambulance which I took then and there.

Then I was asked to go up one evening for an interview or so I was led to believe. It turned out to be a test, part practical – putting together a spring clothes peg, an electric torch, a car plug (I didn't even realise it was a plug) and a bicycle bell and electric light plug thing. I worked on the principal that it was correct if it fitted and got it all done. I rang the bell loudly and switched on the torch. However the next part of the test was a written paper with simple questions but a time limit to each page and you never had time to finish before the woman in charge said turn over. The questions were easy if you didn't get rattled, such as a child could do. But I believe they use these tests even for pilots for intelligence. Anyhow I felt so depressed after that I felt sure I should not get through, though actually after I heard I had done well, as Helen one of my friends I have made in the Corps said she saw the list as those high up were watched to see if they'd make NCO's. We then had about three days to get things ready to go to a training camp in Herts. It was divine like a summer holiday and I never thought I'd get one. We were under canvas and I had taken my own tent and shared it with Helen who was then a stranger but luckily we get on very well together.

The MTC is not really Government and is different from FANYs and ATS but we wear khaki which I always swore I wouldn't and now I realise what a passport it is I put up with it. But we had to buy our own uniform and did not get paid till we got here.

At camp both Helen and I were made Deputy Head Drivers to learn to be a Head Driver, and then in London we had a week's course rather interrupted by air raids learning about car insides and having lectures on tropical hygiene by Professor Buxton who was both good and entertaining.

The voyage was a mixture of good fun, boredom, annoyance and illness (of a sight kind)... The boat was crowded, many of the passengers being women and children so until the warmth made it possible to use the decks all the time it was very crowded in the smoking room. We were drilled, lectured and inspected as well as leading a normal boat life. I had the horrid and impossible job as HD of finding and seeing that all my sub-section of which there are 13 were always there when they should be. It is not easy to find a person on board as there are too many places to look.

Do write to me as I believe Kenya is the one place from where letters don't take too long.

Much love and all the best

From Sybe[32]

GREECE

Nazi Germany's territorial expansion across Europe was envied by their fascist ally Italy. The Italian leader Benito Mussolini regarded much of south-eastern Europe and the Mediterranean as lying within Italy's sphere of influence, and therefore targeted Greece as a candidate for invasion. He was anxious to prove that Italy could match the military successes of the German army.

Italian forces began to invade Greece on 28 October 1940, but the Greek army proved to be a formidable opponent and successfully held off the invaders by taking advantage of mountainous terrain. A counter-attack with the aid of Allied troops forced the Italians into retreat, and by mid-December the Greek army had even occupied a significant part of neighbouring Italian-occupied Albania.

RAF ground crews assemble in lorries outside Athens before travelling to a port in southern Greece for evacuation.

Their success was to be short-lived, however. On 6 April 1941, Germany came to the aid of Italy and invaded Greece through Bulgaria and Yugoslavia. Greek and British troops fought back, but were overwhelmed. Athens was captured on 27 April and the rest of Greece was soon under Axis occupation.

Winifred Bowman received the following letter from her husband, a Captain in the Royal Army Medical Corps. Attached to the Royal Artillery in Greece, he describes the fighting that his unit experienced prior to their evacuation.

April 1941

The last fight was a good scrap, though their planes were a nuisance. We were able to stand and fight and inflict casualties before moving on, according to plan. A lovely place in an entirely gracious country, we must visit after the war. Whistle down in a car, along roads that Hitler will build for us. The road ran along a narrow coastal strip flanked by hills and mountains. Sometimes just beside the water, dead clear as it rippled over grey pebbles, pine trees near; sometimes flat land edged by tall rush. We first hitched up in a good olive orchard. Magnificent cover, where Jerry couldn't see us but he came along, systematically, each bomber going another mile along the coast wise strip. Rather dull. We being in the path of their passage, had to lie down and take cover every ten minutes, when we would have liked to have done something, or nothing, or sleep. I tired of the business and laid a blanket in a shallow trench, where I could watch him and write up my diary, which had got behind hand. Quite difficult remembering what happened two hours or two days ago.

One lucky bomb hit one of our ammunition lorries that caught fire and the shells started popping off 150 yards away. Not really disturbing, but each shell made an embarrassing puff of smoke, that a Jerry bomber lolled down to see and circle. However he must have been bored or forgotten to mention it, for we didn't receive any particular attention. No one hurt, so went for a swim in a stream that coursed down a fissure in the mountain face. Found the water chilly, but sat in the sun and contemplated the figs and Oleanders growing wild. And some white faces, that thought the ravine a quiet spot.

German Panzer III tanks advance along a railway line in pursuit of retreating British troops in Greece, April 1941.

One dealfish lad had been by the lorry when it was hit, and as he couldn't hear the swish of the bomb, hadn't had any preliminary notice and taken a good fright. His face was in the leaves and his hands held by two, over-sympathetic friends. I went and talked to him, slapped him on the chest, and he cheered up and was well enough later. Curious how good the officer class is under fire and how important it is for them to set an example, even to the point of foolishness. And they will always do it. There are no exceptions.

Rather sad this retreat. We felt that we were failing a rather gallant people. We remembered how they had greeted us and our march up, and the flowers thrown in the road; the bay and thyme decorating our trucks. If one wanted a drink in a little poor village, up popped some men who refused to let one pay. You nosed into a shop for matches, and there were some soldiers there, and it was impossible to escape having a drink at three in the afternoon, though I hate drinking then, and feel sleepy and heady for the rest of the day.[33]

Australian troops occupy a front-line position at Tobruk, 13 August 1941.

THE SIEGE OF TOBRUK

Colonial interests remained vital throughout the war, with the key strategic prize in North Africa being the Suez Canal, located in British-occupied Egypt. An initial Italian attack on Egypt on 13 September 1940 was repelled by the British, who then advanced into Libya, but the arrival of German reinforcements at the beginning of 1941 drove the Allies into retreat.

A small garrison consisting mainly of the 9th Australian Division, along with British tanks and artillery, remained in Eastern Libya at the port of Tobruk while the Allies reorganised and prepared a counter-offensive. Tobruk was strategically important for any Axis advance into Egypt, and in April 1941 the German Field Marshal Erwin Rommel made its capture a main objective.

Throughout the siege of Tobruk, the garrison had to cope with constant artillery and air bombardment, and ever-decreasing supplies of food and water – not to mention the overwhelming heat and constant sickness. Yet morale remained high. Finally, the heavy losses sustained by the Germans led to their temporary withdrawal, and on 27 November the port was finally relieved by the British Eighth Army.

Present during the siege was Brigadier Robert Daniell of the Royal Horse Artillery; his 107th South Nottinghamshire Hussars were among the artillery units defending Tobruk.

During the siege, the Germans made three determined attacks on the Perimeter. The first one took place on Easter Monday. The previous night their engineers flattened out the anti-tank wall for about 100 yards. As soon as dawn broke, half a dozen brand new Mark IV tanks approached, each tank carried a machine-gun crew who very efficiently dropped off and set up their machine guns, awaiting an expected counter-attack. They need not have worried, no-one had any intention of staging a counter-attack! It was left to the guns of 1 RHA and the South Notts Hussars as a horde of lorry-borne German Panzer troopers approached, they opened fire, it was devastating. The lorries just disintegrated, the troopers were obliterated. With great bravery, several hundred more made a hopeless attempt to pass through. One of the Mark IVs was burning furiously, a very pleasant sight – the others had disappeared.

The Navy, of course, were a godsend to us. On the four dark nights of the month, they ran the gauntlet from Alexandria bringing letters, ammunition and a few reinforcements. The destroyer only stayed in the harbour for 20 minutes – on one side the wounded were slung aboard, whilst on the other, boxes of all sorts were shot down a chute into small boats. I was lucky, I had met several of their commanders in Alexandria, they invariably brought with them a sealed two gallon tin, filled with very welcome whisky, food and clean clothes, carefully packed by my wife and clearly marked 'Nails of all sizes' to delude the wandering Australians. I only lost one to a looter. I then repaired to the wardroom and downed all the whisky I could before dejectedly throwing myself down the chute.

Then there was a magnificent old sea captain, who probably stole an Egyptian Nile Dhow. It took him a month to crawl along the coast but he always arrived with a plentiful supply of cigarettes, letters and chocolate from the NAAFI. On his last trip, the old Dhow was driven ashore at Marsa Matruh and the Germans got his shipload but kindly sent him and his crew back to Alexandria.

The weather was on the whole brilliant and sunny though every now and then fierce sand-storms tore northwards from deep in the Sahara bringing every movement to a dead halt. The days passed by and the months passed by, more and more crosses appeared in the cemetery. Great hopes were raised by the 1 June attempted relief. A force was prepared to break out and join them. The result was disastrous, all the precious new tanks straight out from England were easily out-powered by Rommel's Panzers and utterly destroyed. Boredom, fatigue, lack of fresh food aided by acute jaundice, took a heavy toll. The future seemed hopeless.[34]

Polish, British, Indian, Australian and Czech soldiers (from left to right)
stand side by side in Tobruk, 22 October 1941.

PEARL HARBOR

Just before 8.00am on the morning of Sunday, 7 December 1941, the Imperial Japanese Navy Air Service carried out a surprise bombing raid on the American naval base at Pearl Harbor, Hawaii. Hundreds of Japanese aircraft attacked in two waves. Of the eight US Navy battleships present at the base, four were sunk and the others badly damaged, along with many other ships that would have seen deployment in the event of war. One hundred and eighty-eight US aircraft were also destroyed, with 2,403 Americans killed and 1,178 wounded.

The damage inflicted on the Pacific Fleet was intended to prevent its immediate response to a number of other coordinated assaults by Japan on both United States and British-held territories in the Pacific. These included invasions of Malaya, Singapore and Hong Kong. The day following the attack, 8 December, marked the formal entry of the United States into the Second World War.

Melville Troy, an American businessman living in London, received a number of letters from relatives keeping him up to date with war news from across the Atlantic. The following letter provides an account of the Pearl Harbor attack.

US President Franklin D. Roosevelt signs the declaration of war against Japan following the aerial bombardment of Pearl Harbor in December 1941.

Greensboro, NC

Jan 27, 1943

Dear Corona

Have I written you since Elizabeth got home from Honolulu? I have written all about it so many times I can't remember whether I wrote you, or not, but I hardly think I have. Honolulu is eleven miles from Pearl Harbor. She said that Sunday morning they were almost shaken out of their beds by the bombing (you know something of that) but at first they thought it was just the usual practice, then she heard someone on the street cry, 'this is not practice but the regular thing, the Japs are really here'.

I suppose you have read in the papers all about the findings of the investigation? You know there are so many Japs in Hawaii and so many of them are not American citizens. Those that were just telling Japan everything about the army and navy, where all the ships were and everything. Of course if they had been on the alert this couldn't have happened but they just thought that they had such a fine army and navy that Hawaii could never be caught. It really is the best fortified place in the world and could not have been caught if the higher ups had been on the job, which they were not.

Most of the bombs fell out at the Army Field and Pearl Harbor. The few that fell in Honolulu fell in the Jap quarter, fortunately. Elizabeth said that she knew only one white person in the city killed and that was down the street where she lived, six blocks, and it happened to be her best friend. This girl had evidently run to the phone to see what was happening, her husband was in the army, and a bomb fell right in the street and a piece of shrapnel went right through the wall, hit her in the chest and killed her immediately, which was fortunate.

E said she would not have come home but all the schools closed and there was no telling when they would open or how many teachers they would need, so she thought she had better get home while she could, not do like Nina, wait until she couldn't. Most of the fleet will be taken up with the army.

She got on a boat. There were three in the convoy, one for tourists, hers, one for the families of the army and navy and one for the wounded from Pearl Harbor. There were four thousand on the three boats. They were led by a big airplane carrier, and the planes were over them all the time, then on each side there were two big battleships. Said there might have been more but that is what she could see. All the time over they had to keep on their life belts for they knew the subs were in the waters between Hawaii and the coast. It took them six days and nights to get over and it was a nerve-wracking time...

Amilie[35]

The USS Shaw *explodes in dry dock at Pearl Harbor. A huge fireball rises after her forward magazine detonates.*

THE FALL OF SINGAPORE

The island of Singapore, located at the southern tip of the Malay Peninsula, was essential to the British as a military base designed to protect their colonial and economic interests in the Far East. As a military fortress it was considered impregnable, and Britain therefore placed greater importance on her naval presence in the region than on defending the island of Singapore itself.

Almost concurrent with their attack on Pearl Harbor, Japanese forces began to invade Malaya on 8 December 1941. While this attack was initially resisted by the British Indian Army and other Empire troops, the speed and ferocity of the invaders meant that they quickly swept southwards. Singapore's main naval force sailed north to oppose enemy landings along the Malayan coast, but was sunk by Japanese aircraft on 10 December.

Forced into retreat, the final British forces reached Singapore on 31 January 1942. Destruction of the causeway linking the island to the mainland delayed the Japanese for over a week, but their invasion proper began on 8 February. Having both air and sea superiority, the Japanese victory was swift, and Singapore fell on 15 February. As the largest military surrender in their history, it remained a massive humiliation for the British Empire.

Smoke billows from bombed buildings on Kallang airfield after a Japanese air raid on Singapore, February 1942.

The following desperate letter was written by Brigadier Lucas to his wife. He was based at Malaya Command Headquarters, and this letter was composed on the very day Singapore surrendered.

15 Feb 1942

My most beloved Irene

The luck is up at last and we have sent in a flag of truce as the water supply is running short – has failed in many places – because Chinatown has been so bombed and shelled that the pipes are all broken and the ruins prevent them being mended. Also the Chinese civilians have had very heavy casualties and it is just murder to go on any longer. Our poor hospitals have had an awful time too. As we closed in more and more on the town we had to move them back and back and even then they were under fire as well as bombs. At present the front line is between Gillman and Alex. Changi and Selarang had to come back quite early on. Tyresall Park was burnt out – frightful. My chaps have played up awfully well and nothing has broken down, thank God. The troops are very tired but still fighting in spite of continuous dive bombing and machine gunning.

The Navy and the Air Force are all gone. They managed to take some technical experts and staff officers with them. All the heads of branches and services stayed. I sent Palmer, Cols Brown and Taylor and Major Heathcote. I hope they will arrange to rescue us soon!

I moved into the office about five days ago as I had a battery on either side of Tanglin house and things were getting a bit noisy. I shot Whiskey who knew nothing; paid off the servants; and brought in my bedding, a suitcase and later retrieved my tin uniform case. Whether the Jap will let me keep any of it I don't know. If he does I will be well off as I have got everything I want including soap, medicines, bandages, etc. Ah Kee very gallantly agreed to stay with me and has been looking after me and waiting in the mess, which we brought to Canning from Sime Road the day I left Tanglin. Sime Road was on fire as a result of enemy fire a few hours after the General left. Singapore has been a bit depressing lately with fires from burning dumps and depots all over the place.

15 Feb 42.

7, ROYAL ROAD,
ALEXANDRA,
SINGAPORE.

My most beloved Irene

The truce is up at last & we have sent in a flag of truce as the water supply is running short — has failed in many places — because China Town has been so bombed & shelled that the pipes are all broken & the ruins prevent them being mended. Also the chinese civilians have had very heavy casualties and it is just murder to go on any longer. Our poor hospitals have had an awful time too. As we closed in more and more on the Town we had to move them back & back & even then they were under fire as well as bombs. At present the front line is between Gillman and Alex. Changi & Selarang had to come back

The Japs, I think, intend to use Fort Canning as they haven't shelled it yet though they have been putting them past each side and over continuously. However I have managed to sleep very well most nights and am very well in myself.

Well old darling take care of yourself and the kids and don't worry about me. God has been extraordinarily kind to me and I'm sure he will go on looking after me... If this gets to you it will be a marvel and a good omen... Keep your chin up and your faith in God. Goodbye for the present my darling.

God bless you and the kids.

Your ever loving Hoodie[36]

ESCAPE FROM SINGAPORE

Those able and willing to escape the island of Singapore had limited opportunities to do so, but the only alternative was to enter captivity, spending the rest of the war behind wire and subject to the harsh treatment dispensed by the invaders. As Japanese troops landed on the island and pressed forward to seize key locations, it was a matter of hours before time ran out and formal surrender was the only option.

Colonel W. F. Page of the 2nd Battalion Cambridgeshire Regiment helped to organise an officially sanctioned escape party, who sought to flee the island shortly before Singapore fell to the Japanese. After an arduous journey, including surviving a submarine attack en route, Page's group eventually arrived in Ceylon, allowing him to take part in the campaign to retake Burma (now called Myanmar).

Japanese troops march through Fullerton Square, Singapore.

Sunday 15th [February 1942]

Awoke to a perfect rain of bombs at daybreak, large formations of Jap planes in perfect formation were dropping bombs from an immense height, not bothering where they went apparently.

By about 11 o'clock I had found a practically burnt out ship in Empire Dock with two sound lifeboats aboard. I accordingly took a party along and launched one – in the middle of which we were shelled again for about a quarter of an hour. We rowed the boat round to where we were and started stocking it up with food and water. We filled patrol cans and almost everything we could find with water, and laid in a stock of tinned food, vast quantities of which could be found in the warehouses quite unguarded. By 2 o'clock all was ready – we had even decided where people were to sit – in addition to our 30 there were 6 RAOC men, 3 Indians and 2 others, 41 in all.

There had been air raids and shelling all the morning, most of the town was a cloud of smoke with a few large fires and debris everywhere in the streets – a most awe-inspiring sight and one which I shall always remember.

It was just about 2 o'clock that a Major from the Australians arrived with the news that a full and unconditional capitulation was to take place at 3 o'clock and if we were to get away we had better leave by daylight instead of waiting for darkness and in fact as soon as we could. So we decided to risk being spotted and moved off about 2.30pm. The rowing was far from brilliant, I don't suppose more than half a dozen were used to any form of boating. We rowed eight oars (four each side and two men on each) in half an hour shifts, then changed over.

We had no maps, knew there were mine-fields all around the place, but had no idea where. We decided first of all to make for the island of Samboe, about 10 miles south. This island had been a landmark for nearly a week as big oil containers were blazing. More than once, while up in the north of the island, I had found my bearings at night by the glow from it.

The hand of Providence was most certainly with us. We saw numbers of enemy planes but they were all too intent on finishing off their work on the town. The last we saw of Singapore island was a positive inferno of flame and smoke, we could still see the glow a day later. The sea was very awkward in places, very choppy near the harbour bar, and pretty strong currents running between the islands. At times we were tossing like a walnut shell, and many a rower had to lean over the side![37]

Lieutenant General Arthur Percival and his party carry the Union Jack on their way to surrender Singapore to the Japanese, 15 February 1942.

THE RETREAT FROM BURMA

Following their successes in Malaya, in January 1942 the Japanese army invaded Burma. The vast Burmese frontier was defended by only two under-strength British battalions, two Indian Army infantry brigades and local Burmese forces. The Japanese invaders advanced rapidly, using their already proven knowledge of jungle warfare and tactics of infiltration.

Japanese troops enter Rangoon station, Burma, in January 1942.

British reinforcements began to arrive, but too late to prevent the fall of Burma's capital city, Rangoon. British and Empire forces under Generals Alexander and Slim began the long and arduous retreat to India. In what became the longest fighting withdrawal in the history of the British Army, the retreating troops faced sickness and disease, having to traverse dense jungle and poor roads while under constant attack by Japanese aircraft. Thousands of civilian refugees were also fleeing northwards to India to escape the threat of Japanese occupation. The last stragglers finally reached Imphal in India in May 1942.

In a memoir written some years after the war, Captain John Hedley described how the 4th Battalion Burma Rifles participated in the general retreat in the face of the Japanese invasion.

Burmese refugees flee along the Prome Road into India, January 1942.

We woke up on the morning of 22nd Feb to the realisation that we had a river behind us but a bridge with two rather important gaps in it! It had by now, of course, been decided that we should withdraw across the river, and the method was quite correct. A box was to be held, while troops got across, and the last troops were to get across the following night. We were to hold on until 7.30 pm.

During the day there was some shelling and sniping by the Japs, but the most unpleasant experience was to see a Jap bomber come over and see the blasted bombs all the way down! A great friend and brother officer of mine, Capt Gemmell was lying beside me, and I thought it was all over. The first was 100 yards short, the second 50 and the third SIX!! Luckily the bombs were diggers and so went in before exploding, otherwise that also might have interfered with the production of this manuscript! By 1pm there were only about 20 of us left in our particular sector, as a large number of troops had been withdrawn and not a few, of all sorts, had withdrawn themselves! However, there were no Japanese attacks, partly because I don't think they were interested after they had failed to save the bridge and partly because we were too far to the Jap left. We did, however, have one incident and I was able to observe one of the most calculatedly brave acts I've ever seen.

During the afternoon we saw a Jap patrol at a range of about 500 yards. They were gloriously outlined against a grass bank and, better still, bunched up to have a confabulation about future patrol policy. We had a Kachin Jemadar of my battalion who was a fine shot, and with one long burst of a Bren he got the whole lot bar one. Did that man beat it? Did he hell. He nipped halfway up the bank and SAT DOWN!!! We fired one shot – a foot left, another – a foot right – a burst – all right – another burst – low. Then and then alone did he beat it, and within three minutes we had grenade dischargers firing at us and had to move. He was NOT going to move till he knew where our LMG was, and he was prepared to offer his own body as a SITTING TARGET in order to find out!![38]

A group photograph of civilian internees in the Far East.

SEPARATION AND LOSS

One of the worst aspects of captivity for those falling into Japanese hands was a lingering uncertainty regarding the fate of friends and loved ones. Those serving in the military became prisoners of war, and were almost always held separately from civilian internees. Families and couples were usually separated and, despite sometimes being imprisoned quite near to each other, might remain unaware of one another's circumstances.

Kenneth Stevens was serving with the 1st Battalion of the Straits Settlement Volunteer Force at the time of his capture in Singapore. During his captivity in Pasir Panjang camp, he wrote a number of letters addressed to his wife, Penelope, who had fled Singapore with their young son before the invasion, hoping that they had managed to reach safety despite his own fate. Tragically, Stevens would die in August 1943 while still in Japanese hands.

October 30th 1942

Penelope my darling

It is only this week, after all this time, that definite news has come in that Bonsteads recently broadcast from home that all the wives of their staff arrived safely in Empire countries. You did say that you and Margaret and Daphne were going to keep together so that it seems now reasonable to hope that you really are safe. What you must have been thro' before you got properly away from this place must have been appalling – if I am right about it, I think you were on the ship that was bombed and went aground close to an island from where you were rescued the next day and taken to Sumatra, from which I hope you got away to India.

The whole time must have been utterly terrifying and what makes me feel even worse about it is that since the capitulation I have never been in any danger and have not even been made unduly uncomfortable – when I compare my experiences with yours it makes anything I say about loving you and caring for you seem so hopelessly untrue. It is awfully difficult to write to you about all those things when it was my stupidity and blindness that kept you here in Singapore when I never for a moment should have run the risk of your staying. So, darling, if I write as if you and our beautiful Christopher are together and happy, don't think that I am forgetful of what you have been thro' – its only that I *must* go on thinking of you two as well and safe, otherwise this being away from you would be unbearable...[39]

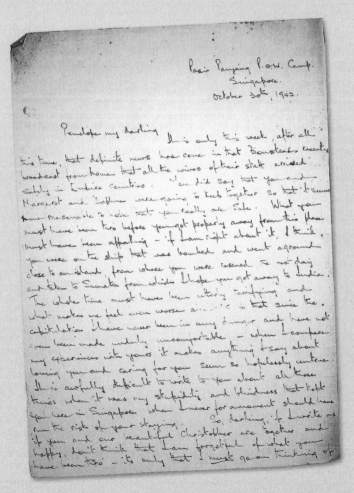

AMERICAN INVOLVEMENT

Until the Japanese attack on Pearl Harbor in December 1941, the United States had maintained an official policy of neutrality, despite supplying Britain, the Soviet Union and China with war supplies through their Lend-Lease scheme.

This changed in 1942, when America began to fight the war in the Pacific against the Japanese. In addition, the first US soldiers began to arrive in Britain, with their contingent forming the bulk of more than two million Allied troops stationed in readiness for deployment by March 1944. The US Army Air Forces based in Britain would also engage in bombing missions over German cities, factories and transportation links. American infantry saw action to a limited degree in Operation 'Torch', the Allied invasion of French North Africa in November 1942, and many were deployed alongside British soldiers in Italy the following year.

The biggest contribution of US troops outside the Pacific, however, would be the D-Day invasion of Normandy on 6 June 1944 and subsequent campaign in north-west Europe. Robert Ware, a surgeon with the 116th Infantry Regiment, US Army, left for England in the troopship *Queen Mary* in September 1942. He wrote the following letter to comfort his family upon his departure. Ware would be one of the first troops to land on Omaha beach on D-Day, only to be killed in action.

Sept 15, 1942

Dear Popa

Received your letter today and was very glad to hear from you. I have been expecting all this to happen for several months, and now it is on the verge of coming true. We don't know when we will leave home, nor where nor when we will sail, nor where we will sail to. But we do know that it won't be long.

I don't feel so bad about going, not near so bad as I thought I would. I was so afraid that Martha wouldn't be able to take it, but thus far she has done

Sept 15, 1942

Dear Popa -

Received your letter today and
was very glad to hear from you.
I have been expecting all this to happen
for several months, and now it is on
the verge of coming true. We don't know
when we will leave here, nor where nor
when we will sail, nor where we will
sail to. But we do know that it wont
be long.

I don't feel so bad about going,
not near as bad as I thought I would.
I was so afraid that Martha wouldn't be
able to take it, but then for she has
done right well. Of course we have no
idea of how long we will be gone.
Even a year is a long time to be away
from home.

I don't know how often I will
be able to write, but will write
Martha as often as possible, and youall
can get the news from her.

right well. Of course we have no idea of how long we will be gone. Even a year is a long time to be away from home. I don't know how often I will be able to write, but will write Martha as often as possible, and you all can get the news from her.

We don't think of the possibilities of *not* coming back, everyone assures himself that he *will* come back. Of course that is a false assurance, but it helps most of the time, but occasionally the other thoughts creep in.

I am so glad that Martha came down when she did. However I hate for her to know when the last time I will see her will be – and she probably won't know. I probably won't know myself. I have always hated to tell *anyone* good-bye. The baby has grown to be so pretty; each time I see him I wonder how big he will be when I come back. I can be sure that they will have subsistence while I'm gone, because I have made an allotment to her. The govt will send her a check each month.

… Well there isn't much else to say. I'll be glad when it's all over. However I am glad in a way that I will be doing my share.[40]

Robert Ware's war grave.

Two British prisoners of war work on the land at Ube prison camp in Japan, supervised by a Japanese guard.

FAR-EASTERN PRISONERS OF WAR

Early successes in Japan's campaign in the Far East resulted in over 190,000 British and Empire troops being taken prisoner. Japan's treatment of its captives was harsh; circumstances varied from camp to camp, but in the worst locations prisoners might suffer under terrible conditions.

Most prisoners of war struggled to survive on a poor diet of rice and vegetables, which often led to severe malnutrition and disease. Food parcels sent by the Red Cross were deliberately withheld by the Japanese and forced labour was common, as were regular punishments for even the most minor breach of the camp rules.

Yet prisoners worked together in order to get through the horrendous experience as best they could. Many shared their meagre rations or risked their lives to barter for extra food outside the camps, while rudimentary medical care was provided by prisoner doctors. Despite such sterling efforts, British and Empire prisoners in the Far East were seven times more likely to die than those captured in Europe.

Peter Lucy was imprisoned in Changi, having been captured at the surrender of Singapore, but soon transferred to a forced labour party in order to work for the Japanese. The following account of his captivity was written after liberation.

8th Sept 1945

... On 16th May 1942 I was sent to Blakang Mati, which as you may remember is a small island (a fortress in our time) about half a mile off the Singapore Harbour front. Our working party comprised about 250 English, mostly FMS Volunteer Forces, and 250 Australians. We were housed in barracks previously occupied by Indian troops, in reinforced concrete buildings which had resisted the heavy bombing pretty well, and we were fortunate in having running water, showers and WCs though overcrowding again was very bad and for the first nine months we had no lighting. However we had a sound roof over our heads, even if we did have to sleep on bare concrete floors, and also the food situation was very much better that at Changi – at first – chiefly because we were given unlimited rice.

We soon found that we were expected to WORK for our living, literally, and Work we did, with a capital 'W', for the next three years and three months; in the main our labours consisted of moving bombs and oil drums backwards and forwards, forwards and backwards, on to the island, off the island, and all over the island all the time being driven on by sadistic Japanese guards. There were, however, a hundred and one other jobs we were called upon to do, cutting grass, digging up the land, making roads, cleaning drains (even cleaning Japanese lavatories), cutting firewood, clearing the jungle, digging pits, carting rice, coal, cement, bricks, timber (in fact anything capable of being carried on the shoulders or in the hands), also all the more menial tasks... sweeping and washing, cleaning, fetching and carrying – in fact, our degradation was complete.

Over us the whole time stood the Japanese soldier, bombastic, taunting, ignorant of the first ideas of decency, cruel, sadistic and, worst of all, empowered to beat a prisoner insensible *without having to answer to anyone for it*. AND I need not say that he took full advantage of his position.

Such was the state of affairs for 39 long, weary months and as time progressed, so the food got worse and worse, and less and less, until it was unbelievable that men could exist on the rations, let alone do hard manual labour, yet we did and survived, so capable is the body of adapting itself to changing conditions. During this time we were allowed no recreation and no entertainment and, to start with, were given one day off every fortnight: this was reduced to half a day off every fortnight with working hours of dawn to dusk (12–13 hours).

The past two weeks have seemed like a dream, knowing that the nightmare of the last three and a half years is over...[41]

A prisoner of war at Changi, Singapore, uses a home-made radio set. If caught by the Japanese, he would face the death penalty.

THE BURMA–THAILAND RAILWAY

Japan relied on the sea to transport supplies to its armies in Burma, but this involved following a long 2,000-mile route around the Malay Peninsula, which was highly vulnerable to Allied attack. To avoid this, they decided to construct a railway linking Bangkok in Thailand to Rangoon in Burma. Work began on building the line in June 1942, with the vast majority of manpower being provided by Allied prisoners of war and co-opted civilian labourers.

For a prisoner of war in the Far East, escape was virtually impossible. Most camps were located hundreds of miles from friendly territory, and captives were far too undernourished to be capable of surviving for long in the harsh jungle. From 1942 until the end of the war, over 60,000 British Empire and Dutch prisoners worked on the railway. Some 16,000 ultimately died, although the death toll among the 270,000 civilians from Thailand, Malaya, Burma and the Dutch East Indies (now Indonesia) who were also forced to work on the project proved to be even higher, with over 100,000 losing their lives.

Captured while serving in the Federated Malay States Volunteer Forces, Alfred Faber was assigned to a working party in October 1942 to assist in the construction of the Burma–Thailand Railway. His experience was typical of that shared by many prisoners of war in the Far East.

Allied prisoners of war construct the Tamarkan bridge over the Kwai Noi River. At this stage the bridge site is covered in scaffolding made from bamboo.

5th October 1945

My dear Hal

... Early in December we moved downstream a little to a camp called Kanu which was roughly 150 kilometres north of Nom-Pladuk where the new railway was being built to Burma. At this time the Other Ranks were building a day weather road near where the Railway would be, but officers only had to do camp work. About February '43 work in earnest started on our section of the line. And an officer's battalion was formed and forced to work. This pleased the Jap 'cooliso' so much that we were given more work and treated more harshly than the OR working parties. Apparently the work was behind schedule, and in addition to that we had about the worst section to deal with as it involved blasting long stretches of rock. The old Kanu camp which was on the River was evacuated, and a new camp started on higher ground where the line would pass; later two subsidiary camps Kanu 2 and 3 were opened, being a few miles north or south of our main camp respectively.

At this stage most people were pretty weak owing to lack of proper food, and a large number had dysentery, fever, tropical ulcers, etc. but the death roll had been light. Now came the period which killed people off like flies. We were worked from an hour before dawn until any time up to 3am the following morning. Food was still only rice and you were driven out whether well or sick. This lasted in this section until about September '43, by which time the Railway had got past us. Our accommodation was leaky huts, and there were practically no washing facilities even if we had ever been in camp during daylight. Also it was the monsoon time.

I collapsed completely with bad dysentery at the end of March. There was a so-called hospital area at Kanu 1, but no drugs and no equipment. Early in April a tent was put up for the worst dysentery cases, so as to isolate them from the rest, and I was the first inmate! The tent should have held about ten, but actually always had 16 in it, and conditions there defy description. No equipment and no light at night, and the occupants lying up against each other. The average time of survival was four days in the tent, and every morning about four corpses were lying among us. In addition to dysentery,

I also had malaria while in the tent, and cellulitis in one leg! Needless to say, I was counted as dead and news reached other camps that I was dead, but that was not the case and about the middle of May I was evacuated by lorry to Tarsao further down river where conditions were better...

My love and thanks to you all.

Alfred[42]

Alfred Faber

Shrewsbury Cottage.
Wellington.
Nilgiris.
5ᵉ October 1945.

my dear Hal,

The time has now arrived when I must attempt to collect my thoughts & give you a precised account of the past, present & future! I am addressing it to you but it is intended for all members of the family as I see no point in writing the same letter, with only slight modifications, to about ten different people; — I only hope that this one will not be too disjointed!!

Obviously, I cannot attempt to give you a detailed account of the last 3½ years, as that would be tantamount to writing a book, so you'll have to be satisfied with a very brief outline.

The last week or so before Singapore fell was truly terrible: continuous air-raids which were virtually unopposed, & continuous shelling. Half the town seemed to be on fire (there was so much smoke you could hardly see the sun), dead & dying everywhere, the water supply cut off, & complete

THE INDIAN ARMY

The British Empire's Indian Army, responsible for the defence of its colonial interests, began the war as a moderate force of just under 200,000 men. By the end of the conflict, it had grown into the largest volunteer army in history, numbering over 2.5 million in August 1945.

Throughout the war, the Indian Army fought on three continents. While they saw service in Ethiopia, North Africa and Italy, their main contribution was to fight against the Japanese Army: first during the British defeats in Malaya and the retreat from Burma to the Indian border, and then during the successful advance back into Burma. Involvement in these campaigns cost the lives of over 87,000 Indian servicemen, while another 34,354 were wounded, and 67,340 became prisoners of war.

Lieutenant Anthony Morris was a junior officer with the 5th Battalion of the 10th Baluch Regiment. Initially stationed on the North-West Frontier of India, he wrote home to his girlfriend's younger sister to tell her about life in the Indian Army.

28/9/41

Dear Sally

I just thought you might like a letter. I'm an officer at last, you see, after training for 6 months at Bangalore, and I've been lucky enough to get into Daddy's old regiment.

The Khyber Pass is a road about 31 miles long which joins India and Afghanistan, and it goes through some of the barest and rockiest country in the world. The pass is very narrow most of the way and there are very steep, high hills of absolutely bare brown rock on both sides. The people who live here are called Pathans, and they

Anthony Morris

28/4/41

5/10th Baluch Regt.
Landi Kotal,
N.W.F.P.
India.

Dear Sally,

I just thought you might like a letter. I'm an officer at last, you see, after training for 6 months at Bangalore, and I've been lucky enough to get into Daddy's old regiment. If you want to know where I am now, I'll tell you how to find out. Get hold of a big map of India. Now look right up in the top corner, above a place called the 'Punjab' (I expect you've done it in geography, anyway) and you'll see a place called Peshawar. Then if you look jolly closely you'll see close to Peshawar it marks the 'Khyber Pass', or it ought to anyhow. Almost at the other end of this pass is Landi Kotal, which is a sort of fort, and isn't marked on most atlases. Well, that's where I am. The Khyber Pass is a road about 30 miles

have dozens of different tribes and clans who are always fighting each other unless we stop them. They are tall, fierce-looking men with... moustaches or beards, and they all walk about with rifles. They don't usually dare to shoot at us in the day-time, but they probably would if we went about at night, so at night the road is closed, and nobody can go along it. We all have to stay inside Landi Kotal [their fortified base] after dark too, and there is a barbed wire fence and sentries all round so that no one can come in and steal things. When you want to go a long walk, or take the regiment out for training, or go riding or shooting, you have to take a man called a 'Khassadar' with you. He is just an ordinary tribesman, but he is paid so much a month to guard you from other tribesmen who might like to take a pot-shot at you. This is all right so long as he doesn't decide to take a pot-shot at you himself! I've drawn some pictures to show you what the men in my regiment look like, and also the tribesmen. A Subedar is a very important person, rather like an English sergeant major, only even more important, and the Subedar-major is very important indeed, more important really than a good many officers like me! Our Subedar-major is called Mustafa Khan, and he has been in the army for 32 years. He has got black hair, but his moustache is dyed red and he looks very fierce. He is very brave indeed,

and he and all the Subedars can remember the time when my father was in the regiment.

In the regiment we have one Company of Pathans and two Companies of Punjabi Mahommedans ('P.M.'s) who are all Mahommedans, and one Company of Dogras, who are Hindus who live in the hills near Kashmir. The Regiment won a big silver cup not so very long ago for being the best regiment in the Indian Army, and we have a very good pipe-and-drum band.

I was lucky to join at this time of year because although it's still pretty warm, the hot weather is over. It's still very dusty though, and it's very hard work climbing about on these steep hills. Lots of them have little tiny forts on top built of stones, called 'sangars', and when they have they are called 'picquets'. They are used as places to watch from to see that the tribesmen don't get mischievous and shoot into Landi Kotal or at people on the road! I don't want to stay here always, though, and I hope we go overseas as soon as possible.

Yours,

Anthony[43]

CHAPTER FIVE

HOLOCAUST

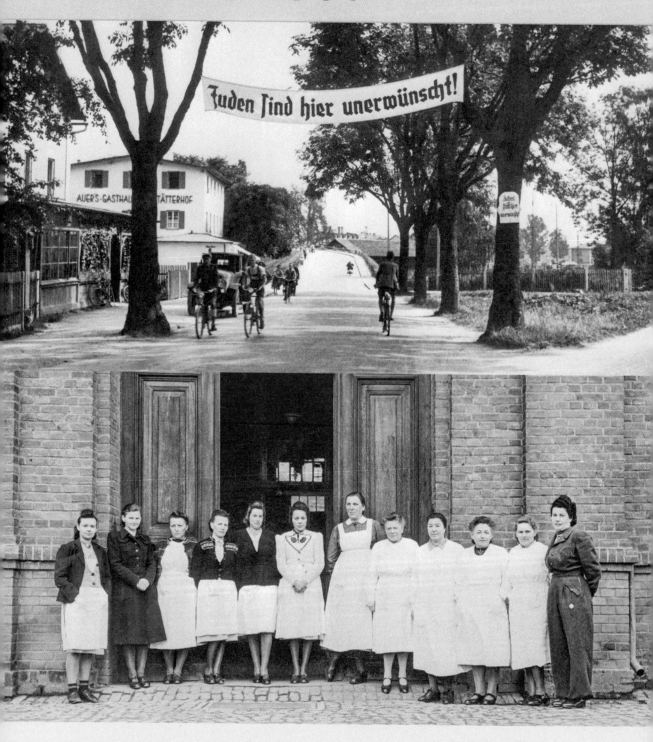

Top: A banner reading 'Jews are not wanted here' hangs over the entrance to the village of Rosenheim in Bavaria. • Bottom: Some of the staff of the euthanasia clinic at Hadamar, Germany, pictured outside the institution after arrival of the US forces, 5 April 1945.

KINDERTRANSPORT

On 9 November 1938, the Nazis staged 'spontaneous' acts of violence against the Jewish communities living throughout Germany. This event became known as *Kristallnacht,* the 'Night of Broken Glass', and served to highlight the level of anti-Semitic persecution that was becoming endemic within Nazi Germany and its annexed territories.

Britain agreed to take in Jewish children fleeing persecution, and in the following weeks and months, nearly 10,000 children arrived in Britain via the *Kindertransport* scheme ('children's transports'). About half of the children were placed with foster families, both Jewish and non-Jewish, while others were grouped together in hostels. In a similar way to the British children who were later evacuated to the countryside, the experience of *Kindertransport* children could vary enormously: while many found valuable

Peter Needham, a Jewish boy from Czechoslovakia (centre), stands with other children at Prague airport before departing on a Kindertransport *flight to Great Britain, 12 January 1939.*

support from their foster parents, others remained deeply unhappy. As the Nazi persecution continued in even harsher ways, most of the children would never see their parents again.

Cecelia Horwitz left Hamburg in Germany on a *Kindertransport* in December 1938. After a brief stay in a quarantine camp (during which she exchanged the letters below with her foster family), Cecelia settled in East London. Cecelia's father died in 1941, but she was reunited with her mother after the war.

Cecelia Horwitz with a canine friend.

January 25, 1939

Dear Cecelia

My Father and Mother have told me that when you come to London you are going to stay with us; I am looking forward to the time as I want to make you feel as if you were at home. My father has seen your brother and he is staying with some very nice people. How do you like the camp where you are and when do you expect to come to London. If you cannot write to me in English write in German and I will get the letter translated. I am 15 years old and have no brothers or sisters.

Best wishes from Mother and Father and myself.

Betty Watts

Dear Betty

I have received your letter and I thank you so much that you have written a letter to me. I am so happy that I can stay with you and your parents near my brother's. I like the camp very much; in the morning we all have three lessons and in the afternoon we can write and do whatever we want. I hope I shall come to London soon but now we are in quarantein [sic] and are not allowed to leave the camp.

Best wishes to your father, your mother and you from

Cecelia Horwitz[44]

PERSECUTION UNDER THE NAZIS

On coming to power, the Nazis began to actively persecute Jews living in German territory through the introduction of discriminatory legislation and vicious anti-Semitic propaganda. With the outbreak of the Second World War, the process escalated and Jews throughout Nazi-controlled Europe came under threat of death, as did other 'undesirables', including political opponents, Roma and Sinti peoples, homosexuals and those with physical or mental disabilities.

While some Jewish families living under the Nazis had been able to take advantage of the *Kindertransport* scheme, there were many more who were forced to remain and suffer the persecution introduced by the regime.

The following letter was written by Liselotte Frensdorff to an American relative. While her husband Kurt had successfully emigrated to the United States, Liselotte and other family members remained in Germany, where they struggled to obtain a travel permit to flee the increasing persecutions. Unsuccessful in their attempts, she and her family were eventually arrested and died in a Nazi death camp.

1 Sept 1941

Hannover

Dear Aunt Jeanette!

I am feeling deeply sorry that I have not heard anything from you for a long time. I am thinking of you and Kurt so much. We are separated two years now, I sometimes cannot imagine that. Please see to my emigration energetically from over there, understand my hurry to come over to you and Kurt. I have always the greatest confidence to you and I am speaking to you like a daughter to her mother. It is not to be conceived to be separated such a long time from my husband who is a piece of myself. I would have born it with Kurt together, but the present condition is unbearable. I know that no other person will understand all as well as you because you are alone too and

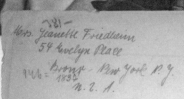

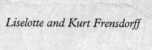

Liselotte and Kurt Frensdorff

Mrs. Jeanette Friedheim
54 Evelyn Place
Bronx - New York N.Y.
N. Y. A.

1. Sept. 1941
Sender: Liselotte Sara Frensdorff
Hannover
Haarsttelsstr. 31
c/o Leonydis

Dear aunt Jeanette! I am feeling deeply sorry that I have not heard anything from you for a long time. I am thinking of you and Kurt so much. We are separated two years now, I sometimes cannot imagine that. Please see to my emigration energetically from over there, understand my hurry to come to you and Kurt. I have always the greatest confidence to you and I am speaking to you like a daughter to her mother. It is not to be conceived to be separated such a long time from my husband who is a piece of myself. I would have born it with Kurt together, but the present condition is unbearable. I know that no other person will understand all as well as you because you are alone too and if one loves the husband so much and as we were always happy, it is all the more difficult. Just now I have helped so many people and am always thinking whether I shall be lucky in coming to you and Kurt. I am feeling that you will not forsake me and putting all my hope and confidence into your hands. Don't forget me and please write to me, I am imploring you with all my heart to do everything for me from over there in order to be united again with Kurt.

Many regards to your dear mother and to yourself.

Yours gratefully
Liselotte

Mein Geliebter! In den bevorstehenden Feiertagen wünsche ich Dir alles erdenklich Gute. Ich bin so sehr über unser Schicksal erschüttert, daß ich keine Worte finde. Wenn

if one loves the husband so much and as we were always happy, it is all the more difficult. Just now I have helped so many people and am always thinking whether I shall be lucky in coming to you and Kurt. I am feeling that you will not forsake me and putting all my hope and confidence into your hands. Don't forget me and please write to me, I am imploring you with all my heart to do everything for me from over there in order to be united again with Kurt.

Many regards to your dear mother and to yourself

Yours gratefully, Liselotte[45]

A German Jewish woman, Dora Francken, standing by notices put up outside a swimming pool at Blaubeuren, Germany, in 1937; one reads 'No entry for Jews', the other 'Dogs not admitted'.

A column of Jews, guarded by German soldiers, is marched through the streets of Warsaw during the winter of 1940.

THE NAZI OCCUPATION OF POLAND

Following their occupation of Poland in September 1939, the Nazis began to impose their strict regime. Squads of *Einsatzgruppen* routinely rounded up and shot Jewish men, women and children, as well as Communist officials and others considered racially or ideologically dangerous. By mid-1941, any surviving Jews had been forced into overcrowded ghettos. The largest of these was located in Warsaw, where 490,000 Jews and a few hundred Roma and Sinti struggled to survive despite extreme hardship.

In larger areas, ghettos resembled prison camps: nobody could enter or leave without a special permit, little food was provided, and diseases such as typhus and tuberculosis were rife. Conditions only worsened once Jews from small towns and other captured territories were squeezed in. It has been estimated that half a million people died in the ghettos from disease and starvation. Many would also perish in nearby slave-labour camps.

The following extract is from a memoir written by Frank Blaichman, a young man living in a Jewish community in Poland at the time of the Nazi invasion.

In December of 1939, the Germans decreed that every Jew over 12 years old had to wear a white Jewish armband with a Star of David. The harassment had just begun. Then the Jews had to put all their money in the bank, retaining only 2,000 zlotys in the house at any time. All Jews had to file a detailed report of their wealth.

The list of forbidden acts grew and grew. Jews were prohibited to assemble for religious services, to travel without a special pass (obtainable only if one worked for the Germans), to engage in business, the arts and teaching. Jewish doctors could not treat non-Jewish patients nor could Jewish lawyers appear in courts.

The Germans targeted the Jewish intellectuals, a group including teachers, artists and musicians, to be the first to suffer. They were rounded up immediately to avert any potential resistance. My uncle, Meyer Levin, was a teacher and *mohel* whom they quickly carted away. Then they began to demand slave labour to work in the fields of the surrounding castles and estates. In the beginning, we were ordered to harvest crops and to do field work twice a week. Then the Germans created work to widen brooks and dry up the wetlands. The only payment we saw was a monthly package of bread, cheese, marmalade and margarine – a package which might last for a week...

In the town, stores were open but were subject to food rationing. No barbed wire surrounded us even though we were in a ghetto. Therefore, we had access to fresh farm food, even though it was officially forbidden. When business was forbidden, I took the risk and travelled to the villages and smuggled food to help my family. I journeyed with neither an armband nor special permission.

In my town, killings were not uncommon. Gendarmes often came unannounced, ostensibly searching for illegal items. When gendarmes detected fresh meat in my uncle Moshe's house, he was taken out and shot behind the local Gentile cemetery. They killed my cousin Brucha because they spotted fresh bread in her home. Family members watched their loved ones being brutally murdered before their very eyes. It was hard to believe that this could get worse, but it did.

We lived from day to day, isolated from the realities we once took for granted. The Germans closed businesses and schools, and tried to divest us of our sense of self. We obtained news only second-hand through rumours from the Gentiles or from the Warsaw Jews who came to us. Life, as we once knew it, was at a standstill.

By the summer of 1942, all remaining Jews realised the fate that awaited them. The Gentiles, travelling freely and transporting the Jews, provided us with more horrible information than we could possibly digest. I knew that at any point I could be deported or sent to a slave labour camp. I grappled with the injustice, and asked everyone the same question – 'Why do they want to murder us?' The answer was always the same. Our sole crime was being born Jewish.[46]

Anti-Jewish grafitti painted on the wall of a Jewish-owned property.

NAZI EUGENICS

Nazism was heavily based on racial beliefs concerning the ideal 'pure' Aryan, which championed the biological improvement of the German people through eugenics, or selective breeding.

This would mean the exclusion of individuals or groups deemed to be 'inferior'. Among those targeted for destruction under Nazi eugenics policies were people with physical or learning disabilities, the 'criminal class', the 'idle or weak', and homosexuals. More than 400,000 people were sterilized against their will, while up to 300,000 were deliberately murdered from September 1939 onwards on the official orders of Hitler.

Dr Ernst Gassen was a medical doctor who fell victim to the Nazi euthanasia policy, as this letter testifies. Although he did not meet any of the criteria outlined above, he seems to have been selected purely on the basis of his criticism of the Nazi regime. Mrs Gassen was informed that her husband had recently died of sickness after being transferred to the state institution at Hartheim, and that his body was cremated immediately to avoid the risk of infection.

10.3.41

Dear Mrs Gassen

We regret to have to inform you that your husband Dr Ernst Gassen died on 10.3.41 of pneumonia and cardio-vascular failure. His transfer to our institution was a war measure and was undertaken for reasons pertaining to the defence of the Reich.

Because our institution is designated as a place of transit for those patients who are destined for another institution in this area, and a stay here is effected only for the purpose of identifying carriers of bacilli (as often occur amongst such patients), the responsible local police authorities in Hartheim have decreed extensive protective measures, in agreement with other parties, to prevent the outbreak and spread of transmissible diseases, and in accordance with article 22 of the Order for the Combatting of Transmissible Diseases have arranged

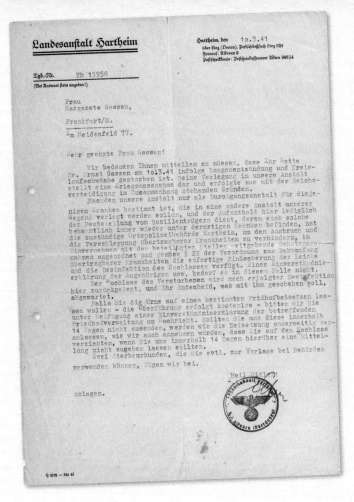

for the immediate cremation of the body and the disinfection of the remaining possessions. In this case the agreement of the next-of-kin etc is not required.

The possessions of the deceased will be retained here following disinfection, and we await your decision regarding their disposal.

Should you wish to place the urn [with the ashes of the deceased] in a particular cemetery (the transfer has no cost to you), we ask that you inform us accordingly, including a declaration of consent from the cemetery administration. If we do not receive this within 14 days, we will make alternative arrangements for the burial, likewise we will assume that you do not wish to have the possessions if we do not hear from you in that regard within 14 days.

We enclose two death certificates which you might wish to present to any relevant authorities.

Heil Hitler![47]

AUSCHWITZ

Located in Nazi-occupied Poland, Auschwitz was originally an army barracks. It was converted in April 1940 to serve as a quarantine camp for Polish political prisoners. From the outset, inmates received incredibly harsh treatment, with beatings, torture and executions being common for the most trivial reasons. Execution of Soviet and Polish prisoners by poison gas began around August 1941. Additional building work then took place to expand the camp to accommodate the huge numbers of Jewish people from all corners of German-occupied Europe, who began to arrive from 1942.

Of the 1.3 million people sent to Auschwitz, all but 200,000 died. Those who were not gassed would usually die of starvation, exhaustion, disease or beatings. Others were killed during medical experiments conducted by Josef Mengele.

Mengele had received doctorates in anthropology and medicine from German universities, and joined the Nazi Party in 1937. At the beginning of the war he was assigned to the SS as a medical officer, and transferred in early 1943 to the Nazi concentration camps service at Auschwitz. There, he found himself with the opportunity to conduct genetic research on unresisting human subjects. His experiments focused mainly on twins, but they were conducted with no regard for the health, safety or physical or emotional suffering of the victims involved. The letter reproduced here, from Dr Johannes Ziegler, indicates a shared interest in Mengele's research.

Auschwitz at the time of its liberation by Soviet troops in January 1945. This photograph shows a transport carriage on the unloading ramp.

9.iii.44

Dear colleague Mengele!

I thank you very much for sending me the findings of your research on twins.

I am in the process of evaluating them.

Perhaps there is the possibility of visiting you in Auschwitz?

Please let me know if that would be possible in the near future.

With my sincere regards

Ziegler[48]

BELSEN

Belsen, a complex of buildings located near Celle in Lower Saxony, was first established as a German prisoner of war camp in 1940. From April 1943, Jewish civilians with foreign passports were also held there as 'leverage' to be used in possible exchanges for Germans interned in Allied countries. Later, many of the complex buildings were allocated for use as a concentration camp.

As with other such camps across Germany and its occupied territories, those held at Belsen suffered from exceptional overcrowding and lack of adequate sanitary conditions, which, when combined with general ill-treatment and poor food, led to outbreaks of sickness. Typhus, tuberculosis, typhoid fever and dysentery were all rife. From 1941 until the end of the war, almost 20,000 Soviet prisoners of war and a further 50,000 civilian inmates died at Belsen. Around half of this total died in the first few months of 1945, when the neglect had reached its peak.

Belsen was liberated by British forces on 15 April 1945. Norman Midgley, a photographer with No. 5 Army Film and Photographic Unit, was allowed special access to the camp in order to record the horrific conditions present there.

In this photograph taken by Norman Midgley at Belsen, women inmates prepare food in the open air, using the boots of the dead (which can be seen piled up in the background) as fuel for their fires.

18th April 1945

Today I visited a German concentration camp at Belsen near Celle. I saw some of the most horrible sights imaginable. No words can describe the horror of this place. It must be seen to be believed. I am now convinced that the Nazis are not human beings but vermin that must be exterminated. This might have happened in England had Hitler's plans succeeded.

The camp is situated in wooded country near to Celle. It looks like an ordinary prison camp – high barbed wire fences with high lookout towers at regular intervals. Over 60,000 men, women and children were herded into this camp. They were political prisoners, mainly Polish, and a large number of them Jews. There were some Hungarians, Dutch and French. The huts in the camp were big enough for 30 people each but as many as *500* had been housed in a single hut. Sanitation was non-existent. The food supplied was meagre to say the least. The object of the Nazis was to slowly starve them to death.

Disease was rampant – typhus, typhoid and dysentery are only a few of the deadly diseases found there. The approaches to the camp were guarded by Hungarian soldiers. Notices warned of the danger of Typhus.

We arrived at the camp and met an officer of the British Army who took us on a tour of inspection. We walked down the main avenue between the huts. The people we saw varied considerably. Some looked reasonably healthy (they were newcomers), others were a shocking sight – mere skin and bone, many with running sores, scabs and ulcers. We left the main avenue to walk between the huts. People were stretched out all over the place. It was difficult to decide whether they were alive or dead. The officer warned us to look where we walked as there were piles of excreta all over the place. The stench was nauseating. Outside some of the huts there were bodies lying in a heap. Three women walked towards the pile dragging a body and dumped it on the heap. The bodies appeared to have been here for a considerable time.

We eventually came to huge pits where our soldiers were organising mass burials. One pit we saw, about 30 yards by 20 yards and of unknown depth, was full of human bodies. Thousands of them just dumped in. This pit was one of many. The bodies were a ghastly sight. Some were green. They looked like skeletons covered with skin – the flesh had all gone. There were bodies of small children amongst the grown-ups. In other parts of the camp there were hundreds of bodies lying about, in many cases piled five or six high. Amongst them sat women peeling potatoes and cooking scraps of food. They were quite unconcerned and when I lifted my camera to photograph them, even smiled... Others burnt the shoes and clothing of the dead to keep warm. There was a huge pile of boots and shoes from dead people. Dotted about the camp were tremendous cess-pools where women washed in the nude and washed clothes. Until our forces supplied water, this was also their drinking water.

At another part of the camp our soldiers had started to organise the removal of piles of dead for burial. They had rounded up several SS men who were caught at the camp and had been there as guards. They were made to load lorries with bodies. They were kept on the move by our soldiers picking up bodies from a heap and throwing them unceremoniously onto the trucks. The other inmates watched the loading, booing and shouting and throwing stones at the SS thugs. When the trucks were loaded the SS men were made to jump on top of the pile of bodies and the trucks drove off to the burial place. On one of these trucks one SS man jumped off and ran away. He only got a short distance – he was shot dead by a rain of bullets, to the cheers of the crowd. The SS men were really being broken down, some cried and sobbed as they were rushed about in their horrible task of picking up the corpses.

We were told that it will be possible to save many of the people but thousands are beyond hope and will surely die. Scores are dying every day. Food is now being supplied by the army but is not much good at the moment, as the people have been so long without good solid food that their stomachs can't cope with it. Milk is now being supplied and this they can take.

I have read about such camps as this, but never realised what it was really like. It must be seen to be believed.[49]

18th April 1945.

Today I visited a German concentration camp at BELSEN near CELLE. I saw some of the most horrible sights imaginable. No words can describe the horror of this place. It must be seen to be believed. I am now convinced that the Nazis are not human beings, but vermin that must be exterminated. This might have happened in England, had Hitlers plans succeeded.

The camp is situated in wooded country near

CHAPTER SIX
FIGHTING BACK

Clockwise: German guards on duty by one of the watch towers at Stalag Luft III, Sagan. • Indian troops inspect a captured German 37mm anti-tank gun, 18 December 1941. • The crossing of the Garigliano River at Lauro, Italy, on 19 January 1944. • British infantry rush an enemy strong point through the dust and smoke of enemy shell fire.

This photograph, taken on 3 December 1941, shows the crew of a Matilda tank being taken prisoner by troops from New Zealand. The tank had been captured by the Germans and used in an attempt to break through the Allied lines, during which it was knocked out by an anti-tank gun.

NORTH AFRICA

The North African campaign fought across Libya and Egypt took place over vast distances and difficult terrain, in an incredibly inhospitable climate. January 1942 marked a resumed effort by the German and Italian armies to push the Allies back into Egypt, and victories were claimed over the British and Commonwealth forces at Gazala and Bir Hacheim before the port of Tobruk was finally recaptured by the Axis powers, along with over 30,000 Allied prisoners. Sustaining yet another defeat at Mersa Matruh, the British Eighth Army withdrew to El Alamein, with disaster looming.

Douglas Wallis was a surgeon attached to the 62nd General Hospital in North Africa. Having experienced the siege of Tobruk, by the end of 1941 he was able to resume more mobile warfare and sent this letter home to his family, recounting some of the conditions experienced while fighting in the desert.

Dec 27th 1941

I have been out several times in the desert. At
one place there had been a tank battle and there
were 25 abandoned Jerry tanks, all shot up and
some burned out; in many cases our shells had
gone right through and exploded inside – not
much hope for the crew. At another place there
were abandoned Italian guns and piles of boxes
of ammo, all sorts of junk and a machine gun
nest nearby with the bodies still lying about.
Once we were looking for a German CCS and
eventually found it – luckily, because a mile
further on there were 70 Germans still
unrounded up and fighting and we should have
driven right into them. In one place the Poles

Douglas Wallis with his wife and daughter.

in lorries went to clear up an old Italian strong point; the Italians came out
and waved a white flag so the Poles got out and walked up to take them
prisoner, when they opened up with a machine gun; all bar one were killed.
He managed to crawl away and eventually found some of his pals in Bren
carriers; they drove the carriers back and forth over the Italians until they
squashed the lot.

Yesterday we had a sand storm – awful things, like a London fog but choking
dust and sand that gets into everything – one's bed, hair brushes, water, food,
eyes – and our planes couldn't take off, so he put on a raid – probably from
Crete. Today it's raining and dull and cold – like an October day at home –
and he sent over a plane or two again. Before, we were relieved when we
really got air raids – anything from two or three to over 20 a day, privates
used to hate it and it was not uncommon for them to ask to be discharged to
the line because they didn't feel safe here!

Now we are slacker but used to get wounded pouring in; one day 700 from a
recaptured Field Ambulance, once 350. We would evacuate 500 by ship and be
more than full again in a couple of days. Thank goodness now we are slacker,
as there are CCS's in front of us. The Italians are awful cowards; the genus like

our fellows never complain of pain, but their officers grumble at our conditions...
There are at the moment over a 100 Italian wounded just arriving. We were
all nearly dropping from sheer weariness at first but are not so bad now.

Well old girl I have told you a little, could tell you about 100 times as much.
Apart from the Far East, the war seems to be going well; I hope we are going
on to Tripoli, and perhaps by next Xmas I may be in Rome. I would love to
see you all.

Lots of love, Old Girl

Douglas[50]

OPERATION 'BARBAROSSA'

After the fall of France, Hitler ordered plans to be drawn up for an invasion of the Soviet Union. He aimed to capture its vast economic resources and enslave its populations, providing the *Lebensraum* ('living space') that he believed Germany needed in the east. Regardless of their recent non-aggression pact, the Soviet Union was regarded as the natural enemy of Nazi Germany due to their 'Jewish Bolshevism'.

On 22 June 1941, Hitler initiated Operation 'Barbarossa'. Germany launched Blitzkrieg attacks towards Leningrad in the north, Moscow in the centre and Ukraine to the south, expecting a swift victory. At first, the invaders enjoyed massive success, but the immense distances and difficult terrain soon created logistical problems. Despite sustaining terrible losses, Soviet troops maintained the strong morale necessary to continue to defend their homeland and German casualties mounted.

Disagreements over strategy delayed a German attack on Moscow, which in turn allowed the Soviets time to consolidate the defence of their capital. As the brutal Russian winter of 1941–2 took hold, the German advance ground to a halt just outside the city and a swift Soviet counter-attack forced them on to the defensive. Serving alongside German troops were the Italian Expeditionary Corps in Russia (CSIR), including Vittorio Caressa, whose unit experienced the cruel winter conditions.

German troops smash their way into a Russian house during Operation 'Barbarossa', summer 1941.

Undated [spring 1942]

Dearest sister Marcella

You asked if I was afraid and... I was angry, more than anything I was angry and, I would say, now that I've heard and recounted many facts I am also afraid. I don't think you have any idea of what winter has done here; don't think that I just have a runny nose at night. When I'm told of certain things it makes me shiver and my white hair shall grow visibly, now that I have short hair you can see lots of it, I'd almost say too much. I heard that this winter more than half [the men]

Vittorio Caressa

were frozen because of the cold, one person lost his foot when he was taking his shoes off, ears and noses fall off at the slightest touch and when pissing many lost everything, these are just a few of the many stories I've been told. You would love it here, seeing as you always feel cold.

We eat fairly well, especially at the hospital I got to eat things that in civilian life, especially now, I could have only imagined. For two whole days I ate fresh butter, about 1 kg and a half and it disgusted me so much I was sick for two days, and then litres of milk that gave me the runs. Wine and plain pasta, every day. Here the food is alright, as I said it could be better but with the mafia ingrained everywhere we are robbed. Every morning a quarter of coffee with plenty of bread, jam or cheese, sometimes, especially on Sundays, a little glass of cognac, the ration consists of soup or plain pasta; we also have lemons, tinned meat, tinned fish and often wine with sweets... but the mafia is intolerable.

Here we don't know anything that's happening in the world, I do not even see the news bulletins, we are only aware of this small area. They give us anti-freeze cream but it doesn't work, actually people who used it froze anyway, it's just a matter of luck. You too believe that there will be a cataclysm but take it from me, it's not going to happen, it is very unlikely.

Kisses, Vittorio[61]

2

Carissimo Renato,

con piacere ho letto finalmente i scritti e notizie di voi tutti; sono contento che ti sei rimessa ma per rimetterti completamente ci vorrebbero i tempi normali, perché altrimenti....... Dopo parecchio che non vai in ufficio, dovrai prenderci un po' di abitudine (mi saluterai la sig. Ada e Bianchi). Mi dispiace molto che Franco stia male meno male, come dici, è una forma blanda, spero che quando riceverai la presente sia completamente ristabilito, andate sempre d'accordo, certo che come coppia siete l'ideale.

Non capisco perché quest'anno 1943 sia così pessimo con noi; non sono del tuo parere riguardo a ciò che mi hai scritto, non vedo, anzi, che prima dell'inverno possa sorgere un fatto nuovo, qui è ben diverso, saperti......... Ormai mi trovo sotto questa stella che mi perseguita e non vedo l'ora di .... levarmela di dorno.

Andrei a fare qualche gita con Franco quest'estate, per godere magari un po' di fresco e penso che tanto volentieri vorrei essere con voi.

Salutami tanto Franco, non posso scrivergli perché non conosco il suo indirizzo, e fargli tanti auguri per la sua convalescenza. Tanti baci e abbracci Vittorio

Carissima sorella (cecepa) Marcella,

Debbo sempre riconosce re, ora che ricevo posta, che tu sei sempre la più .... lunga di mano nello scrivere, te ne ringrazio molto, sai è molto piacevole leggere scritti di care persone quando si è lontano da tutti, e specialmente qui, dove non si pensa nessuno, altro che i .... ruffi. Ti meravigli della velocità della posta, regolarmente deve metterci 6 giorni

Roger Bushell (right) photographed in the North Compound of Stalag Luft III, probably during November 1943.

ESCAPE AND EVASION

It was the duty of all Allied prisoners of war to attempt to escape. If they made it home successfully, then they could resume the fight, but even those who were unable to reach safety might take up the time and effort of the large numbers of enemy police and soldiers sent to track them down. Many airmen shot down over occupied territory would similarly evade capture as best they could, sometimes by taking refuge among local resistance fighters. The War Office department MI9 worked with local contacts to establish and maintain escape and evasion lines within occupied Europe to assist Allied servicemen trying to reach home.

One Allied pilot who was both an escaper and an evader was Squadron Leader Roger Bushell. In May 1940, his Spitfire was shot down over occupied France and he became a prisoner, seizing the opportunity to escape twice from different German camps and living underground in Prague before his recapture. In June 1942, Bushell was transferred to what would be his final prisoner of war camp, Stalag Luft III at Sagan, from where he managed to send the following letter home.

Accompanied by seventy-five others, Bushell managed to break out via a tunnel in the 'Great Escape' from Stalag Luft III on the night of 24 March 1944. Recaptured the next day, he was one of the fifty prisoners who were subsequently executed on the orders of Hitler.

19.6.42

My darlings - Here I am again! I escaped last October, was hidden in Prague during the intervening period, and was unfortunately re-captured last month. That explains everything I think. Further details I will tell you after the war. You will I know have had a very anxious & trying time but I also know that you would not have expected me, in the circumstances, to have done anything other than I did and we will therefore leave it at that. I am quite O.K. and very well so you have nothing to worry about. This is a Luftwaffe camp, with old friends from Dulag of both nationalities here, so I am in excellent hands. At the moment I am in the "cooler" doing my stretch for my escape but I gather there are a number of parcels waiting for me and I have been fitted out with Red Cross clothes & a new uniform so at present want for nothing. There are lots of Red Cross parcels and cigarettes so everything is fine. There is little else that I can tell you except that I love you all very much and feel sure that it won't be very long now before the whole affair is over and we can all start over again with our normal lives. Am naturally bitterly disappointed at having been caught again but my spirits are sky-high & you need have no fear that this life has got me down yet or that it ever will, please God. Give yourselves all a big hug & lots of love

This was the first letter since Sept 1941 and must have been written in Berlin although they made him write Stalag Luft III.

19 June 1942

My darlings

Here I am again! I escaped last October, was hidden in Prague during the intervening period, and was unfortunately recaptured last month. That explains everything I think. Further details I will tell you after the war. You will I know have had a very anxious and trying time but I also know that you would not have expected me, in the circumstances, to have done anything other than I did and we will therefore leave it at that. I am quite OK and very well so you have nothing to worry about.

This is a Luftwaffe camp, with old friends from Dulag of both nationalities here, so I am in excellent hands. At the moment I am in the 'cooler' doing my stretch for my escape but I gather there are a number of parcels waiting for me and I have been fitted out with Red Cross clothes and a new uniform so at present want for nothing. There are lots of Red Cross parcels and cigarettes and so everything is fine.

There is little else that I can tell you except that I love you all very much and feel sure that it won't be very long now before the whole affair is over and we can all start over again with our normal lives. Am naturally bitterly disappointed at having been caught again but my spirits are sky-high and you need have no fear that this life has got me down yet and that it ever will, please God.

Give yourselves all a big hug and lots of love,

Roger[52]

COLDITZ

Colditz Castle, officially designated Oflag IV-C prisoner of war camp, became famous after the war for its well-known prisoners, including Douglas Bader (the double-amputee fighter pilot), Airey Neave (the future politician) and David Stirling (founder of the SAS). Although Colditz was considered a high-security prison, it boasted the greatest record for successful escape attempts. Most of its captives had already attempted to flee from other camps, and were transferred to Colditz for this very reason.

For most prisoners of war, though, there were very few opportunities to escape. Of the 170,000 British and Empire prisoners in Germany during the war, fewer than 1,200 managed to escape successfully and reach home. In addition to the difficulties involved in getting out of a guarded prison camp, any journey to friendly territory was both long and dangerous. Only the well-prepared tended to succeed, although the planning of escapes often provided a popular distraction from the everyday boredom of captivity.

The following letter was written by Lieutenant Anthony 'Jock' Allan to a family friend while he was imprisoned in Colditz. Allan would be remembered for his famous escape attempt, in which he hid inside a mattress that was then carried out of the castle by unsuspecting German troops. Allan went on the run, disguising himself in Hitler Youth uniform before hitching a ride to Vienna, where he was eventually recaptured.

Below left: Colditz castle. Below right: Three tunnellers emerge from a hole in their mess wall, illustrating an unsuccessful escape attempt from Colditz.

Aug 31, 1942

Dear Mrs Gamble

I haven't received any letters from you recently but the parcels have been coming through excellently. Unfortunately out of four hams that arrived three were bad. Your ARX [Red Cross] parcels too arrive regularly. I simply don't know how to thank you for all you've done, but maybe I will be able to one day. My health is really very good and that was the one thing I feared as a prisoner that my health would suffer. But after two and a quarter years I still feel mentally and physically very vigorous.

There are moments of course when one is incurably homesick, where nature cries out against such an unnatural life and when everything around is happening at such a pace we are so inactive. Prison life is a very hard trial of self discipline but if one comes out having profited by what one can learn instead of having a lethargic cynical and warped mind, one can overcome a great deal of life's problems I think. I am continuing my Spanish and French and am making good progress in both. I hope to speak German, French and Spanish with equal fluency when I leave here. I am beginning reading next week a history of the USA. I have just finished Charles Morgan's *The Voyage*.

Please remember me to Mr Gamble and lots of love to all the children.

More again next month.

Jock[53]

THE BATTLE OF EL ALAMEIN

Since the end of 1940, the British Eighth Army had been fighting in the western deserts of North Africa: first against the Italian forces who had invaded Egypt in September that year; then later against the German Afrika Korps, which landed in Libya in January 1941. Pushed back towards Egypt, the British made a stand at El Alamein.

An initial, unsuccessful attempt to force them out of their defensive position took place in July 1942, before the British were reinforced and went on the offensive on 23 October. This, the Second Battle of El Alamein, saw the fighting turn in favour of the Allies, who by 10 November had forced Rommel's army into retreat.

An enemy shell falls short as a British gun is loaded at El Alamein.

Back in London, the annual Lord Mayor's Banquet at the Mansion House was to be held on 10 November. As well as the victory at El Alamein, Allied landings in Axis-controlled North Africa had just begun under the codename of Operation 'Torch'. Prime Minister Winston Churchill would therefore be provided with a valuable opportunity to celebrate the first really significant British victories of the war, and define the moment as a key turning point. Widely reported and broadcast, Churchill's speech at the banquet would be remembered as one of his most famous.

In our wars the episodes are usually adverse, but the final result is satisfactory... In the last war up till almost the end we met with continual disappointments and with disasters far more bloody than anything we have experienced so far in this; but in the end all opportunities fell together and our foes submitted themselves to our will. We have not so far in this war taken as many German prisoners as they have British, but they will no doubt come in in droves at the end, as they did last time.

I have never promised anything but blood, tears, toil and sweat. Now, however, we have a new experience. We have victory. A remarkable and definite victory. A bright gleam has caught the helmets of our soldiers and warmed and cheered all our hearts...

3.

This battle was not fought
for the sake of gaining positions
or desert territory.

General Alexander and General Montgomery
fought it with one single idea -

to destroy the armed force of the enemy,
and to destroy it at the place
where its disaster would be most
far-reaching.

The battle has been fought throughout
almost entirely by British and Dominion
troops on the one hand
and Germans on the other.

The Italians have been left
in the waterless desert
to perish or surrender.

The fighting with the Germans
has been intense and fierce in the
extreme.

The Germans have been killed fought to the death
in great numbers where they stood.

This battle was not fought for the sake of gaining positions or desert territory. General Alexander and General Montgomery fought it with one single idea – to destroy the armed force of the enemy, and to destroy it at the place where its disaster would be most far-reaching.

The battle has been fought throughout almost entirely by men of British blood on the one hand and Germans on the other. The Italians have been left in the waterless desert to perish or surrender. The fighting with the Germans has been intense and fierce in the extreme. It was a deadly grapple...

This is not the end. It is not even the beginning of the end. But it is, perhaps, the end of the beginning.[54]

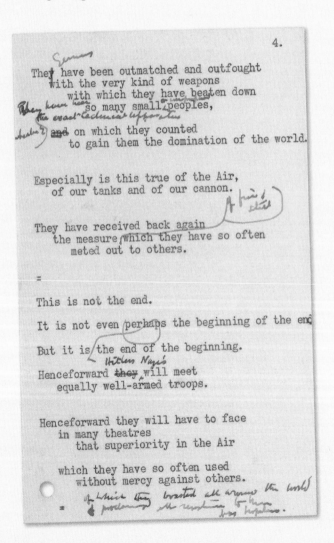

THE BATTLE OF STALINGRAD

Despite the failure of Operation 'Barbarossa' and its massive number of casualties, Hitler launched another major offensive in June 1942 against the Soviet Union, this time further south towards the Caucasus Mountains and the oil fields of Baku. However, the factors that had caused the initial German attacks in 1941 to fail, most notably the logistical problems and immensely strong Soviet resistance, conspired once more to thwart this new attempt.

Stalin demanded that the city bearing his name must be defended at all costs, with every available soldier and civilian mobilised to that end. The Battle of Stalingrad would run for over five months and be remembered as the longest and most bloody battle of the Second World War. The city was heavily bombed by the Luftwaffe, with the ruined buildings becoming the scene for street-fighting. By October 1942, most of Stalingrad was in German hands,

German infantry take shelter behind a wall during street fighting in Stalingrad, autumn 1942.

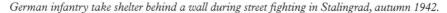

but the Russians clung on, managing to encircle the German 6th Army and 4th Panzer Army by 19 November. Despite repeated attempts to break the stalemate, the battle continued until the beginning of February 1943, when the Germans finally ran out of food and ammunition and had to surrender. From this point on, there was no doubt that the Germans had been beaten on the Eastern Front.

Soviet casualties amounted to 1.1 million, of whom nearly half a million died. The Axis powers also lost over half a million men, either killed or captured. German soldier Fritz Lüderitz was based in Stalingrad in December 1942 when he wrote the letter below to his wife. They had just been married in a proxy ceremony, due to his inability to get home. Lüderitz would be killed in action the following year.

Stalingrad, 27.12.42

My dear little Bunny!

... I was not able to write you a few lines during the holidays, my treasure. We were in our positions until 7pm on the first holiday, and had to repel very heavy Russian attacks. After I had managed some sleep on the second holiday, yet another order to go into action was waiting for me. I had to go back into our positions at 3pm on the second holiday. But we had some luck, as the Russians had been cleared out of the spot they had been occupying within our own lines. That meant I was able to return to our rest area at 4pm today, Sunday. This evening I want to quickly write you a longer

Fritz Lüderitz

letter. I have already given you a short account of my Christmas, I can only say that it was terrible. But we have survived even these days and surely there must come a Christmas celebration that we can experience together. This year Santa Claus was a complete failure, but it was not to be expected otherwise, as he couldn't very well come to Stalingrad.

... So this evening I'm sitting in my bunker at a table that even has a little green pine branch on it, and in this branch I've stuck your photograph and want to be with you alone this evening. After many long weeks it's possible for me to be fully with you in my thoughts, my little bunny. During these hard battles it is surely not possible for my thoughts to be anywhere else but with my men. You won't be able to understand this at once, my darling, but unfortunately it is so. Hopefully the Russians won't launch any bigger attacks in the next few days, so that we can stay in our rest area for a few days, then my thoughts will be only with you my darling. I guess you will have received my short letters in the meantime. Now alas I don't know if you were my little wifey at Christmas, but I very much assume so. You write in one of your letters that I should describe my wedding night to you, which I'll now do.

On the night of the 2nd and 3rd [December] we went into our rest area and were supposed to remain there for 14 days. I was then informed that at 11 o'clock on the 3rd my marriage ceremony was to take place in the bunker, attended by the battalion commander. Our sarge had everything got ready, the Reich flag was put on the table along with whatever else is required for a proxy marriage. In the morning I had my suit cleaned, and at 11 I went to the commander with our sarge and two NCOs as witnesses. I have to say he did it with all due ceremony and after 20 minutes that was it. Unfortunately the NCO who captured the magic on film has been badly wounded, but I assume that I'll get these pictures nevertheless. The table had already been set when we returned, first of all for a small snack with lots of schnapps and lots of bubbly. A large meal had been planned for the evening, but fate had other ideas.

The Russians had made a large-scale attack on the 3rd December at midday and at 5pm we again had to go up to the front, not to our positions but to a ravine where we waited as reserves. This would have been bearable as I had three bottles of schnapps brought along. But at 10pm the commander and I had to have a look at the positions we were to occupy the following day. So we ended up racing around the area the whole night, in our new winter clothing of cotton padded suits and felt boots... So, my treasure, that was my wedding night in Stalingrad, but it doesn't matter, we'll make up for it with the real thing, even if the Devil himself is in attendance.

So, my darling, that's all I know for today... Many thousands of greetings and kisses, and a happy healthy New Year

Your Fritz[55]

Still from the Soviet film The Story of Stalingrad *showing rocket missiles being fired at German positions.*

THE INVASION OF SICILY

Located off the toe of Italy, the island of Sicily would provide an important staging post for an invasion of the Italian mainland, as well as opening up all-important sea lanes in the Mediterranean. Helped by a number of deception plans, which successfully diverted enemy reinforcements away from the island, the Allied invasion of Sicily was launched on 9 July 1943 with airborne landings by gliders and paratroopers, followed early the next day by an amphibious beach assault. Despite poor weather conditions, which affected the airborne operations in particular, it was clear by the end of the month that Axis troops would be forced to evacuate the island. A large-scale German withdrawal from Sicily began on 11 August, and less than a week later the island was fully captured.

The Allied success in capturing Sicily would have major implications. Hitler was forced to move valuable troops away from the Eastern Front in an attempt to reinforce the island, while the Italian failure led directly to the overthrow of their leader, Benito Mussolini. It also effectively marked the beginning of the Italian campaign, with landings on the southern tip of continental Italy beginning on 3 September 1943.

Corporal Harry Chart was involved in the Sicily invasion and recognised that the event would be a key moment in the course of the war.

The landing beaches on Sicily in the early morning of 10 July 1943.

About eight o'clock in the evening as dusk was falling there was a yell from deck, 'Land'. Could it be Malta, we asked ourselves. 'No, Malta was passed hours ago'. Then it can be nothing else but Sicily and we could see it in daylight too! That means if they had been awake they could have seen us too. We could see quite plainly now the outlines of Mt Etna and as dusk finally settled we knew that at last all our suspense was coming to a head. I pass the next five hours; it was hubbub, excitement and even laughter. We, not being the first off, had to go down into the fevered head of below decks and not until the show started did we creep onto deck. It was about 2.30, chilly and with

Harry Chart

a pale moon shining above. The gray shapes of the assault craft were soon disappearing into the distance – and the invasion was on.

I don't know how long it was before they reached shore but I guess we were expecting dive-bombers and all their paraphernalia but save the crump of shells from our cruiser and a belated reply by an Italian coastal battery the whole scene had an eerie stillness. We had an awful moment though, when a searchlight swept the bay and seemed to dwell on the assault craft, but it passed. Now the invasion was on, spasmodic machine gun fire, one or two poofs here and there, a small fire or two maybe and Sicily was on the way. Dawn broke and the whole scene was before us, a sky as clear as crystal and the skyline depicted exactly as we had been shown. That perfect organisation. Not a hitch, not a slip up marred the smooth precision of this machine.

We tucked into a meal of – yes – bully and biscuits and soon it was our turn to disembark. Still no Jerry planes – and then, with our bodies literally weighed down with kit, water cans and bivouacs we clambered into our small craft – the huge liners incidentally had now moved into shore – about 800 yds off – imagine it, only half a mile from the shore of a place which had but been invaded five hours. Confidence – its staggering isn't it. Our kit we dumped as soon as we got ashore and we rooted around for a place to sleep in, trust us to do that first, before we got down to work and you can guess there certainly was plenty to do.

Prisoners were already rolling in – surprised and incredible expressions on their features and with clothes that were in shreds. One or two were badly hurt and covered in blood and were being removed to our hospital, already in action. In fact some of our boys injured in the initial landing were going aboard our troopship before we left. The Sicilians in the little fishing village were at first terrified and to look at them made them put their hands way above their heads like captured gangsters – but the jovial expressions on our faces I guess soon put them at their ease for they were making gestures of the old Victory 'V' sign.

History had been made and I was in on it – if I had thought way back in '39 that I should have been engaged on such a venture I guess I would have passed out and now it was just a normal day's affair.[56]

Following the liberation of Sicily on 17 August 1943, a badly defaced portrait of Mussolini, pierced by a bayonet, hangs from a tree along the road from Messina.

ITALY

The Allied success on Sicily led directly to the collapse of the Fascist regime in Italy and the overthrow of Mussolini, who was arrested by order of King Victor Emmanuel III on 25 July 1943. The new Italian government signed an armistice with the Allies on 8 September, but German forces swiftly took control of the northern and central parts of the country. Mussolini was rescued by German paratroopers and was returned to power, but as a puppet leader, there to oversee German-occupied territory along with his remaining loyal Italian fascists.

The British Eighth Army and US Fifth Army landed in southern Italy at the very beginning of September 1943 and began to work their way northwards to meet

A family places flowers on the grave of an unknown British soldier killed at Cassino.

the Germans, who were still in control. The mountainous terrain of the Apennines proved difficult for the Allies, and a series of offensives throughout the early months of 1944 were necessary before Rome was finally liberated on 4 June.

Jim Fraser was a forward observation officer with the Royal Artillery and, having fought in Sicily, was now involved in the Italian campaign. The novelty of making their way through Italian towns as part of the process of liberation is well-conveyed in this letter, which he wrote to his mother.

6.10.43

Dear Mummy

… We are seeing most interesting sights and having a grand time. I got into a big Italian town a few days ago and found it most interesting. Most of the small towns are filthy but this one was quite clean and had hardly been damaged at all. The shops were open and 'business as usual'. There were some shortages but otherwise it might have been peacetime. I'm afraid I had not sufficient time to buy any presents but will try and get some silk stockings soon as they are fairly plentiful.

It is difficult to get used to the Italian army which is greatly in evidence everywhere. The smartest of officers go about in full uniform absolutely covered in medal ribbons, six or seven rows are quite common. They are immaculate and seem to spend their time being tailors' dummies. The Italian private is still pretty dirty and unshaven in appearance. In fact except for the big towns the Italian towns in South Italy are horrid. Pigs and farm animals wander about in the roads and no-one cleans the streets! The sanitation is primitive and in a lot of the narrow streets there are balconies in the houses and the occupants hurl out their slops and water in to the road below. Some of the villages are almost as smelly as the Egyptian hovels.

Apart from the towns however the country is lovely, enormous mountains with beautiful colours, vineyards, roses and all sorts of flowers. All the farm workers seem to be women, the men are incredibly idle and the women are

B Troop. 110 Med Bty
80th (S.H.) Med Regt R.A.

Dear Mummy.

Letter 8. (9") C.M.F.

I am afraid there is very little news I can give you this week and this letter is more to let you know I am still O.K. than anything else. Your mail has been held up for some time now and I should be getting a big bunch soon as I have had no letters for nearly a month. It usually goes in large bunches unless we stay put for quite a while.

The weather here has left a lot to be desired recently, we are starting the rainy season and it can be most unpleasant. We have had about 48 hours of thunder storms and rain. It is not too bad having rain if we are in billets but if all our clothes and beds get soaked and there is no form of drying wont it gets most annoying. We just plough our way through thick mud. Still we can't complain as up to now the weather has been magnificent and it is quite fine just now.

I am afraid this letter is beginning to sound dreadfully gloomy but actually I don't feel gloomy at all. Rather the opposite. We are seeing most interesting sights and having a grand time. I got into a big Italian town a few days ago and found it most interesting. Most of the small towns are filthy but this one was quite clean and had hardly been damaged at all. The shops were open and "business as usual". There were some shortages but otherwise it might have been peace time.

I'm afraid I had not sufficient time to buy any presents but will try and get some silk stockings soon as they are fairly plentiful. It is difficult to get used to the Italian army which is greatly in evidence everywhere. The smartest of officers go about in full uniform absolutely covered in medal ribbons, six or seven rows are quite common. They are immaculate and seem to spend their time being tailors' dummies. The Italian private is still pretty dirty and unshaven in appearance. In fact except for the big towns the Italian towns in South Italy are horrid. Pigs and farm animals wander about in the roads and no one cleans the streets! The sanitation is primitive and in a lot of the narrow streets there are balconies in the houses and the occupants hurl out their slops and water into the road below. Some of the villages are almost as smelly as the Egyptian hovels. Apart from the towns however the country is lovely, enormous mountains with beautiful colours, vineyards roses and all sort of flowers. All the farm workers seem to be women, the men are incredibly idle, and the women are vastly superior in physique. They wear the sort of native costumes that are usually associated with the Balkans, all bright colours. They seem to keep their clothes quite clean, unlike their men.

The grape harvest is at its height just now and "vino" making is taking place everywhere. The grapes are gathered by the small boys and women and carried in huge barrels on donkeys to large wooden basins where the children and men do their trampling. It

---

vastly superior in physique. They wear the sort of native costumes that are usually associated with the Balkans, all bright colours. They seem to keep their clothes quite clean, unlike their men.

The grape harvest is at its height just now and 'vino' making is taking place everywhere. The grapes are gathered by the small boys and women and carried in huge barrels on donkeys to large wooden basins where the children and men do their trampling. It is a revolting sight as their feet are far from clean. They often jump out and run around in the mud, doing various jobs, and get back in again. One I saw who cleaned out a pig sty in the middle before returning to the squashing!

Love, Jim[57]

THE BATTLE OF MONTE CASSINO

As the Allied armies advanced northwards through Italy, they met with pockets of dug-in Axis defenders, who proved difficult to remove. Approaching Rome, the Allies had to face the German and Italian 'Winter Line', a series of military fortifications that would need to be removed before further progress could be made.

Located in a key strategic position, the ancient hilltop monastery of Monte Cassino was mistakenly identified by the Allies as being a German observation post, and became a particular target. A series of Allied offensives were therefore undertaken against the monastery, and the fortified town of Cassino below it, over four months, beginning on 17 January 1944. Soldiers from the Polish II Corps finally proved successful in their attacks, and in the spring the Allied advance towards Rome could resume. The cost of the battle was immense, resulting in 55,000 Allied casualties and around 20,000 German.

Serving with the Indian Army at Cassino, Captain Rupert Weld-Smith wrote the following letter to his parents describing the final Allied attack.

Troops of the 2nd Polish Corps throw grenades during the heavy fighting around Monte Cassino.

15th May 1944

I am going to lift the veil of secrecy a bit and tell you of our adventures; let me first say that I am quite well and came through it all without being hit.

As you now know the Eighth Army attacked over the Rapido River in the Cassino area. Our Division had the honour of being spearhead and ourselves the assaulting unit. We'd been training for this for weeks... My role was Beachmaster, left beach. Zero hour was 23.45 hrs and we were to advance under a terrific barrage...

By 22.55 hrs we got to where boats, collapsible, were waiting and then Cra-a-a-a-sh bang, thud, wallop, smash, down it came just over the river. No more need for silence. Up went boats onto men's shoulders and on we went, cheering our men onwards. The Sepoys were just grand. Everything was happening, airbursts all round, a terrific noise. I was with the forward assault company on the left. Slipping, sliding, falling into dykes, encouraging, sweating, we approached the river. As I got there a major came up and said, 'Weldy? Good. X (to whom I was understudy beachmaster) has been hit. Take over will you.' I said 'OK' and went off.

The Hun had put down a smokescreen to hinder us so visibility was one yard and less. All boats got to their right place, which was a damned good effort, and we all lay flat to wait for the barrage to lift. X crawled past on his way to the stretchers; said he, 'Hullo old man, how're things? 'Fraid I'm out. Hit in the hand, two fingers gone. I shall probably collapse soon.' He was hit again in back and thigh. I had time to think a bit for three minutes... I remembered that when I wanted Him, the Almighty was not so far off. Verily hell was raging all round, then red tracers from Bofors soared skywards, the barrage moved on and into the river went the boats and started across. Something went wrong on my side so I only had two boats working – but WORKING. There should have been four. Conditions were bad. I was groping my way round, rather a dangerous operation as the air was very thick with other things than smoke, and fell twice into slit trenches in which Sepoys were huddled, one of them moaning gently from a shattered forearm, another with a broken leg. Then, after what seemed an interminable time of helping people into boats, I heard the Sikhs give their battle cry as they stormed the first enemy positions at bayonet point. One fellow chanted the refrain and they all roared back the answer as they charged. This chant they used several times. It sounded marvellous. Then came machine gun fire, h-r-r-rr, h-r-r-r-r, h-r-r-r-r, and so on. The Ghurkhas must have crossed by 05.00 hrs and dug in under smoke on the far bank.

By 07.30 it was still pea-soupy fog but daylight and odd pockets of enemy were popping up and sniping us with machine guns. So we collected ourselves and a few casualties and went back to report to Brigade. We were told that we had 'done our jobs'.[58]

An American B-17 Flying Fortress bomber photographed over Monte Cassino during the first Allied air raid on the monastery, 15 February 1944.

THE SPECIAL OPERATIONS EXECUTIVE

Violette Szabo, GC

The Special Operations Executive (SOE) was formed in Britain in July 1940 to assist local resistance fighters in conducting espionage and sabotage in occupied territory. Under high levels of secrecy, recruits were trained in unarmed combat, firearms and sabotage. SOE agents would be dropped behind enemy lines throughout occupied Europe, and also operated in the Far East as a branch known as Force 136. Their work was extremely dangerous, with the consequences of discovery potentially fatal; of the 470 agents sent into France, 118 failed to return.

One such SOE agent was Violette Szabo, a British woman recruited for her fluency in French. She and two other agents parachuted into south-west France on 7 June 1944 to set up a new network with local resistance groups. Three days later, her car was stopped at a roadblock and a gun battle took place that led to her capture. Brutally interrogated in Paris before being moved to Germany, Violette was executed at Ravensbrück concentration camp in early 1945. After the war, she was posthumously awarded the George Cross, the highest civilian honour. (As a woman, she was not allowed to be a front-line combatant, and so was awarded this civilian distinction, which has the same level of importance as the Victoria Cross.)

Violette's husband, Etienne Szabo, was killed in action in North Africa, just four months after the birth of their daughter Tania on 8 June 1942. The following note was written by Violette shortly before she embarked on her first SOE mission.

Violette Szabo's daughter, Tania, receives her mother's posthumous George Cross.

17 Nov 1943

I Hereby appoint Miss Vera Maidment and her Mother Mrs Alice Maidment
the legal guardian of my child Tania Damaris Desiree Szabo, in the event of
my death.

V. Szabo[59]

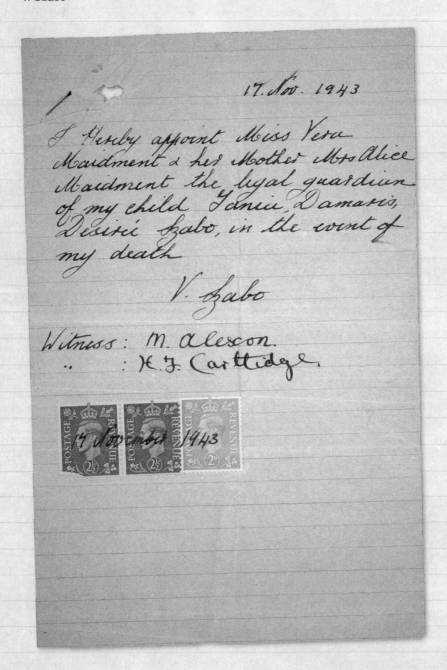

CHAPTER SEVEN
HOME FRONT

Clockwise: A British officer inspects the wreckage of Rudolf Hess's Messerchmitt Bf 110 that has been removed to an RAF depot in Scotland, 13 May 1941. •Working on the land was an alternative to military service. • Conscientious objectors attend a course in mechanised agriculture at a school in Essex, under the Ministry of Agriculture's labour-training scheme. • Soldiers of the Home Guard being inspected, 1941.

CIVIL DEFENCE

By September 1940, it was clear that
the German Luftwaffe had failed
to destroy RAF Fighter Command.
Instead, London and other key
locations would now be targeted with
a campaign of regular night bombing.
Very significant damage and high
casualties resulted, with Glasgow,
Bristol, Plymouth, Liverpool,
Birmingham and Exeter experiencing
particularly devastating raids.

*Women were encouraged to take on
new wartime roles.*

Even before the outbreak of war, the
British government had begun to
prepare its civilian population. Air-
raid shelters were distributed from
1938, while from 1 September 1939
the 'blackout' was enforced to prevent
the light from towns helping enemy
bombers. With the risk of the enemy
dropping poison gas, over 44 million
gas masks had been distributed across the nation by the beginning
of September 1939.

Air Raid Wardens were appointed, and were responsible for reporting
incidents, reassuring the public and providing Air Raid Precautions (ARP)
advice. They were also expected to extinguish smaller fires, administer first
aid and follow up on reports of unexploded bombs. Fire fighters, police,
ambulance drivers and rescue teams were also essential elements of Civil
Defence; almost 7,000 such workers would be killed during the war.

Winifred Musson served as an ARP Warden in the London Borough of
Fulham, and in this letter to her sister recounts Londoners' ability to 'keep
calm and carry on'.

25.9.40

Dear Alix

Here's a note in between yawns to let you know we're still surviving and the flat too. We seem to have come a long way the last fortnight and any normal life seems almost forgotten; one can only be trite and say it's like a horrible nightmare, with this terrible destruction spreading every night, no district has escaped. We've had 18 nights now without a break, starting with sickening regularity at dusk and going on until dawn... We're at the stage now when all

Winifred Musson

we want is to sleep, and how thankfully we crawl up the stairs and into our beds when we find the flat still intact every morning after the all-clear. Even if we come off duty at midnight, as we sometimes do now, we never get undressed or sleep in the flat, as the guns are very near us and the shells just seem to skim over the roof above our beds, not to mention that everlasting droning overhead and the rocking and swaying if anything falls near. Either we stay out all night or sleep round at the Warden's post on camp beds, and latterly a fellow warden opposite has invited us into his basement and we sleep on a divan in our trousers and jumpers, with packed cases beside us which we bring over from the flat in case of hurried departures.

I stood beside a man in pyjamas and a borrowed overcoat in the road last night, or rather this morning at 4.0, while the AFS [Auxiliary Fire Service] pumped gallons of water into his flat to put out incendiary bombs and smashed the remaining windows to let out the smoke, and he was darned lucky compared with many other people nearby, or at any rate the ones who were still alive to worry.

I forgot to tell you that I'm an Air Raid Warden now, volunteered a fortnight ago, mostly because I just couldn't face another night alone up in the flat...

we can't do much patrolling as the shrapnel just pours down and bounces off the roads, great jagged pieces, so we foregather in small groups in each other's halls or friendly basements, and drink Oxo and tea until there is a quiet interval. Sometimes we are round at the Post, or on duty at one of the shelters, and you just ought to see – and smell – those shelters. They were made gas-proof, which seems to mean no ventilation whatever, and with well over 100 people inside and the only air coming from a very narrow opening off the street upstairs, no running water, with people already installed early in the afternoon to get a place, you can perhaps imagine the conditions.

Had another very bad time last night with a lot of bombs near us... We were supposed to go off duty at 12 but had a report of a woman screaming for help to be let out and as we couldn't find any damage just there, couldn't track down the noise. Finally did, and she was dead drunk, and the neighbours had locked her in and retreated to their shelter. Then we had to fetch the police. What a life!

Love, Win[60]

Many cities suffered from the Blitz. Here, firemen direct their hoses on burning buildings in Manchester.

THE BLITZ ON SHEFFIELD

While London was bombed more heavily and more often than anywhere else in Britain, the Blitz was effectively an attack on the entire country. There were very few areas left untouched by air raids and, especially in smaller cities, the impact of severe bombing could be truly devastating. From mid-November 1940, the Luftwaffe targeted major provincial cities and industrial centres. Early the following year, another wave of attacks began, with targets including ports. This continued until the summer months.

Damaged tram cars in one of the main streets in Sheffield after the raid on 12 December 1940.

The industrial city of Sheffield, famous for the production of steel, was a key centre for armaments manufacture. It was hit by two major bombing raids on 12 and 15 December 1940, which together left 750 dead. Damage to the city's industrial areas was, fortunately, relatively light, but the city centre was devastated in the raid, and nearly 3,000 homes and shops were destroyed.

Annie Fewkes lived in Sheffield and wrote to her nephew shortly after the two big raids to tell him of the devastation inflicted on the city, while reflecting on the fortitude of British people during the height of the Blitz.

27/1/41

Dear R.

Sheffield is in ruins. It is impossible to make one realise, we must see it to believe it. Can you imagine the Moor practically without a shop and the centre of the city just as bad? Whole estates were practically wiped out. What hasn't been blown up has been burnt out. L's wood yard was fired and that of course fired the brewery. Uncle's shop was like an inferno. Then after nine hours of continual bombing, we were left alone and went out to find fires everywhere. We never thought but that our house would go up in flames, but luckily our windows at the back hadn't been blown out and the wind changed, but the house opposite our kitchen window was on fire, also the houses in Cherry St South – that's opposite the cricket pitch – were burnt out. How we come to be alive beats me.

Nine high explosives were dropped on the football ground, a huge bomb was dropped in L's wood yard and had it exploded neither we nor the place would have been here. Do you remember St Mary's Road? They dropped a land mine there, people were blown to bits, trapped by fire. David, in fact all the soldiers were doing rescue work for a fortnight after, and occasionally they let things out. This came out yesterday. They were digging for five people, they got one, tried for hours to find signs of the others when someone noticed a body on the roof opposite and on investigation found the other four had all been blown up there. Now do you remember the old man at the greengrocer's shop opposite the bus shed beyond where Mr Bell lives? His house got a direct hit and they haven't found a sign of him or his wife, the woman next door had her head blown off and the child an arm off, the husband went insane. Can you wonder. In spite of this the only thing we suffered was two panes of glass gone and the bathroom roof damaged by shrapnel and all around us is in ruins. Everybody else seems to have their windows blown out, frames too. Streets of houses are uninhabitable.

I used to think I'd take all and say nowt, but I now think everybody ought to know what war really means today. I really feel, too, everybody ought to go through it, then we shall really know what Poland, France, Belgium and all German occupied countries are suffering. But mind, it's marvellous how the people take it. One shop which is almost down to the ground has a notice up 'Business as usual. We have just had one lousy customer'. Another 'It's too draughty here, so we've gone round the corner'.

We had a soldier staying with us one night who was at Dunkirk and he said we in Sheffield must have gone through far worse than they did, also I heard of a man who had been living in Liverpool and they have had nearly 300 raids, but he says there's nothing anywhere in Liverpool like the devastation in Sheffield. We were without water a fortnight, electricity three weeks, in fact the Brewery offices (that's all that's left) have only got light today, and we had no gas for nearly a month, but we are all smiling yet. I had a house full. The brewer and his wife and maid stayed with us for a week as there was a time bomb near their house and every night the kitchen was full of soldiers having a wash and shave. You see they were all disorganised like everybody else and the poor devils were working so hard, but nobody went without food or money or shelter. Some of the lads, RE's, were drafted in to dismantle time bombs of which there must have been hundreds.

Well, what a life. One's afraid to take one's teeth out at night in case of having no time to put 'em in, but after all it wouldn't matter as I expect they'd still drop bombs not sandwiches.

All my love[61]

A section of the London underground system was converted into an air-raid shelter by tearing up the tracks.

THE BLITZ ON LONDON: 1941

By the end of the war, over 40,000 civilians had been killed by German bombing. Almost half of these were in London, where more than a million houses were either damaged or destroyed.

Molly Fawcett-Barry worked as secretary to the editor of *The Listener*, a weekly magazine published by the BBC that transcribed recent broadcasts and reviewed new books and musical performances. Molly was based in the offices at Broadcasting House, located in central London, just off Oxford Street. The building lay in the main target zone for many German air raids throughout the war, and had already been badly damaged in a raid during October 1940.

This letter from Molly to her mother, undated but almost certainly written on 17 April 1941, reflects the way in which civilians had to cope with the regular threat posed by bombing.

The morning after a night raid, a café proprietor in a London side street carries on.

Dear old Thing,

I think I'd better take back my invitation to you in my last letter! What a night! They say it was the heaviest yet and I can believe them, altho' of course first thing next morning always seems 'opeless. I think Margaret slept right thro' it! At any rate there wasn't a sound or a light from her room the whole time.

I went to bed about midnight, during a lull in the gunfire, and was wakened just before 2 by a terrific barrage. Then all our guns went quiet and our fighters went up and there seemed to be a terrific air battle going on just over our heads. The wretched things were dive-bombing, which made it sound much worse. Then about 2.15 a 'plane zoomed down close to us – I thought it sounded as if something was wrong with it – then it roared up again and a few seconds later there was a sickening thud and the whole world seemed to shake, followed by several explosions. It was a Heinkel down on Campden Hill, just behind Patrick's place! Hammersmith suffered badly again, up by the Broadway, and Oxford St is closed from Marble Arch.

B.H. [Broadcasting House] itself is all right, but all round it again caught it badly. Our building structure seems to have stood firm, but the inside is just blown out. We clambered up to our offices, over blown-down walls and doors, and floors littered with glass and rubble, and have spent the morning salvaging. I got busy with brooms and duster and actually our office doesn't look so bad. The telephone had been blown right out of the window, hanging

Thursday, 12.45 p.m.

Dear old Thing,

I think I'd better take back my invitation to you in my last letter! What a night! They say it was the heaviest yet and I can believe them, altho' of course first thing next morning always seems hopeless. I think Margaret slept right thro' it! At any rate there wasn't a sound or a light from her room the whole time. I went to bed about midnight, during a lull in the gunfire, and was wakened just before 2 by a terrific barrage. Then all our guns went quiet and our fighters went up and there seemed to be a terrific air-battle going on just over our heads. The wretched things were dive-bombing, which made it sound much worse. Then about 2.15 a (plane zoomed down close to us - I thought it sounded as if something was wrong with it - then it roared up again and a few seconds later there was a sickening thud and the whole world seemed to shake, followed by several explosions. It was a Heinkel down on Campden Hill, just behind Patrick's place! Hammersmith suffered badly again, up by the Broadway, and Oxford St. is closed from Marble Arch. B.H. itself is all right, but all round it again caught it badly. Our building structure seems to have stood firm, but the inside is just blown out. We clambered up to our offices, over blown-down walls and doors, and floors littered with glass and rubble, and have spent the morning salvaging. I got busy with brooms and duster and actually our office dowsn't look so bad. The telephone had been blown right out of the window, hanging down its cord, and when I rescued it and put the receiver back on it rang - still working! It was P., to know if I was all right. The City apparently didn't get it so badly, altho' it was pretty widespread. They're still digging for people under a pub just opposite our windows - it's rather sickening, but how those A.F.S. men do work!

Ah well, A I didn't waste my sleepless hours -

down its cord, and when I rescued it and put the receiver back on it rang – still working! It was P, to know if I was all right. The City apparently didn't get it so badly, altho' it was pretty widespread. They're still digging for people under a pub just opposite our windows – it's rather sickening, but how those AFS [Auxiliary Fire Service] men do work!

Ah well, I didn't waste my sleepless hours – I darned all the stockings I could find, and plucked my eyebrows and made some tea! But I would have liked someone with me, all the same. One thing I'm thankful for – I didn't shampoo my hair last night as I intended to do – I'm covered with white dust now! It seems so heartbreaking, just as people were getting tidied up and rebuilt, to have the whole lot devastated again. But I suppose that's war – or this kind of war anyway.

... Lots of love to you all

Molly[62]

THE FLIGHT OF RUDOLF HESS

After Hitler became Chancellor of Germany in 1933, he appointed Rudolf Hess to be Deputy Führer of the Nazi Party. Upon the outbreak of war, Hitler's attention became focused on foreign affairs, and as a result Hess found himself increasingly sidelined and being replaced in many of his duties, most notably by Martin Bormann as the Führer's Private Secretary. Feeling increasingly distanced from Hitler and the conduct of the war, Hess grew concerned that Germany would face a war on two fronts as plans began to be made for the invasion of the Soviet Union. He felt that a deal with Britain might be feasible, and took it upon himself to pursue this by travelling to negotiate in person.

Rudolf Hess having a meal during his trial at Nuremberg.

Hess's sources mistakenly believed that King George VI was in disagreement with Churchill over how the war was being conducted, and that the Duke of Hamilton could serve as an appropriate contact through whom Hess could reach the King. Hess therefore took off in a Messerschmitt Bf 110 aircraft and flew to Scotland, parachuting out just south of Glasgow. He was arrested by a local farmer and handed over to the local Home Guard for interrogation, at which point he encountered Major Graham Donald of the Royal Observer Corps, as described in the letter below.

Hess's mission was in vain. Upon learning of his actions, Hitler stripped Hess of all his party and government offices and branded him insane in the German press. Hess was tried at Nuremberg after the war, where he was convicted of war crimes. He served a life sentence in prison in Germany, until his death by suicide in 1987 at the age of ninety-three.

19/5/41

Dear Sir Harry

I enclose a small piece from the Me 110 kindly flown into my area by
'Captain Alfred Horn' on the night of May 10th. I thought it might interest
you to have this as a memento of a most historic flight.

I had the privilege of apprehending him and later in the evening, after
checking over his plane, the unusual distinction of being the first (and only)
person to identify him as Rudolf Hess. After interrogating him for about 5
mins and getting his signature, I recognised him easily. This was easy. My
difficulty lay in getting one sensible individual up here with enough eyesight
to bear out my identification! Fortunately I was able to contact the Duke of
H about 2am and finally things started moving, slowly.

On Sunday I damned nearly phoned you to ask you to let Mr Churchill know
personally, but I knew it would sound such a cock-and-bull story over the wires.

I hope to see you
shortly up here again.
With best regards,

Yours sincerely

Graham Donald

P.S. When Adolf himself
arrives, I shall definitely
phone you this time,
even if it is at 3am![63]

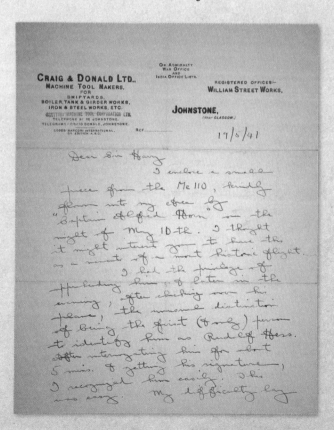

THE HOME GUARD

With German invasion a distinct possibility for the first few years of the war, a home defence force was set up in May 1940 as Britain's 'last line' against the invaders. Originally called the Local Defence Volunteers (LDV), recruits were usually men above or below the conscription age, plus those unfit or ineligible for front-line military service. By July 1940, nearly 1.5 million men aged between seventeen and sixty-five had enrolled, and the force's name was changed to the more inspiring Home Guard.

At first, the Home Guard were rather a slipshod militia, rarely in proper uniform and often bearing ancient or home-made weaponry. Yet they would soon evolve into a well-equipped and well-trained army. As well as preparing for a potential invasion, units of the Home Guard also performed other important roles, including bomb disposal and the manning of anti-aircraft and coastal artillery. Throughout the war, over 1,200 members of the Home Guard were killed. Once the likelihood of invasion receded following the Allied invasion of Normandy, the force was stood down on 3 December 1944.

Members of the Local Defence Volunteers being taught simple German phrases.

Regular training was undertaken during the war to provide local Home Guard and Civil Defence workers with realistic scenarios in which to hone their skills. One major training practice was undertaken in Oxford in January 1943. Student David Raikes wrote home to describe the strange events in which he was involved.

31/1/43

My dear Mummy

...Oxford was preoccupied with the great invasion exercise which for weeks had filled columns of the local press, announced itself from walls and doors and windows, occupied the mind of the local officialdom and spurred the Home Guard and local militia to the highest pitch of enterprise and cunning; while hard working civilians looked forward with mixed feelings to a weekend which they would probably spend as messengers, wardens, firemen, drivers, spies, refugees or as 'casualties' in some ARP clearing station; and while the RAF looked forward to a gala day of fun and games. In fact, a good time is being had by all.

The 'invasion' began at 1.30pm today. At 6.0pm a halt is called until 9am tomorrow morning. Closing time is 3.30 tomorrow afternoon. It is a very big affair, and probably much more realistic than the actual thing. I was just a humble fire watcher, and as such was relieved after a bit. But for the Home Guard and other defence forces it is a whole time job, and aeroplanes have been strafing the city non-stop since the outbreak of hostilities; bombs have been 'set off' in the streets, incendiaries have been lit, smoke from bombs has shrouded the city and bells and whistles have accompanied fire engines and ambulances through the streets. Meanwhile enemy ground forces are trying to occupy Oxford, and the Home Guard are, I hope, resisting.

An incendiary bomb appeared on one of the roofs and we were very prompt in reporting it on the telephone. Our promptness was not so very virtuous, as for at least ten minutes we had watched a party stealthily creeping along the roof, choose a site, place their firework in position and use a number of matches in lighting it. One of us stood by the telephone while the other

Tel. 3116.

TRINITY COLLEGE.

OXFORD.

31/1/43

My dear Mummy,

I wouldn't, for choice, have spent the last two hours on Trinity tower, with a North west gale blowing extremely cold air round me, and with intermittent showers of rain adding a great deal to the fun. But being in no position to choose, I made the most of it, appreciated to the full the panorama of towers, steeples, pinnacles, roofs, chimneys and fire escapes, viewed with detached amusement the comings and goings of the feverish little men below, and generally let nothing escape me of the drama that was being enacted around me, of which I was the reluctant but interested

watched for the first trace of smoke; we thought of ringing up to say where the bomb was as soon as it had been positioned, but we felt we'd better maintain the principle of realism...

Best love from

David[64]

CONSCIENTIOUS OBJECTION

The National Service (Armed Forces) Act introduced conscription during the war for all men aged between eighteen and forty-one. This would be extended by 1942 to include men up to the age of fifty-one, as well as women aged between twenty and thirty. Candidates could be rejected for medical reasons, while those already employed in vital industries and 'reserved' occupations might also avoid enlistment. From 1943, some conscripted men were also put to work in the mining industry as 'Bevin Boys'.

Provision was also made for conscientious objectors – those who held a moral or ethical objection to fighting in the war. These men would be forced to face a Tribunal, where they would be given the opportunity to present their case. Throughout the war, over 60,000 individuals registered in this way. The vast majority would be given non-combatant work of some nature, which might mean civilian work on the land or in a hospital, or a role in military units such as the Non-Combatant Corps.

However, the social stigma attached to holding a conscientious objection was ever-present. Despite the undoubtedly genuine reasons behind refusing to fight, accusations of cowardice were common. Chris Smith was a student at Cambridge University when he applied to be exempt from military service on religious grounds.

A conscientious objector facing a Tribunal.

16.4.43

Dear George

... Everybody has been so kind and helpful during the last week... I saw the Joint Recruiting Board yesterday and re-registered, this time as a C.O. I shall get a Tribunal – when, I am not quite sure – and as far as I can make out will be able to stay up here until then. Isn't that wonderful? You know, this is a remarkable country – so much so, that it is not easy to refuse the service they demand of one!

But of this one thing I am quite sure, if my duty to God and my duty to my country conflict, I must obey the call of God. I know that all Christians have not been led to make the same choice as myself, and I know they are just as sincere as myself. I tried to persuade myself for long enough that my way was the same as theirs, but it isn't, and I shan't be much of a witness for Christ if I fail him now. You know, I don't think I had ever realised before what strength God puts at our disposal, but I am convinced that through those who honestly and sincerely offer their lives to him – whatever way they may be led and however they choose to answer this particular question – God can work, God will work and is working, and through them his power, which is almighty, can change the world.

How did I give you the idea that I could not do Red Cross work? Have I left out a negative somewhere? On the contrary, I feel I cannot stand aside from all the dreadful suffering in the world and do nothing. Since the Christ upon the Cross is not suffering passively, since the cross is not the end, since the love of God is not negative, but active and dynamic and redemptive, that same action must typify our lives. To do nothing is never the right attitude for the Christian as he faces evil, sin and suffering.

But since RAMC work involves some training of a combatant nature, I cannot conscientiously do this and have applied to the Friends' Ambulance Unit to see if I can get in there. The one thing I am anxious to avoid is comfort and security, and I can best bear my Christian witness by sharing in the suffering and pain of the world, and by doing all in my power to alleviate it.

... Remember me in your prayers. I know there are many who are doing the same, and it makes all the difference.

Yours ever

Chris[65]

13 Warkworth Street,
Cambridge
16 : 4 : 43

Dear George,

Note the address please! It was grand to get your letter and the lithograph. Just like you to remember such a thing at this time!

Everybody has been so kind and helpful during the last week. Gordon Bennett, Mr Walker, my old School Chaplain & Headmaster, & Welbourne — all have been doing all they can for me. And things haven't been so black as I had expected. After enquiries had been made in London by Alex Wood and I had interviewed many people many times, I saw the Joint Recruiting Board yesterday and re-registered, this time as a C.O. I shall get a Tribunal — when, I am not quite sure — and as far as I can make out will be able to stay up here until then. Isn't that wonderful? You know, this is a remarkable country — so much so, that it is not easy to refuse the service they demand of one! But of this one thing I am quite sure, if my duty to God & my duty to my country conflict, I must obey the call of God. I know that all Christians have not been led to make the same choice as myself, and I know they are just as sincere as myself. I tried to persuade myself for long enough that my way was the same as theirs, but it isn't, and I shan't be much of a witness for Christ if I fail him now. You know, I don't think I had ever realised before what strength God puts at our disposal, but I am convinced that through those who honestly & sincerely offer their lives to him — whatever way they may be led and however they choose to answer this particular question — God can work, God will work and is working, and through them his power, which is almighty, which change the world.

How did I give you the idea that I could not do Red Cross work? Have I left out a negative somewhere? On the contrary, I feel I cannot stand

THE WOMEN'S LAND ARMY

As a nation, Britain had traditionally imported much of its food. When war broke out, and the Battle of the Atlantic limited the arrival of supplies into British ports, it was therefore necessary to grow more at home. With many male agricultural workers transferring to the armed forces, women were needed to provide a new rural workforce. The Women's Land Army (WLA) had originally been set up during the First World War, but reformed in June 1939. Initially consisting of volunteers, conscription was introduced in December 1941. By 1944, there were more than 80,000 Land Girls in uniform.

WLA Land Girl Margaret Scott brings in the harvest with a local villager near Rockingham, Northamptonshire.

Land Girls did a wide variety of jobs, ranging from traditional farm work to rat-catching and irrigation. They had to work in all weathers and conditions, and could be posted to any corner of the country. Many had originally lived in London or one of the other large cities, and therefore had to come to terms with a new outdoor lifestyle.

Mary Tetlow was a Land Girl based at RAF Catterick in Yorkshire.

Tues, Jun 1st 1943

Dear all

Your letter came this afternoon at five o'clock. We were hoeing potatoes in long rows before our house, and it was raining – just the right time to get a letter. The last half hour soon passed afterwards. How kind Valerie is to spend her Sunday afternoon writing. I must assure you we don't starve. This is the tea we ate today - three slices of spam, two tablespoonsful of peas, as much of carrots, some beetroot, a great slice of cake. Enough was left for our supper. So don't trouble to send a parcel, it was good of you to think of it, and thank you, but we are well fed.

Yesterday morning I was pulling up cabbages when Doreen came to say I had to go to the rabbit-hut. It was Sarge's idea that I should care for them when she left. Someone had told him I coveted this task very much, it was revealed later – someone who dislikes rabbits. Sarge began demonstrating how to clean out hutches. 'The main thing', he said, 'Is keep 'em dry. And it's an 'ell of a job.' Doreen and I continued cleaning all day, and she reminded me this meant staying indoors all the time. This depressed me so much, I wept on the rabbits, secretly. But a word here and there, a hint to Sarge led him to draw up a rota. Everyone is to do rabbits one day a week.

Out with my hoe again this morning into the fresh air.

Love,

Mary[66]

Women's Land Army
A. M. Q 45,
R. A. F. Station.
Catterick.

Tues. Jun 1st 1943.

Dear All,

Your letter came this afternoon at five o'clock. We were hoeing potatoes in long rows before our house, and it was raining. – Just the right time to get a letter. The last half hour Doreen passed afterwards. How kind Valerie is to spend her Sunday afternoon writing. I must assume you we don't starve, this is the tea we ate to-day. – three slices of spam, two tablespoonsful of peas, as much of carrots, some beetroot, a great slice of cake. Enough was left for our supper. So don't trouble to send a parcel, it was good of you to think of it, and thankyou, but we are well fed.

You had a pleasant week-end. On Saturday I did nothing particular, but on Sunday Ida and I went to Aunt's again. It had been a grey, chilly day but the evening was splendid. Mr. A. suggested a walk round Brough. – you would have enjoyed it. He pointed out a white horse on the farthest hill, (a land-mark, done in chalk or paint) and roads through the fields that leads to the sea. We sat on the bridge opposite Brough Hall, which is three hundred years old, and built of stone. Ida said she liked to look at it, it reminds her of a house in a story. She is collecting flowers, we found a wild strawberry flower. Yesterday morning, I was pulling up cabbages, when Doreen came to say I had to go to the rabbit-hut.

Left: 'Make Do and Mend' became one of the key Home Front campaigns of the war. Right: Repairing and refreshing older clothes was one way of coping with the rationing restrictions.

CLOTHES RATIONING

The war saw a huge demand for uniforms and other military uses of fabric, ranging from tents to parachutes, and civilian clothing production was therefore curtailed in order to reserve both materials and garment workers for the war effort.

In order to ensure that the limited civilian clothes available were distributed as fairly as possible, clothes rationing was announced on 1 June 1941. The 'Make Do and Mend' campaign was also launched to encourage people to make existing supplies of clothing and materials last longer. Posters and leaflets were distributed with advice on how to repair, renovate and make one's own clothes. Such information proved extremely important: as the war progressed, buying new clothing was severely restricted by the numbers of ration coupons made available to each person. Another solution was the Utility Clothing Scheme introduced in 1942, which offered consumers a range of standardised clothes affordable to all.

In the extract below from a letter written to her husband, who was serving overseas, Eileen Gurney described how she had fully embraced the 'Make Do and Mend' scheme.

I'm rather pleased about the clothes rationing as I can easily manage on the coupons allowed. I've got heaps of materials and all sorts of old things I can renovate. As it limits the extravagant business girls who spend about thirty bob a week on their clothes the competition won't be so great for although I can't be as well-dressed as a girl who spends lots of money on her clothes, I'm second to none when it comes to dressing for nothing, and looking well turned out in renovations, wangles and oddments pinched from your old suits.

I was going to ask for another pair of trousers but of course you'd better keep them now and I have now got two pairs of slacks so I don't really need another. I've got heaps of clothes and several lengths of material that I shan't even begin to make up till next year. So I'm not worrying. Joan's granny sent her two enormous winceyette night gowns. Real outsize they were and of good material. Joan gave them to me and from them I have made Richie three pairs of pyjamas. He looks sweet in them, they are like this with a little round collar and bell-bottomed trousers. When he's just had a bath and is all golden and rosy and is dressed up in them he looks good enough to eat.[67]

Eileen Gurney with her children in August 1944.

Left: New recruits to the WRNS arrive at the gates of the Drafting and Training Depot, suitcases in hand, where they are greeted by existing members. Right: WAAF personnel assist new recruits with their enrolment forms at a depot in Innsworth, Gloucester.

NEW ROLES

In order to free up men for combat roles, women were also conscripted into the three branches of the armed services to take on non-front-line duties. This would involve coming to terms with a new wartime way of life – wearing uniforms, following orders and completing tasks that, until now, few women would have been asked or expected to undertake.

Maureen Bolster wrote regularly to her fiancé Eric during the war. This letter, dating from her service while training as a Wren, illustrates the novelty of carrying out duties previously only performed by male sailors.

Jan 23 [1944]

Dearest Eric

Sunday morning – quiet sunshine after a stormy night, bacon and ersatz eggs for breakfast, went to communion – and here I am. I'm sitting on Margaret's bottom bunk, writing on a chair drawn up as a table – beside our cabin window. It's quite a pleasing view – over the city to the country, with a fair amount of trees here and there...

However – for the news: My love, I nearly had kittens on Friday pm! We were out in the 48 ft long Diesel, a rather cumbersome affair but fairly reliable. I was at the engine room controls (gears and throttle) when suddenly the Naval Officer aboard shouted out – 'Boggis, take over from Bolster – Bolster, take the wheel and be coxswain for half an hour!'

My love – I've *never* had charge of a boat in my life! And not a thing that size into the bargain – and a mixed crew, to make it worse. I didn't know *what* to say! I climbed tremblingly up to the wheel – the other Wrens all agog with amusement – and off we went. I just *can't* tell you the heart attacks I had that afternoon! I had to go alongside all sorts of things – do all sorts of manoeuvres – shouting instructions to the stoker – 'Half Ahead' – 'Astern' – 'Full Astern' – 'Easy' – 'Full Ahead'.

I then had to answer the Officer's questions – 'Yes Sir, full amidships' – 'Steamer on the starboard bow, Sir' – 'more than two points abaft the beam'. I was *exhausted* by the time we'd got in! One day, I'd love to be a coxswain – but I want to prove myself an efficient stoker first!

Love, Maureen xxxxxxx! Xxx[68]

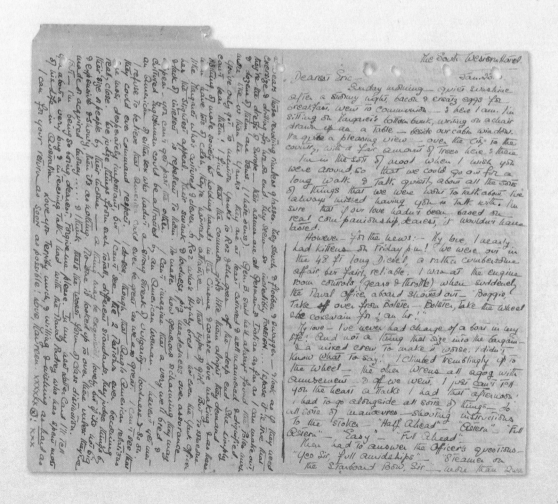

THE WOMEN'S ROYAL NAVAL SERVICE

As with other branches of the military staffed by women, the Women's Royal Naval Service (WRNS) was created during the First World War, but disbanded shortly afterwards. It reformed in April 1939 with the aim of recruiting women for shore-based jobs, and by 1943 there were around 74,000 'Wrens' in Britain and overseas. They would play a crucial part in duties including intelligence work and the planning of naval operations. Many also served at Bletchley Park and its outstations, where code-breaking was undertaken.

Stephanie Batstone was a Wren signaller. Her letter home below, written from the Lancashire shore establishment HMS *Cabbala*, illustrates that the Royal Navy was not yet quite fully equipped for women.

Recruitment campaigns played on the glamorous side of life in the forces.

Monday 17:15 [14/6/43]

Dear B

... I am now a *real Wren*! I am actually writing this in my bell-bottoms! I expect you heard when I rang up that everything is simply miles too big, but as there is no way of getting things altered we are all having to wear them as they are.

When we came to be kitted up, we were all completely flabbergasted to discover that the bell-bottoms issued to us are actually sailor's trousers, and not made for girls at all. We each had two pairs – enormous thick things, all padded with lumps of wadding, hundreds of buttons, blue and white stripe linings and an enormous let-down flap in front, just on the stomach. I was lucky, and got two pairs of 6's, but some of them, no bigger than me, were given 12's and cannot change them... The only thing to do is to just take in an enormous tuck each side and hope for the best – but you will have about four thicknesses of stuff on your stomach... Still, as we only wear them in the camp I suppose it doesn't much matter. Mum will probably get led in for altering two pairs when I come home on leave.

I also wear that ridiculous hat, and it isn't as bad as I had expected. I am getting quite used to putting it on over one eye. Yesterday, Sunday, seven of us went out together in full glad rags for the first time. We were simply terrified we should meet an officer and have to salute, but luckily we didn't. We went and had tea at the 'White Swan' – Baked beans on toast, toast and jam, tea, damsons and custard. Afterwards we walked miles, trying to break our shoes in. When we were all quite lame we got on a bus and went to Earlstown where there is a good services canteen. We asked for whatever they had got, and they brought – baked beans on toast, peas, chips, toast, jam, cake, tea. This lot, which took us hours to eat, cost 6½ d. It's certainly cheap to be a Wren. When I came back I felt as if I had been working in a baked bean factory all my life...

Must stop now. Love from

Bunny[69]

FOOD RATIONING

Britain introduced food rationing in January 1940 to ensure that the limited supplies available in the country were shared out as equally as possible. Every man, woman and child was given an individual ration book containing coupons that had to be exchanged before rationed goods could be bought.

Basic foodstuffs, such as sugar, meat, fats and cheese, were directly rationed, while other items, such as tinned goods, dried fruit, cereals and biscuits, were allocated using a points system dependent on availability and demand. Priority for particular items, such as milk and eggs, was given to select

Customers queue up outside a bakery and confectioner's on High Road, Wood Green, in London.

groups, including children and expectant mothers. Fruit and vegetables were not rationed, but remained in short supply, with imported items such as bananas proving incredibly rare. As part of the 'Dig for Victory' campaign, people were encouraged to grow their own produce in gardens and allotments, with many public parks converted for this purpose.

In letters written to her daughter in the United States, Mrs Rickman recounted aspects of her wartime life in Sandon, Hertfordshire. She was particularly concerned by the shortages of food on the Home Front.

December 16, 1940

For the first time since the war began I am finding blanks in the simple menu I usually live on. Cheese is very difficult to get and Stilton (at 3/- a pound) was literally the *only* cheese Selfridges had in stock last week. I bought a large chunk and shared it with the Evans's [at Danyells] when I got back as they also go in for cheeses and fruit and nuts instead of desserts. There are no dried fruits of any sort to be had and no marmalade anywhere. Selfridges are sold out of tinned fruit but one can still get it in smaller shops. Sweets have completely disappeared in all forms from small shops but I got a stock at Selfridges so as to have some to hand out at Christmas. I also got a pound of crystalised ginger for a Christmas present. Chocolate you can get only if you happen to get in on the day the shop gets its monthly ration from Cadbury's.

I can't be bothered to make cakes and puddings for myself so I find I have difficulty in absorbing all the fats of the ration (which most people have difficulty with) though I try, for health's sake. The margarine is very good if you don't spread it on too thick and gets its texture. I can hardly tell it at all at cold temperatures from most of the butter now distributed, but if it *were* butter I could paste it thick on hot toast and enjoy it as I can *not* enjoy margarine that way. The 'cooking fat' supplied at first was awful, but I was able to get lard locally till lately and still have some. Now only 'cooking fat' is available and I was surprised today on frying some potatoes to find it was as good as lard.

Bananas are off the map, so are lemons and a very few oranges are being distributed; dates and figs, usually a standby at this time of year, and also raisins, are not to be had. Tomatoes are still to be got, not very good, and ⅛ a pound. I managed to get a couple of pounds of onions before the shortage got so acute they were not to be had at all, and am using these very sparingly for flavouring only.

I have written all this at length so you can get a picture of what the shipping crisis means to such a family as us. In short, it isn't bad *yet* at all for us, but is on the verge of being very unpleasant, though not serious.[70]

Growing your own was a preferred alternative to relying on rationed food.

FACTORY WORK

From early 1941, it became compulsory in Britain for women aged between eighteen and sixty to register for war work. That December, the conscription of unmarried women under the age of thirty also began, offering them a choice between military service or employment in factories. Women who were pregnant or had young children were exempt, but could still volunteer, while women classed as 'immobile' (meaning that they had a husband at home or were married to a serviceman) were directed into local war work.

Civilian war work might include employment in factories making munitions, vehicles, aircraft or other supplies to keep the nation's economy and war effort going. Other vital work was undertaken outside on the land, as well as on Britain's transport network. Britain managed to mobilise its civilians more effectively than any other combatant nation, and by 1944 a third of the civilian population was engaged in war work, including over 7 million women.

Nancy Ridgway was conscripted to work on aircraft production in Cheshire.

Female workers have a quick cup of tea before the dinner-time rush begins at this works canteen in an aircraft factory, somewhere in Britain.

I was working on a milk round for the Co-Op, horse and cart of course... One day we all got letters to say that we would have to do war work and I was to go and build aeroplanes... I was to go to Broughton at Chester to learn about Wellington aircraft, Vickers Armstrong's as it was known. I had to get digs in Chester so got them in North Street, 10 shillings per week got just a piece of toast and a cup of tea for breakfast, but at least they had a canteen for dinners. I was to be taught how to do flotation. This it seems was if a plane got into the sea they pulled a stopper out and 12 bags blew up on the floor of the plane and helped to keep it afloat. I was put with a young bloke called Carl and his mate Aggie. To do this job you sat on a stool underneath the plane, it was marked off where the bags would go and little straps were riveted in and the bags were on plastic trays, sort of...

One day a hammer fell out of the plane where we were sitting and hit Carl on the head and knocked him out. I said to Aggie, come on then we can get on with the job. I don't know what to do, she said. I was disgusted – she'd worked with Carl for three years. We are expected to learn this job in a month... You'll not learn it here, she said, as the men have said they're not going to tell you anything 'cos you'll only be taking work away from us here.

I went down to the Foreman's office and played hell about this. He knew about this attitude but would do nothing about it. Don't fall out about it, he said, just keep your eyes open and see what you can pick up... I was glad when the month was up. I thought, I'm not going to like this job. I wish I was back on my milk round with my horse and cart.[71]

This campaign harked back to female employment in the First World War.

WE **NEED** THE WOMEN BACK AT WORK AGAIN

Help to make the goods we want

Join your friends at work

Put more money in your bag

WOMEN WORKERS ARE WANTED
IN THIS FACTORY
come in and talk to our Labour Manager

EVACUATION

The first official civilian evacuations had begun on 1 September 1939, shortly before the outbreak of war, when almost 1.5 million people were moved away from larger cities in order to protect them from the expected bombing. Among the groups to be evacuated to the countryside were school-age children, pregnant women, mothers with toddlers and those with disabilities. In many cases, the experience was a traumatic one, especially for children who may never have spent time away from their parents before. It could also be difficult for the foster parents, who were sometimes unsuited to looking after young children.

When enemy bombing failed to occur, many returned home at the beginning of 1940, thereby exposing them later that year to the very dangers from which the government had hoped to protect them. Further rounds of official evacuations occurred across Britain in the summer and autumn, when a German invasion seemed possible and the Blitz brought devastation to the cities. But the scheme was voluntary, and many children remained at home with their families. The German V-weapon attacks on the south-east of England, which began in June 1944, prompted a final wave of evacuations from those areas.

Graham Willmot was evacuated to Devon with the rest of his primary school in June 1940, and sent home the following note to his parents to announce his arrival.

A group of young female evacuees from Bristol carry their suitcases and gas masks as they are led along the platform upon arrival at Brent Station in 1940.

12.6.40

Dear Mummy and Daddy

I am happy in my billet the people are nice but at school it is horrible everything is different we have French names sing French songs. Three other boys are billeted with me the name of the landlady is Mrs Milbourne. I have a lot off [sic] homework to do so I will write a longer letter later on.

Yours,

Graham

PS the dinners are horrible there is not [a] lot of cutlery, so I had to eat my first course without a knife and my second without a spoon.[72]

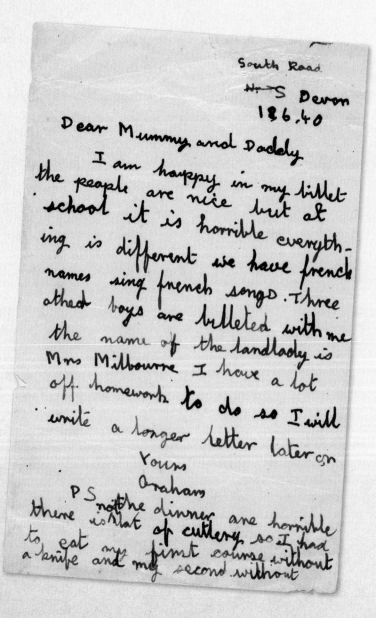

CHAPTER EIGHT
NORTH-WEST EUROPE

Clockwise: Paratroops of 22 Independent Parachute Company, British 6th Airborne Division, wait to board the aircraft that will drop them over Normandy on D-Day. • Follow-up troops from the US 1st Infantry Division disembark onto Easy Red beach, Omaha area, 6 June 1944. • HMS Warspite, *part of Bombarding Force 'D' off Le Havre, shells German gun batteries in support of the landings on Sword area, 6 June 1944.*

OPERATION 'OVERLORD'

As early as December 1941, the western Allies were all in agreement that the defeat of Nazi Germany should be their main war aim. A successful invasion of France and north-west Europe would open a second front and relieve pressure on the Soviet Union, which was fighting in the east. It would also help to drain Germany of valuable resources and key strategic sites.

The invasion, named Operation 'Overlord', would require an unprecedented level of cooperation between the Allies. It was led by the Supreme Headquarters Allied Expeditionary Force (SHAEF) under General Dwight D. Eisenhower of the United States. Secrecy was an essential part of the operation, and elaborate deception plans were developed in order to draw German defences as far away from the Normandy landing sites as possible. Massive resources were prepared for the invasion, with over 2 million troops held in readiness.

'Overlord' would begin on D-Day, 6 June 1944. The Allied invasion force was a truly international one, consisting largely of American, British and Canadian troops, but also Australian, Belgian, Czech, Dutch, French, Greek, New Zealand, Norwegian, Rhodesian and Polish naval, air or ground support. The following message from Eisenhower was distributed to troops at the final moment.

Eisenhower gives a last minute talk to paratroopers of the US 101st Airborne Division as they prepared to take off from their base at Greenham Common, Berkshire.

SUPREME HEADQUARTERS
ALLIED EXPEDITIONARY FORCE

Soldiers, Sailors and Airmen of the Allied Expeditionary Force!

You are about to embark upon the Great Crusade, toward which we have striven these many months. The eyes of the world are upon you. The hopes and prayers of liberty-loving people everywhere march with you. In company with our brave Allies and brothers-in-arms on other Fronts, you will bring about the destruction of the German war machine, the elimination of Nazi tyranny over the oppressed peoples of Europe, and security for ourselves in a free world.

Your task will not be an easy one. Your enemy is well trained, well equipped and battle-hardened. He will fight savagely.

But this is the year 1944! Much has happened since the Nazi triumphs of 1940-41. The United Nations have inflicted upon the Germans great defeats, in open battle, man-to-man. Our air offensive has seriously reduced their strength in the air and their capacity to wage war on the ground. Our Home Fronts have given us an overwhelming superiority in weapons and munitions of war, and placed at our disposal great reserves of trained fighting men. The tide has turned! The free men of the world are marching together to Victory!

I have full confidence in your courage, devotion to duty and skill in battle. We will accept nothing less than full Victory!

Good Luck! And let us all beseech the blessing of Almighty God upon this great and noble undertaking.

Dwight Eisenhower

Supreme Headquarters Allied Expeditionary Force

Soldiers, Sailors and Airmen of the Allied
Expeditionary Force!

You are about to embark upon the Great Crusade,
toward which we have striven these many months.
The eyes of the world are upon you. The hopes and
prayers of liberty-loving people everywhere march
with you. In company with our brave Allies and
brothers-in-arms on other Fronts, you will bring
about the destruction of the German war machine,
the elimination of Nazi tyranny over the oppressed
people of Europe, and security for ourselves in a
free world.

*Major General Dwight
D. Eisenhower*

Your task will not be an easy one. Your enemy is well trained, well equipped
and battle-hardened. He will fight savagely.

But this is the year 1944! Much has happened since the Nazi triumphs of
1940–41. The United Nations have inflicted upon the Germans great defeats,
in open battle, man-to-man. Our air offensive has seriously reduced their
strength in the air and their capacity to wage war on the ground. Our Home
Fronts have given us an overwhelming superiority in weapons and munitions
of war, and placed at our disposal great reserves of trained fighting men. The
tide has turned! The free men of the world are marching together to Victory!

I have full confidence in your courage, devotion to duty and skill in battle.
We will accept nothing less than full Victory!

Good Luck! And let us all beseech the blessing of Almighty God upon this
great and noble undertaking.

Dwight D Eisenhower[73]

OPERATION 'NEPTUNE'

Nearly 7,000 naval vessels, including battleships, destroyers, minesweepers, escorts and assault craft, took part in Operation 'Neptune', the naval component of the D-Day operations. This huge armada was responsible for escorting and landing over 132,000 ground troops on the beaches, while also carrying out intense bombardments on the Normandy coastal defences to remove key fortifications. Once the troops began to land on the beaches, the ships anchored off the coast assisted with continued artillery to support the move inland.

On D-Day, the cruiser HMS *Belfast* was the flagship of Bombardment Force E, supporting troops landing at Gold and Juno beaches. Her first target was the German gun battery at La Marefontaine, which was successfully put out of action. Over the following thirty-three days she remained in support of the Normandy landings, and in that time fired over 4,000 six-inch and 1,000 four-inch shells. Able Seaman Arnold Jones was serving in the *Belfast* throughout that time.

An aerial photograph of Allied ships gathering off the Isle of Wight before setting off for the Normandy beaches.

7/6/44

Dear Nell and Kath and Kev

By now you will have realised why I have not wrote before. I guess you have heard on the news that the *Belfast* is in the Cruiser 'Invasion Force'. As I am writing this, the sun is beating down and it's a glorious day, as I look to my right I can see the green fields and small forests of Cherbourg which is just about a mile away from the ship, and just over the hill you can see small bursts of smoke where a kind of tank battle seems to be in progress.

When we came along the English Channel on our way here, we passed thousands of Landing Craft of all shapes and sizes and as we passed them all the boys were cheering, and as we approached the coast of France we could hear thousands of bombers overhead and then all along the coast there were loud explosions, and great fires. We went in first with the invasion barges behind us, and then came the great moment when we opened fire. When we had finished shelling the beach, all the invasion craft surged forward and landed on the beach and they seem to be making splendid progress.

All yesterday there were ships full of army wagons moving towards the beach and I was wondering if Bert was there. If you were here right now you would be amazed at the number of ships there are here, and every now and again you can see streams of landing craft and amphibious tanks going ashore. We haven't seen any U-Boats or E Boats yet but we had a few air attacks, which are soon drove away. All yesterday we shelled the German shore batteries and put nearly all of them out of action.

We are just going to start another bombardment so I shall have to close now, hoping that everything is OK with you and that you have heard from Lew, and that Bert is OK wherever he may be. I am still keeping swell. Cheerio for now!

Your loving Brother and Uncle

Arn[74]

4/6/44.

PJX 521173
28 MESS
HMS. Belfast
C/O GPO
LONDON.

Dear Nell, Kath, Ken,

By now you will
have realized why I have not wrote
before. I guess you have heard on the
news that the "Belfast" is in the
Cruiser "Invasion Force". As I am
writing this, the sun is setting down,
and its a glorious day. As I look to
my right I can see the green fields
and small forests of "Cherbourg" which
is just about a mile away from
the ship, and yet over the hill you
can see small bursts of smoke, where
a kind of tank battle seems to be
in progress. When we came along
the English Channel on our way
here, we passed thousands of landing
craft, of all shapes and sizes, and
as we passed them, all the
boys were cheering, and so was

D-DAY: THE AIRBORNE LANDINGS

D-Day was conducted in two main phases, with an initial airborne assault preceding the amphibious landings on the beaches. Allied aircraft also supported the operations, having already secured air superiority prior to the invasion.

Shortly after midnight on 6 June, over 18,000 men of the British 6th Airborne Division and the United States 82nd and 101st Airborne Divisions were dropped into Normandy by both parachute and glider. Their objectives were to capture key sites behind the beaches and to secure the flanks of the assault areas.

On their night-time approach, the transport aircraft faced heavy cloud and enemy ground fire. As a result, many of the airborne units were dropped some distance from their target areas, yet this scattering of forces actually proved beneficial by causing confusion among the Germans, who refused to accept that a major invasion was happening until it was too late. Despite heavy resistance in places, the airborne forces largely achieved their objectives.

Gerald Ritchie was a company commander in the 12th Battalion Parachute Regiment, part of the 6th Airborne Division, and sent this letter home shortly after D-Day.

Sunday

My dear Muriel

... The days before the party started were, as you may imagine, rather hectic ones. We were cut off from the outside world completely and spent our time going over our little bit of the operation over and over again with maps, photos and models, until everyone knew their piece backwards. We emplaned late in evening of the Monday and it all seemed very unreal, it was difficult to imagine that by dawn on the next day, we should have been tipped out of our aeroplane over France and should have landed in a place where they were quite a number of evil minded Bosche, whose one object would be to liquidate us before we could do the same to them. It all seemed so like an

Depot + School Airborne Forces

Chesterfield

Derbyshire

1

Sunday

My dear Muriel

Thank you so much for your letter received some time ago when I was in hospital, as you see I am now out, thank goodness & am more or less alright again, I have still a bit of a ~~whole~~ hole in my arm but nothing to speak of. I must say I was terribly lucky as the bit of shrapnel missed everything important, it went in about four inches below my shoulder, rather

Gerald Ritchie visiting the Imperial War Museum during the 1970s.

ordinary exercise, and this illusion (very fortunately) went on for me right up to the moment I landed with a bump in a field.

The doors of the aircraft were opened while we were still over the sea and being No 1 to jump in my aircraft I had a grand view as the coast of France appeared below us. I could see no sign of life below us, thanks to the RAF, and although I believe a few shots were fired at us I never saw any... A few moments more and the red light came on and then the green, and out I went, my mind a complete blank as usual when I jump. I can remember very little of my descent, it didn't take long anyway. I did rather a poor landing, my own fault entirely and bruised my knees which made crawling most painful, and I had a certain amount to do during that day! Anyway I scrambled to my feet and unhitched myself from my parachute and took a look round. I knew I was more or less in the right place as others were coming down in the vicinity, but I was not exactly sure where. There was a horse grazing in the field where I was, who didn't seem to like my presence much, so I went off in the direction where I thought our rendezvous was...

On the other companies' areas, things were more exciting and quite a number of enemy with some tanks had got right up to our line and had over-run one position, but they were beaten off. By this time however the sea landing had been made, in fact some time before. The barrage put down on the coast was terrific and was just one continuous explosion and noise for some time, quite indescribable really, and most cheering to us. A few hours after the sea landing the commandos got up to us and came across our bridges, again most cheering, and things were a bit hectic just then. I remember that our lot had a piper with them, which was the first thing we heard of them, and a very pleasant sound it was, and I have taken a better view of bagpipes ever since!

A lot of it I've given rather sketchily and I could never hope to give you the atmosphere, as it were, it is really quite indescribable. The extraordinary smell of broken buildings and explosives; the countryside, very like the Cotswolds really, littered with gliders and parachutes; gliders everywhere, in hedges and fences, some broken so much that it looked that no one could have survived... It was really an amazing but very unpleasant and tragic two days...

Yrs ever,

Gerald[76]

This oblique aerial photograph shows parachutes and Horsa gliders on one of 6th Airborne Division's drop zones between Ranville and Amfreville, 6 June 1944.

GLIDERS

While gliders had already been used to land troops and supplies during the war, D-Day would see these aircraft employed on an unprecedented scale to transport both men and equipment to Normandy.

One of the most common forms of glider was the Horsa, first built in 1942. They were particularly useful when heavier equipment unsuitable for delivery via parachute, such as vehicles, needed to be transported. Gliders were towed by transport or bomber aircraft before gliding silently into the landing zone, their hinged noses and removable tail sections allowing cargo to be unloaded relatively easily after landing.

Glider troops of 6th Airborne Division beside their Horsa, which crashed through a stone wall on landing near La Haute Ecarde, 6 June 1944.

However, such gliders were relatively flimsy vehicles, being mainly built from wood and fabric. They were also difficult to steer when compared to a standard aircraft. As this letter from Captain Cross of the 2nd Battalion Oxfordshire and Buckinghamshire Light Infantry illustrates, a landing by glider could often prove dangerous.

23rd June 1944

The glider flight was bloody! It was, of course, longer than most we've done before because of the business of getting into formation, collecting fighter escort and so on. After about quarter of an hour I began to be sick and continued until we were over the Channel where the air was much calmer. The Channel was a wonderful sight – especially the traffic at this end – Piccadilly Circus wasn't in it. We were not over the coast this side long enough for me to be sick again and we were pretty busy thinking about landing. The landing was ghastly.

Mine was the first glider down though we were not quite in the right place, and the damn thing bucketed along a very upsy-downsy field for a bit and then broke across the middle – we just chopped through those anti-landing poles (like the ones I used to cut during my forestry vac) as we went along. However the two halves of the glider fetched up very close together and we quickly got out ourselves and our equipment and lay down under the thing because other gliders were coming in all around and Jerries were shooting things about at them and us so it wasn't very healthy to wander about. Our immediate opposition – a machine-gun in a little trench – was very effectively silenced by another glider which fetched up plumb on the trench and a couple of Huns – quite terrified – came out with their hands up!

Having discovered that we were all there and bound up a few scratches we then set off to the scene of the battle. I shall not tell you about that except that apart from a bar of chocolate and half the contents of my whisky flask I had no time to eat or drink for a very uncomfortably long time – too much else to do, but it seems incredible now. From my last meal in England to my first cup of char and hard ration in France was very nearly 48 hours! But I've been making up for it since.

Somebody once said that war was composed of intensive boredom relieved by periods of acute fear. That is it in a nutshell. The boys used to hate digging themselves trenches on Salisbury Plain but you should just see how fast they do it now! And we've had a good many to dig in various different places since we came here. My hands are not what they were![76]

D-DAY: THE BEACH LANDINGS

On the morning of 6 June 1944, ground troops landed on five assault beaches codenamed Utah, Omaha, Gold, Juno and Sword. Despite facing different degrees of resistance, and in some places suffering significant casualties, by the end of the day the Allies had established themselves on shore and could begin the liberation of France.

Captain Hugh Collinson came under heavy fire when landing on Sword Beach with the 1st Battalion South Lancashire Regiment, part of the British 3rd Infantry Division. Sword was the easternmost of the landing beaches, and rising tides and the local terrain created a narrow front. This, along with the strong German resistance, hindered their assault. Congestion on the beach then caused delays in landing the armoured support needed for the advance inland.

Troops of the 3rd Infantry Division on Queen Red beach, Sword area, early in the morning of 6 June 1944.

Although successfully repelling a German counter-attack, the 3rd Division failed to take their key objective for D-Day, which was the city of Caen. The capture of Caen would therefore become a focal point for British strategy over the coming weeks and, due to strong resistance from the Germans, would not be fully achieved until mid-July 1944.

10.6.44

5.45 down we went in our assault boats and it *was* rough... I knew we were due for an unpleasant run in to the beaches. Luckily, common sense had prevailed amongst the higher-ups and we were allowed to stand up until quite close in-shore, which made a big difference and only about 25% were sick... It really was a wonderful sight and I hope to see it again in comfort in the pictures. The hosts of small landing craft, the flag ships, the landing craft tanks, the rocket craft, the destroyers, cruisers and battleships firing

Hugh Collinson

away, and the continued drone of aircraft overhead. In fact I was so lost in admiration that I had almost forgotten that this was not an exercise and was only brought back to reality when a few bullets started whistling over our heads. Then we got down. A few minutes wait, then the ramp went down and we were up to our waists in water with bullets whistling round our ears.

I got to the edge of the water, looked round and found my Tels [Army Telephonists] were just behind me, then made for a tank which had been knocked out – afforded some cover whilst I took stock of the situation. Paused there, saw my CO 30 yards ahead on my right and followed. We were getting across the beach nicely when I heard the whine of a shell, shouted 'get down', and fell flat on my face. There was a bang and I felt something hit my side. I put my hand down, felt it was wet, looked at it, no blood. Then I realised what had happened. A shell splinter had hit my water bottle and had broken it. Then I saw something much worse. My best Tel, a chap called

Harrison of Preston, was lying in rather a peculiar attitude. He was a grand little chap, and landed in West Africa, Sicily and Italy, always doing something useful, and I'm sure he would have gone to the top in the Navy if he had stayed in it. He was only 21 and I had to leave him there and get on with the job. I feel awful whenever I think about it and I have to write to his mother.

Well, I got up to the cover of the sand hills and then we found that we had been put down on the beach 300 yards too far north, right opposite a strong point. The CO tried to find a way out, exposed himself for a second and was killed. And all the time shells, mortar-bombs and bullets were flying around on the beach; craft bringing vehicles ashore were arriving, vehicles coming ashore... We found a dug-out – kindly dug by Jerry – about 300 yards off the beach, and after some time under continuous shell fire we managed to get a message through to the *Virago*...

Hugh[77]

Canadian troops of the 3rd Canadian Infantry Division disembark from an LCA (Landing Craft Assault) on to Juno beach while under fire from German troops in the houses facing them, 6 June 1944.

D-DAY: OMAHA BEACH

Troops from the United States 1st and 29th Infantry Divisions landed on Omaha beach. This proved to be the most heavily defended of all the landing areas, and casualties were correspondingly higher than in any other sector. Unexpectedly, the highly experienced German 352nd Infantry Division had been taking part in anti-invasion training in the area, and was therefore able to reinforce the coastal defences near Omaha. Additionally, the preliminary air and naval bombardments had failed to knock out the strong German defences along that part of the Normandy coast.

The Americans experienced great difficulty in getting off the beach, yet were able to gain a small foothold by the end of the day. At the nearby Pointe du Hoc, US Rangers managed to destroy German gun emplacements at the top of the cliff, despite sustaining heavy casualties.

Lieutenant Commander Robert Macnab began this letter just a week after D-Day, writing it entirely at his action station as Torpedo Officer in the cruiser HMS *Glasgow*. This was the only British ship in an otherwise American naval squadron, and their particular responsibility was to support the landings on Omaha.

A survivor from a sunk American landing craft is given first aid on Omaha beach, 6 June 1944.

14th June '44

My dear Mummy and Daddy

A signal has been made that we can 'relate our experiences' in this operation – astonishing, but there it is!

At nightfall we... began the approach to the French coast. The Padre read Lord Nelson's prayer over the loudspeakers... But all was not quiet ashore during this ponderous approach. The RAF 'whom God preserve' (!) had been giving their biggest and best to the beaches, batteries and entire defences. A pyrotechnic display such as this has, I believe, seldom been seen before – it was splendid... One six inch gun battery on Pointe du Hoc in particular came in for a terrible time; enormous explosions rent it continuously for about 20 minutes and later it received many broadsides from the US Battleship *Texas*. Almost the entire point is now crumbled into the sea and the battery never fired a shot.

... Our Squadron was supporting the landing of the 2nd American Army on the stretch of beach from Vierville sur Mer to Port en Bessin... At 0640 after an intense bombardment by Rocket Craft, the first wave of the invasion landed – against heavy opposition – and it was here that things first took a more sombre turn. There was rather too much sea and the enemy were strongly positioned in fox holes in the cliffs and high ground beyond the beaches – and these positions had not been neutralised by the bombardment. The destroyers now all closed in to point blank range and plugged away at these hidden positions with all their guns; the effect, however, was disappointing and the troops were held on the beaches all that day, under a heavy fire. It was only at night that they managed to break out. The enemy brought up artillery and kept up a continuous fire, which soon had some good old blazes going on the beach. The ships tried to locate and destroy these batteries but of course this was not as easy as dealing with the fixed defences.

I think the story of the landing is just one of gigantic organisation and effort – which succeeds in planting many thousands of tons of soldiers and equipment on French soil each day...

Much love to all

Yrs ever, Robert[78]

H.M.S. Glasgow,
c/o G.P.O.
London.

14th June '44.

My dear Mammy & Daddy,

A signal has been made that we can 'relate our experiences' in this operation – astonishing, but there it is! I expect you'll have had it all already from the B.B.C. and newspapers – however, another 'eyewitness account' may be of interest.

Anchored here off the coast of France (Isigny), our reaction at the moment is one of complete and utter boredom; all is perfect peace – but this is a good sign, so we mustn't grumble.

We knew it was coming about a fortnight before; tension was growing, movement increasing – and then we all sailed for our assembly ports. The ships were now "sealed" and the orders opened – about a ton o' them! Here we met our American squadron, of which we are the only British ship. U.S.S. 'Texas', 'Arkansas' and 'Nevada' were, I think, all mentioned by the B.B.C. and are the same ships that formed the American Battle Squadron over here in the last war. (And, incidentally, are the ships which put up the incident of the drunken commander for you at Portsmouth!) There are several U.S. cruisers, many destroyers and the two French cruisers 'Georges Leygues' and 'Montcalm', both of which I dined in during the time of waiting; these which were both at Dakar during the battle in the 'Dragon' took part. We exchanged quite

NORMANDY

While the importance of D-Day was crucial in establishing a position in north-west Europe from which to launch a larger campaign, it was just the first step in liberating France and the rest of the continent. During the three months following 6 June 1944, the Allies launched a series of additional offensives throughout Normandy in an attempt to advance further inland.

Sherman tanks of the 10th Armoured Cavalry Brigade (1st Polish Armoured Division) advance through open fields in support of the 2nd Canadian Infantry Division during the Battle of the Falaise Gap.

German resistance was both strong and determined, and as a result the Allied campaign in Normandy took much longer to succeed than had been expected. The Normandy landscape was characterised by the *bocage* – sunken lanes bordered by high, thick hedgerows – which proved difficult to penetrate, yet easy for the German occupiers to defend.

Thomas Green served with the 7th Battalion Hampshire Regiment in Normandy, and here describes the street-fighting in which they were involved in the French village of Maltot in July 1944.

I found myself behind a Churchill tank which was firing at something at the end of the orchard. The something turned out to be a dug-in Tiger tank. Its first shot blew up the Churchill and then, ponderously it backed out of its emplacement and disappeared into the village. I joined the section, who had lost the rest of the platoon. They were trying with a mixture of A Coy and C Coy riflemen to clear the house at the end of the orchard. Three or four dead, including a C Coy officer lay in front of the door. I had the only Bren. Sergeant Miller came up and acted as my No 2 while I sprayed the whole of the front of the house. Under cover of my fire, Francis, Aggie and Wally rushed in the front door. A smattering of shots, and two sullen SS appeared. Seeing us confronting them they stopped on the top step. Aggie promptly kicked them down the steps and they shambled to the rear at a jog trot.

We worked our way round to the front garden of this house, the garden which butted on to Maltot's main street. Beyond that we could not go. A fusillade of burst after burst of machine gun fire swept down the street, mainly coming from a large eight wheeled armoured car to our right, parked by the low stone wall of the church. From the church tower a brisk sniper fire coming straight down into the garden was rapidly making a shambles of it. Here, in this laurel bushed garden, among many others died my old companion of QM days, Charlie Jenner, and his inseparable companion, L/Cpl Downs was so enraged that seizing a Piat mortar he rushed into the street and was shot down immediately by the armoured car. Clearly, unless we could dispose of the car, we would all be shot down as we crouched in the earthy garden.

At this juncture, B Coy's 2" mortar man, a giant named Bayliss walked deliberately through the hail of bullets and lay down with his weapon in the road. He placed a bomb in the barrel and fired. The bomb soared up in easy flight, turned at the top of its trajectory and plummeted down. The hatch in the turret of the car opened and a German officer looked out. As he did so, the bomb swooped in. There was a muffled roar, and the car rocked on its springs. White smoke poured out of it. I gave it a long squirt from the Bren, and we surged out of the garden and across the road. Our friend in the church tower lost his nerve and ran when he saw the car blow up. He dashed through the tombstones, and as he drew way Aggie contemptuously brought him down with a snap shot, and fired again and again into the place where the Nazi fell.[79]

A German prisoner captured by Canadian troops of 1st Battalion, North Shore Regiment, at Langrune-sur-Mer, 7 June 1944.

British airborne troops move through a shell-damaged house in Oosterbeek, 23 September 1944.

OPERATION 'MARKET GARDEN'

As the advance in Normandy slowed due to German resistance, the Allies decided to try to regain the advantage in north-west Europe by concentrating their resources on a narrow assault into northern Germany via the Netherlands. Codenamed 'Market Garden', this would involve some 35,000 troops of three Allied airborne divisions dropping into Holland to secure key locations and bridges in and around the towns of Eindhoven, Nijmegen and Arnhem.

*Vehicles of the Guards Armoured Division of the British XXX Corps pass through the Dutch
town of Grave, having linked up with 82nd (US) Airborne Division.*

The first Allied landings by parachute and glider occurred on 17 September 1944, and a corresponding British ground assault sought to quickly link up with the airborne troops. Some initial successes saw the liberation of Eindhoven by the US 101st Airborne Division the following day, while the bridge at Nijmegen was captured on 20 September. Yet poor weather meant that Allied air support was limited, and strong German resistance prevented the important capture of Arnhem and the final bridge across the Rhine. The costly British defeat at Arnhem meant that Operation 'Market Garden' was ultimately considered a failure, yet the Allies had now established themselves in an area from which they could launch a future offensive into Germany's Rhineland.

The following letter was written by a member of the Dutch resistance in Arnhem, and describes the intense fighting in that area during September 1944.

Oosterboek, 16/10/45

Dear Sir

We are quite aware that some kind of history has been made in the last years and though a large part of our village is in ruins, we don't think the price too high for the final result: Liberty. Liberty is, for us, who for five years were under the yoke of the Germans, the finest word in the world.

Many things happened since September 17th last year... As our shop is in Arnhem and I am mostly there I was connected with Arnhem resistance group, so I establish telephonic contact with them (some of our men occupied the telephone office and made the necessary connections – during the last year all telephonic communications was restricted by the Germans for a few privilege people) and soon we could forward to your HQ all German movements in Arnhem. They reported the arrival of the Tiger tanks, gun positions, etc. They also [had] a telephone communication with Nijmegen over a secret line, which the Germans never discovered.

The things which hindered us most and must have given you a good deal of worry were the snipers. From the first day or so everybody seemed a good target for these good for nothings. When the firing became so heavy that only the cellar was comparatively safe we retired there. All of a sudden we became German again. With Indian war cries they probably attacked your position and though I had often told my wife that this war would be fought out in our garden I had not expected that our living room should also be included. One thing we positively understood that before this little skirmish was over, all our belongings would have gone to pieces. The German war lords kicked the front door open, searched the house, started pillaging and took a door to carry wounded away. We were very depressed for the taste of liberty had been very good. The next day the Germans made a Red Cross Station of our house and used all our linen, blankets and mattresses. All was soaked with blood. There was only a 19 year old medical student to care for the wounded and not many will have stood his treatment.

In the evening I went to the farmhouse to see if my neighbours were still alive. The scene was most horrible there. Several of your men were lying in the kitchen, dead or wounded, unattended in a most pitiful condition. The farmers were in the cellar, very frightened of course and as they did not speak English they could only [offer] little assistance. We did in the evening light what we could, gave them a drink, a cigarette, bandaged some and fetched some blankets for the night. The shooting was very heavy and it was acidly unpleasant. Early the next morning I went back to see how matters stood. The Germans had robbed the dead and wounded and were busy with your supplies in the jeeps.

At the beginning of August I had recovered so far that we returned to Oosterboek and now we are busy repairing the damage done... Yesterday we got electric light again. Our shop has opened for sometime: business as usual. Life returns to normal. We are free – thank you – we won't forget.

Sincerely yours,

A. G. Van Daalen[80]

THE ALLIED ADVANCE IN NORTH-WEST EUROPE

Casualties were heavy on both sides throughout the Normandy campaign. However, the Germans were constrained by Hitler's refusal to let his commanders make tactical withdrawals when necessary, which meant that the bulk of their forces were eventually outflanked and destroyed. By the end of August 1944, the Germans were in full retreat out of France. A desperate last-ditch attempt at a counter-offensive in the Ardennes in December failed to stop the ongoing Allied advance towards Germany.

Ron Gardiner was a signaller attached to the British 56th Infantry Brigade in Normandy. In this letter written home to his sister, he reflects on the Allied determination to reach Germany and 'finish the job'.

A landing beach in France bustles with activity as reinforcements arrive to back up troops advancing in Normandy.

Sunday, 17 Sept 44

My dear Phyllis and Peter

… After the miles upon miles of endless waving and cheering, the operations in Germany will be a very different story. The flags on this side of the border are an inspiring sight. Our arms are tired with acknowledging salutes, and our stomachs well lined with apples, pears, plums, greengages, tomatoes and peaches. We had a glut of fruit, mostly given us in convoy en route. If we didn't look like stopping the people threw it in to the cabs or the back of the trucks. This is 90% applicable to Belgium, and 10% to France where the people were just glad. There is precious little for them to give us, but in Belgium they certainly gave what they could. They are not starving to any degree, but they have been doing without a great deal, notably their national beverage – coffee, a fact which has hit them as hard as tea would affect us.

… I may say that after Normandy it has been a refreshing change to travel through countryside untarnished by battle, littered only with wrecked German tanks and vehicles. These were to be seen at regular intervals. Really it is pitiful to see what they were obliged to use in their retreat, and shameful to see literally dozens of dead horses. In the famous Gap, the litter and wreckage was a sight to be remembered. The loot which the filthy Bosche had taken from the French was most outstanding among piles of ammunition, uniforms, documents to say nothing of guns and trailers and sidecars and lorries. It infuriated me to kick among the rubbish of German photographs and letters and shaving kit and papers, to reveal dresses and shirts, toys, dolls, corsets and such like. The stuff they had started to cart off to the Fatherland was unimaginable and in such contrast to the Allied armies. We carry nothing but essentials.

Since then we have swept through town after town and village after village with little pause. Soon we shall be on the last lap. It will be more dangerous then even, with everyone a potential enemy, but with the tools firmly grasped, the job looks like being finished decisively. Any ill-feeling on their side of their precious frontier will be mutual and we shall not be slow in demonstrating which boot is on which foot if necessary. They have certainly asked for it and if you could only see what we have in this tremendous mobile army alone, you would know that they are most certainly going to get it!

All the best, love

Ron[81]

Sunday 10 Sept. '44

2582349 L/Cpl. Gardiner R.S.
"Q" Section, H.Q. Coy.
50(N) Divisional Signals
B.L.A.

My dear Phyllis & Peter,

I think that you have both been having something of a holiday and a celebration, which I should say you both heartily deserve. Later on I expect to hear all about it. By that time who knows, I may be in Germany. The momentum of the advance has slowed a little, but I fancy this check is only temporary.

Remembering what a pleasant surprise I had when I met Neil the day he came back from the East. I feel disappointed that I was cheated of a similar meeting with Pete in the same circumstances. Never mind, you are home at last, and I hope it has been as much a joy as I feel it would be for me, after so long.

I would love to have recorded your impressions on such a great occasion. Neil was so pleased — if my memory serves me aright — that he was restless and refused to settle for very long at anything. At least we got him to talk and he was most interesting. You have been so long away that you may not find, or realise that everybody wants to know!

The lads here all wear the Africa Star and most of them spent 2 or 3 weeks in South Africa. Without exception they speak in majestic terms of the hospitality of folks in Cape Town and Durban. This goodwill is on such a bountiful scale that it seemingly dwarfs anything which England offers to its heroes. Perhaps a longer association however, does not agree with these views.

Many thanks for continuing the newspapers which I still read when time permits. As you will appreciate, the time factor is more important than ever now. There isn't much leisure at present. Any there is comes in the evening, when it is too dark to see. Fortunately I have been able to fix up a crude light in the back of the truck with cell and hulb out of the stock I control, with a blanket for black-out. Others less fortunate have nothing more to do after dark but go to bed in their bivouacs of every size, shape, and description.

With the alteration in summer time you can imagine what a depressing difference it will make to the fighting

THE LIBERATION OF NORTH-WEST EUROPE

While the D-Day landings and the campaign in Normandy did not bring an immediate end to the war in Europe, they did begin the process through which victory would eventually be achieved the following year. While much fighting was still expected, the end was in sight as the Allies moved slowly towards Berlin and the heart of Nazi Germany.

Many soldiers, such as Stewart Irwin, writing here, who was serving with the 1st Battalion Rifle Brigade, took delight in seeing the reaction of the local populations in France and Belgium as towns were slowly liberated from German occupation.

Sherman tanks drive through Douvres-la-Délivrande, 8 June 1944.

July 12 44

Dear Ma

... I have seen a few more of the civilian population since I last wrote and found them very interesting. I saw a child of five the other day smoking a cigarette!

The other day a couple of old peasant women came along and gave me some red currants, black currants and white currants – they were very welcome and much appreciated. I thanked her in my best pidgeon French and she seemed to understand. Sometimes we manage to buy milk from a neighbouring farm which costs about five francs a litre (roughly fourpence a pint).

We carefully camouflaged our truck the other night with large branches from nearby trees – early the next morning I heard what sounded like someone drinking soup through a moustache but it turned out to be a cow chewing the camouflage a few inches from my left ear! I couldn't pluck up the energy to get out of bed and chase the wretched creature away – besides it was too cold at that time of the morning to dance around in one's underclothes in pursuit of trespassing cattle, and so I returned to sleep to the musical munching of a cow chewing its cud – fortunately it wasn't near enough to dribble down my neck! By breakfast time our camouflage was the merest skeleton of its former self. This process will probably continue as the beasts have not as yet been discouraged from this form of early morning meal.

Some of the smaller children near here come up to us and in all innocence give us a very promising version of the Nazi salute. One or two of them wear clogs and the majority some form of pinafore.

With much love from your loving son

Stewart[82]

Rfn Irwin S. 14241994
A Coy. 1st Btn Rifle Brigade
B.W.E.F.
July 12 44

Dear Ma,

I hope my letters to you will not take too long to get to you but we have been told that they take rather a long time — I have not received any of your letters yet, the last one I received was when I was still at Bury St Edmunds but I expect they'll soon reach here once they are forwarded. I have written to Dick since I got over here — I suppose he is still out in Italy. I should imagine Ralph is over here somewhere by now. I have just finished supper (cooked by myself and the Platoon Sergeant who by the way went to King's College Wimbledon and knew George Dann) it consisted of sardines and crushed Army biscuits mixed into a stodge and fried — I found it quite palatable but have not heard the rest of the communities opinion of it. I have attempted to paint an alluring female on the bonnet of our truck with red and white paint and turps to put it on with! — earlier in the proceedings attempts were made to make paint brushes out of any thing from rope ends to a lock of my rampant hair but all was in vain and I returned to a broken twig. However I never finished the said female and this evening she was wiped out with a drop of petrol and a jack knife. I have seen a few more of the civilian population since I last wrote and found them very interesting. I saw a child of five the other day smoking a cigarette!

The other day a couple of old peasant women came along and gave me some red currants, black currants and white currants — they were very welcome and much appreciated I thanked her in my best pidgeon French and she seemed to understand. Sometimes we manage to buy milk from a neighbouring farm which costs about five francs a litre (roughly fourpence a pint) We carefully camouflaged our truck the other night with large branches from nearby trees — early the next morning I heard what sounded like someone drinking soup through a moustache but it turned out to be a cow chewing the camouflage a few inches from my left ear! I couldn't pluck up the energy to get out of bed and chase the wretched creature away — besides it was too cold at that time of the morning to dance around in ones underclothes in pursuit of trespassing cattle and so I returned to sleep to the musical munching of a cow chewing its cud — fortunately it wasn't near enough to dribble down my neck.!

Stewart Irwin

Russian soldiers raise the Soviet flag in victory on the top of the ruined Reichstag building following the fall of Berlin, 2 May 1945.

THE BATTLE OF BERLIN

With the western Allies advancing towards Berlin and the Soviet Union doing so from the east, the final battle to seize control of the city would be played out in April 1945. The Soviets were particularly keen to advance west as far as possible before meeting the British and American armies, in the hope of retaining their occupied territory after the war. The chief Soviet ambition was to occupy Berlin, the symbolic capital of Nazi Germany, where Hitler was located – along with potentially valuable intelligence and research.

The western Allies assisted the Red Army by launching regular intensive bombing raids on Berlin, which only ended in the early hours of 21 April, prior to the Soviets entering the city later that day. The 1st Belorussian and 1st Ukrainian Fronts advanced into the city, engaging in street-fighting until much of the suburbs were captured. The remaining German garrison consisted only of depleted and disorganised Army and SS divisions, along with poorly trained *Volkssturm* (Home Guard) and Hitler Youth.

German Jew Max Bock was still resident in Berlin as the Allies repeatedly attacked the city throughout April 1945, and kept a detailed record of how the Soviet troops gradually advanced into the city. Most of the German defenders would surrender on 2 May.

Sunday, 29th April 1945

Today hell is let loose in all its variations. Since 5am Russian gunfire has been such that one must assume we are approaching the last battle. Soon and from very nearby this is joined by heavy rifle and machine gun fire. At about 6 the planes which did not put in an appearance yesterday, are back in force.

I go up to the flat to see if all is well, have a wash and a cold drink of coffee, as it is impossible to go out onto the balcony because of passing

Max Bock

bullets. In the street, lorries and other vehicles are parked under the trees. The infantry have laid telephone wires along the pavement, and troops, rifles at the ready, are advancing in the direction of the Ranke Platz. Above the din, the piercing bangs of the aforementioned nearby gun, and all around intense activity. Soon it becomes necessary to seek shelter again as bombing is getting dangerously close. Again columns of smoke from the city centre. Gunfire thundering from all directions, and one has the impression that the Russians are making an all-out attack. Planes flying overhead unceasingly, leaving us alone but dropping their bombs elsewhere.

In the direction of the Zoo hell is let loose. Round after round of ammunition is fired in that direction, probably aimed at the big bunker, probably leaving little intact of the Zoo and its gardens. One thinks with horror of the suffering of the poor helpless animals, probably running loose so that one might find oneself face to face with a lion or a jaguar in the street. And poor Lissy, the big elephant who used to stand at the entrance, might well be dead, the last of her family, the others having died in an air attack in November 1943. Was it really not possible to find another spot for the big bunker, not so close to such a famous cultural institution. Typical of the Nazis, 'We are so strong – impossible that an enemy could get so close!' Yes, gentlemen, he is coming and he is here, and the rest of the world is no longer going to listen to your bragging and your provocations, and is now united to beat the daylight out of you, and that moment is imminent.

... At lunch time I saw them bury a soldier in the grass verge outside my house. A simple mound and a few shrubs is all that remains – an unknown soldier who has given his life for a lost cause. Later I notice another dead soldier lying in the entrance hall, apparently bled to death from a stomach wound. So we are now on the battlefield – a battlefield among streets and buildings. The devastation in the street is constantly increasing – rubble lying around, buildings in ruins everywhere.

... So it seems the end is imminent... Another night approaches. We have had a terrible Sunday and lying down to rest, one thanks God that one has managed to survive it.[83]

CHAPTER NINE

RESOLUTION

Left: In Britain, news of victory finally arrives. • Right: Two internees are seen in a room at Stanley Civil Internment Camp, Hong Kong, photographed after liberation. Such a room would normally be occupied by seven.

THE LÜNEBURG HEATH SURRENDER

With Berlin surrounded, Adolf Hitler took his own life on 30 April 1945. His named successor was Grand Admiral Karl Dönitz, who swiftly entered into negotiations with the Allies to end the war, seeking to save as many Germans as possible from falling into Soviet hands.

On 4 May, a German delegation arrived at the headquarters of British Field Marshal Bernard Montgomery at Lüneburg Heath, near Hamburg. There, Montgomery accepted the unconditional surrender of German forces in the Netherlands, north-west Germany and Denmark. Three days later, at his French headquarters in Reims, General Eisenhower accepted

Field Marshal Bernard Montgomery signs the Instrument of Surrender of German forces in north-west Europe at Lüneburg Heath.

the unconditional surrender of all German forces. Another, more formal, surrender ceremony was held in Berlin on 8 May, with delegates from the Soviet Union in attendance.

Flight Lieutenant George Attenborough was based at Lüneburg when he was ordered to fly out a number of very senior German officers to discuss the surrender, as related below in an account written soon after the event. Despite a surrender having been signed, pockets of resistance still made Germany a very dangerous place to be.

At midnight on May 5th, I received another call from Ops informing me that in the following morning I was to take some more important passengers from Luneburg to Flensburg (the seat of the German Government) where I was to wait until necessary tasks had been performed by them in the town. There were no British forces near Schleswig-Holstein and the aerodrome was completely under Luftwaffe control. The Germans had promised to ground all their aircraft and guaranteed my aircraft a safe passage. I was informed by Ops that if I were to be fired upon, I must immediately return.

With mixed feelings, my navigator and myself, each armed with a revolver (scant protection if there was any trouble) found ourselves waiting by the aircraft on the morning of May 6th... just then our passengers arrived. This time we were favoured by the presence of the C of staff German supreme command, General Keitel. Soon we were airborne and when Hamburg passed by on the port we realised that we had left behind all friendly forces. Although we kept our eyes open, especially over aerodromes which had a surprisingly large number of aircraft parked on them, everything was quiet and we soon reached Flensburg aerodrome. As we circled the 'drome preparatory to landing, a green Very light was fired from the ground which we presumed was a signal authorising us to land on the runway which had a white T beside it. On the approach I watched for any sign of trouble, but all was quiet below so we touched down and taxied to Flying Control where we were marshalled in by a duty crew and switched off.

Three hours after we had landed, the carts returned with a plenipotentiary of the German Government, General Jödl and his ADC, whereupon we immediately started up the engines and taxiing out we took off for Luneburg with all speed... Our task was then finished: shortly before another day was out, Geberal Jödl was to sign the surrender document of all German forces to the allies, but our experiences were not over in that I had the great honour to meet and be introduced to F/M Montgomery at a dinner at the Luneburg HQ.[84]

Location: landing Strip about 14 miles south east of Luneburg.

Job: Aircraft attached to F.M. Monty's field H.Q. Light A/c stationed on strip with crews living in a requisitioned house next to strip. One Anson stationed at Luneburg aerodrome.

Story: Just before midnight on May 4th 1945 I received a phone call from G (ops) informing me that the German forces opposed to 21 Army and that hostilities in the areas concerned would cease at 0800 hrs on May 5th. At that time I was to fly some important persons down to our main landing strip at Brust, where another aircraft would be waiting to take over my passengers and convey them to Rheims (H.Q. of S.H.A.E.F.). ... phone communications to the aerodrome to go there by car, ... find the ground crew of the Anson and warn them that the aircraft would be needed early that morning.

That morning the navigator and myself had just completed our necessary pre-flight details and waiting by the A/c when two staff ... and

VICTORY IN EUROPE

Anticipation of Germany's surrender had been building for some months. The decisive radio announcement that the war in Europe had ended was broadcast in Britain late on the evening of 7 May 1945. The following day would be a national public holiday, to mark Victory in Europe, or VE Day. Special editions of newspapers were printed to carry the long-awaited headline, and news that the war against Nazi Germany was finally over spread rapidly across the world.

After years of suffering – whether from wartime restrictions, air raids or separation from loved ones – people could finally put their troubles to one side and begin to enjoy themselves. Colourful bunting and flags soon lined the streets of villages, towns and cities across Britain. Bonfires were lit, people danced and the pubs were full of revellers. London, the centre of the Empire that had experienced such intense bombing, was the prime location for the greatest of celebrations, as Elizabeth Tate described in her letter home opposite.

Yet for those in the forces who were still serving overseas, soldiers in captivity as prisoners of war, and relatives awaiting the return of their loved ones, VE Day proved to be somewhat bittersweet. Although it meant victory in one theatre, the war was not yet over in the Far East and Pacific.

A victory bonfire burns at night while people celebrate.

May 10th (1945)

My dear Mum

… I can't realise Germany really is done for – can you? I was going to write to you today anyhow to tell you and Dad about our excursion last night. It was simply marvellous. I've never had such a time!

We got transport to Hyde Park Corner and walked to Buckingham Palace. We just pushed our way through the crowd till we got to a good place! It was huge, all over everywhere, a very patient and good-humoured crowd. Occasionally someone raised the chant of 'We want the King!' in which we joined lustily. We waited like this about 20 mins perhaps, quite prepared to wait for hours; we didn't really think we would see anything because other people were so much taller and there were some in front lifting children up, and added to all this we were in our flattest of flat heels in preparation for walking home.

It wasn't quite dark yet, but at last a light went up in the room behind the balcony and everyone shouted; nothing happened; then the floodlights went on, and it was the most *lovely* sight, the huge white palace against the dark blue sky, and the Royal Standard (lovely colours) lit up above it – a tremendous burst of cheering, of course, when this happened and then out they came on the balcony and I just wish Hitler had heard the cheering. The King in naval uniform, and the Queen in white evening dress with a tiara, the 2 princesses in blue or grey. They stood waving for several minutes and we sang 'For they are jolly good fellows'… We saw it all perfectly even if we did have to stand on tiptoe.

Finally when they went in the crowd broke up, and we decided to go to Westminster and see the floodlighting. We took our time, as every step further from the Palace we had to keep looking back to see how it looked from the new angle, and even dilly-dallied to admire the chestnut trees silhouetted in front of it. We went down Birdcage Walk, with a horde of people, a few cars were struggling through and most of them had self-invited passengers on the roof. A party of servicemen joined hands round a policeman and we left them mobbing him. We could see Nelson lit up in Trafalgar Square and hundreds of buildings all round – one of the best things was to see the flag floodlit by itself there, so that it seemed to be shining and flying unsupported in the sky.

It was a marvellous warm night and just the right amount of wind to make the flags look perfect.

When we came into Parliament Square, still gaping foolishly at everything and not hurrying at all, we heard terrific cheering in front of us. We ran like mad to see what was happening, and arrived *just* as the Prime Minister had appeared on a balcony! It couldn't have been better timed if it had been a Cook's tour. We saw him perfectly. It was the big building on the corner, I think it's the Ministry of Health but I'm not sure – it was floodlit and flying the biggest and best flags, scores of them... Everyone shouted of course and at last Mr Churchill made us a speech which I'm sure was impromptu – I wish I could remember it all... He was thanking London for their courage, but nobody wanted to be serious and he knew just the right jokes to make... He had terrific applause, doubled when he waved his hat and puffed his cigar – which he did deliberately at well-chosen moments throughout his speech. It was wonderful to have seen it and so completely by chance!

Love from

E.[85]

Women inmates prepare a meal at Belsen while the dead lie abandoned in the background.

THE LIBERATION OF BELSEN

The British 11th Armoured Division liberated Belsen concentration camp on 15 April 1945. The situation greeting them was appalling. An estimated 13,000 bodies lay unburied around the camp, and some 60,000 starving and seriously ill people were packed together in terrible conditions without adequate food, water or sanitation. Many were badly sick from typhus, dysentery or simple malnutrition.

Additional military and civilian medical personnel were brought in quickly to support the relief effort. Their initial priorities were to bury the dead and contain the spread of disease, restore the water supply and arrange for the distribution of food suitable for starving people in various stages of malnutrition. The medical response to the crisis proved to be an immense challenge, and help arrived too late for many - nearly 14,000 prisoners would die soon after being liberated.

The horrors of Belsen, documented on film and in photographs, would ensure that its name became synonymous with Nazi war crimes. Arnold Horwell, himself a Jewish refugee from Nazi Germany, served as an interpreter with 102 Control Section of the British Second Army, and happened to be located at Belsen when news arrived of the end of the war in Europe.

8 May 45

My only dearest darling

Now, this is VE Day, and what a wonderful day it is – sunshine all day, and hardly a cloud in the sky.

Darling, it is a great thing that we have survived to see the end of all this – the Hitler regime and all the vileness, cruelty and wickedness it stood for, the war, at home and over here. I was happy in a feeling of overflowing gratitude. And the company around me contributed so much to my happiness, the fact that in this unit amongst officers of standing and understanding, not one I could not call my friend.

Arnold Horwell

There were only two guests in the Mess – Levy and Hartman, the two Jewish Chaplains. This mere fact, that one should be happy together in a Mess, where there is no risk of discrimination, in the contrary where the Jewish padres were the most honoured guests, it made me realise it again: it *was* worthwhile to be in this war, it *is* an honour and distinction to wear this uniform... And a third thing contributed to my happiness: the fact that the great day should be spent by me in this camp – surrounded by the living proof that thousands of lives were saved, thousands of tormented bodies given comfort and healing. The phrase 'That's what we are fighting for' never had so deep a meaning for me as last night.

... And now Good Night, dearest.

All yours,

Arnold[86]

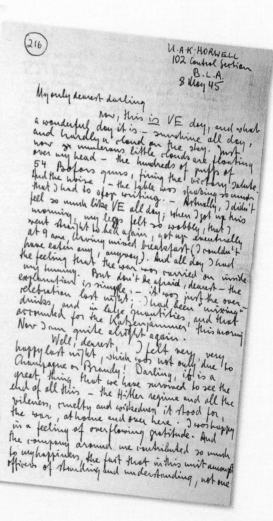

HIROSHIMA

The war in the Pacific, largely fought between the Japanese and the Americans, had begun with Japan holding the clear advantage after invading the Philippines, as well as British and Dutch territory. It was the Battle of Midway in June 1942 and the sinking of Japan's main aircraft carriers that proved a turning point in the Allies' favour. US forces seized the initiative, and the campaign became one of island-hopping, establishing air bases ever nearer to Japan so as to strike at the heart of their enemy. The severe aerial fire-bombing of Japanese cities began in June 1944.

Hiroshima following the dropping of the atomic bomb on 6 August 1945.

The Allies were expecting to launch an invasion of the Japanese mainland, which would undoubtedly have resulted in extremely high casualties on both sides. But another option presented itself: a fierce battle might be avoided by bringing the war to a swift conclusion through the use of atomic weapons. The first atomic bomb was dropped on the Japanese city of Hiroshima on 6 August 1945, delivering the equivalent of around 12.5 kilotons of TNT. The explosion reduced five square miles of the city centre to ashes and caused the deaths of an estimated 120,000 people in the first four days following the blast.

Father Siemes was a novitiate of the Society of Jesus in Nagatsuka, located some two kilometres from Hiroshima. The day after the bombing, he and his colleagues took it upon themselves to enter the city to offer assistance to the wounded.

We take off again with the handcart. The bright day reveals the frightful picture which last night's darkness had partly concealed. Where the city stood, everything as far as the eye can reach is a waste of ashes and ruins. Only several skeletons of buildings, completely burned out in the interior, remain. The banks of the river are covered with dead and wounded, and the rising waters have here and there covered some of the corpses. On the broad streets in the Hakushima district, naked, burned cadavers are particularly numerous. Among them are the wounded who still live. A few have crawled under burned out autos and trams. Frightfully injured forms beckoned to us and collapsed. An old woman with a girl whom she was pulling along with her falls at our feet. We place them on our cart and wheel them to the hospital, at whose entrance a dressing station has been set up. Here, the wounded lie on the floor, row on row. Only the largest wounds are dressed. We convey another soldier and an old woman to this place, but we cannot move everybody who lies exposed in the sun. It would be hopeless and it is questionable whether those whom we drag to the dressing stations come out alive, because even here, nothing effective can be done. Later we ascertain that the wounded lay in burned out hallways of the hospital, and there they died.

The magnitude of the disaster which befell Hiroshima on August 6th was only slowly pieced together in my mind. I lived through the catastrophe and saw it only in flashes, which only gradually emerged to give me a total picture.

What actually happened simultaneously in the city as a whole, is as follows. As the result of the explosion of the bomb at 8.15, almost the entire city was destroyed in a single blow. Only small outlying districts in the southern and eastern parts of the town escaped complete destruction. The bomb exploded over the centre of the city. As the result of the blast the small Japanese houses within the diameter of five kilometres which comprises 99%, collapsed or were blown up. Those who were in the houses were burned in the ruins. Those who were in the open sustained burns resulting from contact with a substance or rays emitted by the bomb. Where the substance struck in quantity, fires sprung up. These spread rapidly. The heat which rose from the centre created a whirlwind, which was effective in spreading fire throughout the entire city.

How many people were sacrificed to this bomb? Those who had lived through the catastrophe placed the number of dead at at least 100,000. Hiroshima had a population of 400,000. Official statistics placed the number who had died at 70,000 up to September 1st, not counting the missing and 130,000 wounded, among them 43,500 severely wounded.

We have discussed among ourselves the ethics of the use of the bomb. Some consider it in the same category as poison gas and were against its use on a civil population. Others were of the view that in total war, as carried on in Japan there was no essential difference between civilians and soldiers, and that the bomb itself was an effective force tending to end the bloodshed, warning Japan to surrender and thus to avoid destruction. It seems logical to me that he who supports total war in principle cannot complain of a war against civilians. The crux of the matter is whether total war in its present form is justifiable, even when it serves a just purpose. Does it not have material and spiritual evil as its consequences which far exceed whatever the good that might result? When will our moralists give us a clear answer to this question?[87]

The aftermath of the atomic bomb on Hiroshima.

Hiroshima, a city of both industrial and military significance, suffered mass devastation as a result of the bomb.

THE ATOMIC AGE

Just after 11am on the morning of 9 August 1945, a second atomic bomb was exploded above the Japanese city of Nagasaki. Although this particular weapon was even more powerful than that dropped on Hiroshima, the destruction caused at Nagasaki was somewhat less, due to the nature of the terrain. However, it still resulted in over two square miles of the city being pulverised, and some 73,000 people killed

The use of atomic weapons proved as controversial then as it still does today, with many debating the justification or otherwise of using such weaponry on largely defenceless civilian targets, and at such a terrible cost. The ever-present threat of a nuclear option became the key factor in the superpower stand-offs of the Cold War, and remains highly relevant to the global politics of today.

The following letter was written to Captain Victor Ramsden by the Assistant Chief of the Intelligence Section of the US Strategic Bombing Survey, whose team was tasked with investigating the effects of the atomic bombings.

Tokyo, 1 Nov 1945

Dear Rammie

I'm just back from Nagasaki and Hiroshima and it is in order that I write
you my promised impressions of the effect of the atom bombs.

I've been through Tokyo, Yokohama, Nagoya, Osaka, Kobe, Kure and Sasebo,
all of which are 60% to 80% burned down by fire bombs. The effect here is
quite different from the bombed cities of Europe for most of the buildings
were of flimsy, inflammable construction, and without basements, so that
in each city there are square blocks running into square miles showing just
broken roof tile rubble with occasional twisted small steel girders and the
now mushrooming squatter shacks of rusted corrugated iron which the
returning populace are putting up to live in.

I have also been through Kyoto, ancient and reputedly beautiful capital
of Japan, which is un-bombed and which I found interesting more for the
contrast than the supposed beauty or the ubiquitous and ever present
oriental smells.

And lastly I have spent four days at Nagasaki and one at Hiroshima. It is
hard to describe the complete devastation of these two places but here goes.
Hiroshima was first and it's easier to tell about. The city is located on a flat
plane along a river just a short way from the Inland Sea. It's rather like the
situation of London. The bomb you will recall was dropped about eight in
the morning and exploded roughly about 2,000 feet above the city. The result
is four square miles of houses and factories flattened to the ground with the
exception of about eight reinforced concrete, or sturdy structural steel
buildings... Significantly every glazed tile wall, and every polished tombstone,
which faced the direction of the explosion for a distance of a couple of miles
is thoroughly sand blasted. Moreover, in several spots, particularly on one
bridge paved in a light grey asphalt, the flash of the explosion has burned in
outline the forms of the bridge rail palings and the forms of two men, a horse
and a cart. To be more specific, where these objects protected the surface
paving from the diagonal flash of the bomb overhead the asphalt is not scorched
and the outline is just as clear as a shadow on a bright moonlight night.

The effects on the people were awful. About 80,000 were probably killed or died subsequently in Nagasaki and about 50,000 in Hiroshima. Many died outright from direct effects. Those near the source were scorched... but... the flash seems to have had more of a disintegrating effect than a combustible one.

Nagasaki is a more industrial seaport town situated in a Y shaped valley. Although the bomb used on this town was larger and of a different and more potent character the overall effect to the city was not as devastating... [yet] all of this concussive power was greater than anything I witnessed from even close strikes by the big Ten-tonners the RAF dropped in Germany.

... I have the utmost appreciation for the power of this new weapon, and if combined into the warhead of a V2 like carrier, an aggressive, vicious and opportunist nation could knock out an opponent before it knew that a war was on.[88]

The atomic mushroom cloud over Nagasaki, photographed from an escorting American B-29 aircraft on 9 August 1945.

THE JAPANESE SURRENDER

The American strategic bombing of Japanese cities had caused huge casualties and massive devastation to Imperial Japan's infrastructure, while the two atomic bombs dropped on Hiroshima and Nagasaki on 6 and 9 August clearly illustrated the extent to which the Allies were prepared to go in order to end the war. The United States captured Okinawa by the end of June 1945, while the Soviets invaded Manchuria in August. Bombed into submission and its resources to wage war fast dwindling, Japan could no longer continue to fight a losing battle and finally offered to surrender.

Servicemen read about the Japanese surrender while perching on traffic lights in Oxford Circus, London.

The news quickly travelled around the world that the war was finally at an end. Some, however, still expressed doubts that the fighting had really finished after all this time, as Captain Denis Howard implied in a letter written home during his Royal Artillery service in Calcutta.

13 Aug 1945

Dear Parents

The Japanese Surrender. I heard the first news of it in the train on the way from Delhi to Calcutta. Of course I went wild with excitement.

But know we don't know what the situation is, one minute it looks as if the war is over and the next as if it is going on, and while the politicians are wavering a lot of wretched fellows are getting killed. But anyway I reckon it must be officially over in a few weeks, but the big question arises as to whether the Jap army will give in. Someone will have to be very clever in making them believe that their government has surrendered. A Jap officer recently captured was firmly of the opinion that they'd captured Sydney! All this worry about the rightness or otherwise of using the atom bomb is a bit foolish. No one seemed to worry when a bomb became a block buster and then a b-b turned into a Ten Ton Tess nor when hundreds of these were dropped. But now we've found a bigger and better explosive everyone is horrified!

... With love,

Denis[89]

189476 Lt D. HOWARD
115.
13/Aug/45.
%o LLOYDS BANK
CALCUTTA.

Dear Parents,
The Japanese Surrender. I heard the first news of it in the train on the way from Delhi to Calcutta. Of course I went wild with excitement. But now we don't know what the situation is, one minute it looks as if the war is over and the next as if it is going on, and while the politicians are havering a lot of wretched fellows are getting killed. But anyway I reckon it must be officially over in a few weeks, but the

big question arises as to whether the Jap army will give in. Someone will have to be very clever in making them believe that their government has surrendered. A Jap officer recently captured was firmly of the opinion that they'd captured Sydney.!!! All this worry about the rightness or otherwise of using the atom bomb is a bit foolish. No one seemed to worry when a bomb became a block buster and then a b-b turned into a Ten Ton Tess nor when hundreds of those were dropped, but now we've found a bigger and better explosive everyone is

PRISONERS OF WAR: RENEWING CONTACT

Many prisoners of war, but particularly those who had been held captive in the Far East, had been imprisoned for several years without much idea of how the war was progressing outside their small prison environment. They were therefore surprised to hear the news that the conflict was finally over and that they would soon be on their way home. In some cases, captives had not seen their families for many years, nor even been able to exchange letters with them; in some cases those at home might even have considered them missing in action or even dead.

After being liberated, and while waiting in Mukden, Manchuria, for transport home, Brigadier Sam Pearson wrote to his wife to let her know the difficulties he had experienced when trying to communicate with home while imprisoned by the Japanese.

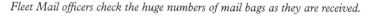

Fleet Mail officers check the huge numbers of mail bags as they are received.

19.8.45

My darling Aythel

The great moment has at last arrived
and I find it almost impossible to find
words adequate to express my
feelings, so I'm not going to try.

First and foremost let me say I am
absolutely fit and well. I am a little
underweight owing to 3½ years of
living, or rather existing, on Japanese
subsistence scale of rations as a result
of which we are all undernourished
and in a weak state. But now we are
rapidly putting that right, helped
tremendously of course by the terrific
moral uplift which the staggering
news of the last few days brought us.

Sam Pearson

You cannot imagine to what extent we have been cut off from the rest of the
world, living in abject poverty. I got my first letter from you in July 1944,
over 2½ years after I left you. Since then I have had a few, but my total
bag from all sources including those handed over two days ago after the
armistice is about two dozen. We have undergone a form of mental torture.
For a while we were allowed... propaganda newspapers with news about two
months old but that stopped in April 1944 since when they think we have
had no news at all. Nevertheless, from time to time we have managed to
keep in touch in broad outline with world affairs...

For a time we were allowed to write roughly one letter a month in which
most subjects of interest were unmentionable. It didn't even pay to try and
be subtle so that folks at home might read between the lines because our
captors were so darned suspicious that on the slightest provocation, or rather
the slightest thing of which they were a bit suspicious, would confine the
letter to the wastepaper basket and that would mean that our loved ones

at home would be so much longer without news of us. About a year ago we were reduced to sending six letters a year! I have felt very keenly at not having written to Mother and Aunt Charlotte, especially, but I feel sure that when they know the above facts they will understand...

Love to all the family and friends

Sam[90]

We hope to get this away by one of the relieving planes which are bringing us very welcome supplies etc. Love Sam.

Mukden, Manchuria
19. 8. 45.

My darling Aythel,

The great moment has at last arrived & I find it almost impossible to find words adequate to express my feelings, so I'm not going to try. First & foremost let me say I am absolutely fit & well. I am a little under weight (11 stone 8 lbs). owing to 3½ years of living, or rather, existing, on Jap bare subsistance scale of rations as a result of which we are all under nourished & in a weak state. But now we are rapidly putting that right, helped tremendously of course by the ~~terrific~~ terrific moral uplift which the staggering news of the last few days brought us. You cannot imagine to what extent we have been cut off from the rest of the world, living in abject poverty. I got my first letter from you in July 1944, over 2½ years after I left you. Since then I have had a few, but my total bag from all sources, including those handed over 2 days ago after the armistic is about 2 dozen. The "nips" have behaved towards us like absolute swine. We have undergone a form of mental torture. For a while we were allowed nip propaganda newspapers with news about 2 months old but that stopped in April 1944 since when they think we have had no news at all. Nevertheless, from time to time we have managed to keep in touch in broad outline

VICTORY OVER JAPAN

The president of the United States, Harry S Truman, announced the surrender of Imperial Japan to the American people on the evening of 14 August 1945. For many British people, the first knowledge they had of the war ending for good was from newspaper headlines the following morning, 15 August, which was deemed Victory over Japan or VJ Day in Britain. People celebrated just as they had done for VE Day in May.

The news that Japan had finally surrendered brought massive relief to Allied servicemen. Many who had been serving in the Pacific and Burma cherished the hope that they would soon be able to return home, while others were grateful that they would not be sent out to the Far East as planned. The formal signing of the surrender terms by Japan occurred on 2 September, aboard the battleship USS *Missouri*, which was anchored in Tokyo Bay.

Betty Ellis was a student at Reading University when the Japanese surrender was announced, and couldn't resist travelling into London to see the mass celebrations.

A Chinese soldier carried shoulder-high by American soldiers in Piccadilly Circus, London.

Friday, 17 Aug 45

Dear Mummy and Daddy

... Fortunately I went to bed early on Tuesday evening so I had had about two hours sleep before I was woken by singing, shouting and banging dustbin lids along Elmhurst Road, and at first I thought it was drunks, but then I thought it couldn't be or they would have been cleared off by the police for such a row. It must be that Japan had accepted surrender! ... By this time people were moving about on the corridor, going out of their rooms to consult one another about what was happening. Fortunately someone had heard the midnight news so we found that it really was true. Isn't it amazing to think that the war really is over – the penny hasn't dropped yet.

And gosh, am I glad we went [to London]! I wouldn't have missed it for anything. For once we enjoyed being in a crowd – it was a crowd in The City at a time when London was the focal point of all the world. We were too late to see the King and Queen going back from Parliament, but after waiting outside Buckingham Palace about an hour – no, longer – in the biggest crowd that I have ever seen, they (and the Princesses) came out on to the balcony... then to Westminster Abbey for a Thanksgiving Service at 6 o'clock... Westminster Abbey seemed one of the most appropriate places to be at for the Thanksgiving Service – as the Dean said, 'One of the most sacred spots in the British Empire' and certainly right at the heart of the Empire.

The view from Waterloo Bridge was indescribable. Up the river there was the Houses of Parliament with Big Ben standing out against the dark sky, the detail showing up even more than in the daylight, and searchlight shining on a Union Jack on one of the towers – far more beautiful to see it lit up like that and waving, just that one spot lit up, against the dark night...

Love, Betty[91]

Crowds shown dancing in Oxford Circus, London, on VJ Day.

Emaciated former prisoners of war sit on the steps of an ambulance in Singapore following their release from captivity in Sumatra.

BEGINNING THE JOURNEY HOME

Once Japan had surrendered, it was time to begin the long process of bringing home Allied prisoners of war and civilian internees. But with camps scattered throughout the Far East, sometimes in remote areas of inhospitable jungle, it was extremely difficult for the recovery teams to reach them all immediately.

Accompanied by a parcel of food, the following letter was dropped by an American B29 bomber over a prisoner of war camp in the Far East on the morning of 7 September 1945.

In Flight

7th September 1945

Hello Fellows

I happen to be Co-pilot, but I am trying to express the thoughts and feelings of the whole crew – many of them could probably do the job more eloquently.

We sincerely hope you won't need these supplies but if the same conditions prevail in your camp as has been reported about others you are sorely in need of them. Already some PWs have been liberated and I want to assure you every effort is being put toward getting you back home, to rest camps and to hospital. Some crew members from our own bomb group have already been liberated and we are hoping that more of them, several close friends, are still interned.

Since you have sacrificed so much it is with humility that I offer a short record of our crew. We arrived in the Marianas in the middle of March '45 and since that time have flown 33 combat missions, with this 37 missions, we have had our share of the rough ones but by the Grace of God our original crew remains intact with no Purple Hearts to our credit.

Again we wish you all the best of luck in everything you undertake and if any of you live near any of our crew or ever come close to where we live we want you to drop in and will treat you as royally as possible.

Best of luck to all of you, would appreciate hearing from you if possible –

Lt Joseph Rose (Bombardier), 414 S. Ashfield, La Grange, Illinois[92]

Letter dropped with foodstuffs from
B.29. morning of of 7th Sept, 45.

IN FLIGHT,
7th September, 1945

Hello Fellows,

I happen to be Co-pilot, but I am trying to express the thoughts and feelings of the whole crew — many of them could probably do the job more eloquently.

We sincerely hope you wont need these supplies but if the same conditions prevail in your camp as has been reported about others you are sorely in need of them. Already some PWs have been liberated and I want to assure you every effort is being put toward getting you back home, to rest comps and to hospital. Some crew members from our own bomb group have already been liberated & we are hoping that more of them, several close friends are till interned.

Since you have sacrificed so much it is with humility that I offer a short record of our crew. We arrived in the Marianas in the middle of March '45 &, since that time have flown 33 combat missions, with this 37 missions, we have had our share of the rough ones, but by the Grace of God our original crew remains intact with no Purple Hearts to our credit.

Again we wish you all the best of luck in everything you undertake & if any of you live near any of our crew or ever come close to where we live we want you to drop in & will treat you as royally as possible

Best of luck to all of you, would appreciate hearing from you if possible — Lt Joseph Rose (Bombardier), with S. Ashfield, La grange, Illinois.

Capt. John F. Mapes (Pilot)
Monticello, N.Y.

Sgt. James Firetakis,
9144. E. Outer Dr.
Detroit, Mich.

F.O. Harvy Gordon (Nav).
2-782, Somerton Rd.
Cleveland Heights, Ohio.

Lt. Joseph Andrews (Navigator),
2062 Swansberg Av. N.S.
Grand Rapids, Mich.

S/Sgt H. A. Heckworth (L.G.)
2405, Washington Av.
Knoxville in Tenn.

S/Sgt Samuel Brawer. (R.Gnr)
2057. S. Maxwell Av.,
Knoxville in Tenn.

S/Sgt. O.C. Cushing (Rad. Op.)
310 College Av,
Fort Worth. Texas.

M/Sgt. Ardie R. Vorley (Eng)
Sacup, Texas.

THE LIBERATION OF FAR-EAST PRISONERS OF WAR

For many who had been held captive by the Japanese, the physical and emotional impact of such brutal treatment would remain with them for the rest of their lives. Those former captives may have considered themselves fortunate to have been alive at all, since almost a quarter of all Allied prisoners held in Japanese camps had died during captivity.

For newly liberated prisoners, such as John Harris, who had suffered captivity in Borneo for the last three years, the sense of sudden freedom was astonishing and certainly something to be savoured.

An Indian prisoner of war from Hong Kong is attended to by nursing staff on board the hospital ship Oxfordshire *after liberation.*

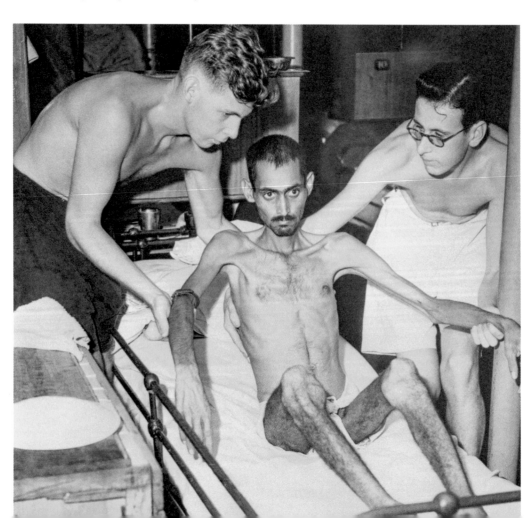

13 Sept 45

My dear John

You have no idea what it means to me to write this to you, to be free, to have enough to eat, to be surrounded by friends who do not resemble mechanical corpses – if ever there was a heaven on earth, I am right in it now. Our guardian angels have been the US Navy and now an Australian general hospital. This letter will be like my mind – an incoherent medley of happiness.

I left the prison camp at 11am yesterday, was on board the USS *Doyle C Barnes* (an 'escort' vessel of 1600 tons) by 16.30 and came here on her. Last night the American sailors just showed us what they could do. Everything was ad lib – food – clothes – toilet things and such friendship and welcome. I ate as much fricassee of turkey as I could at supper, but two hours later I knocked back three huge bacon and egg sandwiches and 'cawfee' and about a pint of tomato juice. I could hardly sleep for joy and roamed the ship chatting to everyone. Breakfast was the next highlight (you will observe my obsession about food! It is a common complaint amongst prisoners!). I ate a large plate of porridge, followed by one of cornflakes, then a big ham steak with six fried eggs, followed by at least the equivalent of six scrambled eggs and rounded off with four slices of toast with lashings of butter and marmalade. For lunch I stuck to peas and ice cream – oddly enough I was not very interested in a huge beef steak that was offered to me but the ice cream was just the stuff. I had to take to chewing gum to keep off smoking – I think that on average I was offered one cigarette per minute throughout.

Medically I have really kept surprisingly fit. I only weighed 8st 10 at the end: I survived what was believed to be diabetes which looked gloomy but suddenly stopped for no apparent reason - that was in March '44. I have had dysentery, worms, piles, tropical ulcers, scabies and last of all I went a bit crackers towards the end. That was brought on by overwork. I rather foolishly used to flog myself in the garden and after so doing I just used to go nuts for an hour or two – until I dropped off to sleep and woke up OK! Fortunately I realised what was about to happen and could get organised in time, though occasionally I was caught on the hop. I found that vitamin B1 was the best answer to this! It was a long time coming though. I will be able to give you some real hot stuff medical data, but would rather do that over a gallon or so of beer than here. Suffice to say that I have seen men die of starvation, but not until you could get your thumb and forefinger round their thigh and easily surround his abdomen with two thumbs and forefingers.

I want to forget the past and live in a glorious future...

Yours ever,

John[93]

A group of Royal Air Force prisoners cheer for the camera following their release from Changi Prison, Singapore.

CHAPTER TEN
AFTERMATH

No. 4
MILITARY
DISPERSAL
UNIT
REPORT HERE

Clockwise: Arriving at Charing Cross railway station in London, soldiers gather at a notice board, ready to be sent home. • British soldiers of the 7th Armoured Division talk to German children in Berlin. • Josef Kramer, Camp Commandant, photographed in irons at Belsen before being removed to the POW cage at Celle.

THE ALLIED BOMBING OFFENSIVE

By the end of the war, the RAF's bombing offensive against Nazi Germany had proved to be one of the longest, most expensive and controversial campaigns of the conflict. Its aim had been to severely weaken Germany's ability to fight, and, in those terms, it could be considered a success.

Yet in accepting that precision bombing was incredibly difficult to achieve, the War Cabinet had sanctioned the targeting of whole cities, to destroy both factories and their workers. Industrial towns were pounded to rubble,

Bomb damage to Mannheim, photographed from a B-17 Flying Fortress of the 94th Bomb Group.

with a record 4,851 tons of bombs being dropped on Dortmund alone in a single night. German war production was massively disrupted, and in some places ceased altogether. Controversially, large urban areas were also razed to the ground in an attempt to destroy German morale. Dresden, Pforzheim and many others were consumed by fire, and the mass damage to civilian housing resulted in homelessness for many Germans.

Having served as a bomb aimer for much of the war, Flight Lieutenant Geoffrey Dawson had the opportunity to fly over liberated France and Germany after the armistice, witnessing the devastation that his own bombing missions had caused to cities such as Mannheim.

25th May 1945

And now I have a tale to tell. Yesterday I did a thing which I have wanted to do ever since the war ended. I went on a cross-country flight over Germany.

We crossed the Mozelle and pressed on through the Ardennes towards St Vith. Here, as you know, there was much fighting... consequently there was more damage to property than anywhere we had seen previously. There is not a village which is not wholly or partially wrecked. There is not a farm house that has not been fought over, got holes in its roof, had a wall knocked down and hardly a field where the savage tracks of manoeuvring tanks do not still show in dark twin gashes slashed across the green growing acres.

We then turned south-east and headed into Germany itself...

Mannheim used to be a city, a thriving city, otherwise it would not have got what happened to it and it would still be a city. Mannheim is nothing more than a grey smudge on the bank of the Rhine. Mannheim is a total loss. There is not a building left intact. There is hardly a set of four walls standing in a rectangle. Most definitely there is not a single rook or first storey left. If four walls stand linked in a shell they were stark drab ruins rearing out of the dust. Mostly it is undulations in rubble, in the desert of rubble, which indicate the plan of once prosperous streets. And it is all grey, light dirty grey dust like the ash of Forest of Dean coal, acres of grey rubble and dust with the odd chimney rearing up, the occasional bulldozer pushing some dirt from one place to another, a lonely group of figures grubbing about with shovels and spades, a few wagons filled with rubbish. There no longer is a city Mannheim. It has gone. It just simply does not exist anymore. I really mean it. A city as large as Manchester has gone, has been utterly and hopelessly wiped off the map. Without seeing it I could not have believed it.[94]

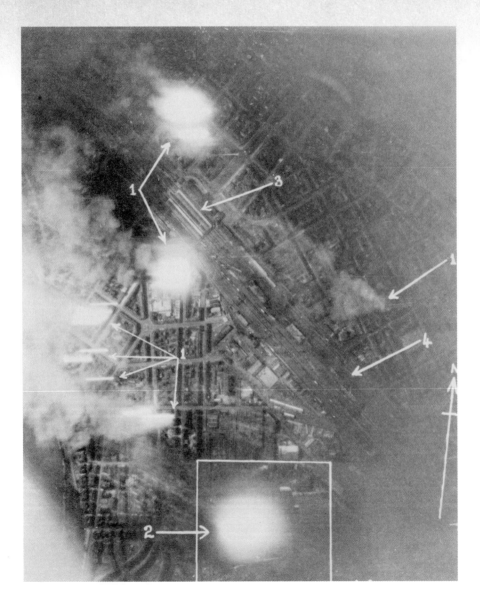

This annotated vertical aerial photograph was taken during the first concentrated Allied night bombing attack on Mannheim, Germany.

THE ARREST OF NAZI WAR CRIMINALS

The end of the war in Europe saw key figures within the German military and Nazi Party apprehended to face trial for war crimes. Many went into hiding or sought to escape capture by fleeing overseas under false identities, but very few were successful in getting away.

Joachim von Ribbentrop was the Minister of Foreign Affairs in Nazi Germany. He lost this position following Hitler's suicide and went into hiding in Hamburg under an assumed name. On 14 June, some weeks after the German surrender, Ribbentrop was identified and arrested by a French sergeant, who handed him over to the British occupation forces. As the following letter describes, the British medical officer Robert Thompson was sent along to inspect the captive and ensure that he was in a fit state to face trial.

Ribbentrop was ultimately convicted at Nuremberg and became the first Nazi war criminal to be sentenced to death by hanging.

Sat 16 Jun [1945]

My Darling Sally

... As you will have heard, Ribbentrop was captured in Hamburg on Thursday morning. A message was sent to our HQ asking for a senior medical officer to go and examine an important person. I was sent along. When I got there I was told who it was. In a way I had guessed who it might be. What a thrill!

I told them what I intended to do – our fear was, of course, that as soon as he knew he was going to be examined, he would try to swallow poison. In we went and there he was – much fatter than he used to be, and plus a moustache. First I stuck my fingers in his mouth and had a good look around – nothing there. Then I ordered him to take off his

Von Ribbentrop, former Foreign Minister, in his cell at Nuremberg.

jacket, waistcoat and shirt. As he took his things off I sent them out of the room (Two security officers were present with me while all this was going on). He didn't like parting with his shirt.

I examined him very carefully. He kept on saying 'What are you looking for? Are you looking for poison?' I didn't answer him, but just went on. Then I told him to take his trousers off. I got the two security officers to hold his hands, but he suddenly pulled one hand away and pushed it down between his legs! I grabbed hold of his wrist and he said 'if you are looking for poison, I will save you the trouble – there it is'. He opened his hand and there was a little round sealed tin with adhesive plaster on it. It had been strapped to an intimate portion of his anatomy and must have been very painful, judging from the appearance of the skin. The atmosphere was absolutely terrific, and I have never been so excited in all my life! I then got his socks and shoes off, and made him get down on his hands and knees, stark naked, and examined him per rectum. There was no poison there! He didn't like that a bit. As I was doing this examination I thought to myself that this was the man who said we were a decadent, degenerate people, and that this was the man who gave the King the Nazi salute, and I wasn't very gentle in my examination. He groaned and moaned, and made a fuss, but that didn't stop me!

We then gave him a pair of long pants and a vest – his own, which I had previously inspected. He also got a pair of thick pyjamas to put on, but they offended his dignity too much, and he wouldn't wear them. I said to him 'if you feel cold, you'll be glad to put them on.' I left him sitting there in a chair, with his head sunk in his hands, a tragic figure if ever there was one.

Ribbentrop doesn't seem to think that he will be treated as a war criminal. Despite his tragic position, he is still arrogant. It was only when we took all his clothes off, and submitted him to the close, personal examination, that he lost his arrogant bearing. It was my big moment, and I shall never forget it. Both the security officers and I were literally trembling with excitement when we found the poison!

All my love, sweetheart, Yours ever

Bobbie[95]

H.Q. 8 Base Sub Area
B. L. A.
Sat 16 Jun

My Darling Sally, I had no letters yesterday - only the Sphere, which, of course, was much appreciated.

As you will have heard, Ribbentrop was captured in Hamburg on Thursday morning. A message was sent to our H.Q. asking for a senior medical officer to go and examine an important person. I was sent along. When I got there I was told who it was. In a way, I had guessed who it might be. What a thrill!

I told them what I intended to do - our fear was, of course, that as soon as he knew he was going to be examined, he would try to swallow poison. In we went and there he was - much fatter than he used to be, and plus a moustache. First I stuck my fingers in his mouth and had a good look around - nothing there. Then I ordered him to take off his jacket, waistcoat, and shirt. As he took his things off I sent them out of the room. (Two security officers were present with me when all this was going on.) He didn't like parting with his shirt! I examined him very carefully. He kept on saying

THE ALLIED OCCUPATION OF GERMANY

Upon the defeat of the Nazis, Germany was occupied by the Allies, who asserted joint authority over the entire country. For administrative purposes, it was divided into four occupation zones, each run by one of the three western Allies (the United Kingdom, France and the United States) and the Soviet Union. As Germany's capital, Berlin was a special case – although wholly located inside the Soviet zone of occupation, it was subdivided into four sectors in order to mirror the division of the entire country.

While the occupying powers sought to remove any last vestiges of Nazism, their immediate concern was to feed and house the population, who had been suffering from terrible living conditions. Germany had thrown all of its resources into fighting the war, and as such the country's civilians were struggling to survive by the time of the surrender. Homelessness was common, and many were feeling the effects of hunger. The adult population was provided with food ration cards in exchange for work, but a great deal would need to be done in terms of post-war reconstruction.

During the period of Allied occupation, Michael Singer served as an interpreter with the British Military Government in the Berlin-Tiergarten district.

British and Russian soldiers on the balcony of the captured Berlin Chancellery, the spot from which Hitler made many of his speeches.

10-7-1945

Dear Jack

... I have seen a lot on my
journey across Western
Germany, and I think it is
about the same there, as it is
here; there are, of course,
differences in degree,
according to the severity of
war damage, and a few other
circumstances, [on] which I
cannot elaborate at present.

Michael Singer

Well, the first outstanding thing is, there are no Germans living in the whole
of Berlin, if you listen to the many people who try and talk to you; they are
Britishers, Americans, Canadians, Australians, Dutch, Swiss, French, Belgians,
Italians, Jews, their descendants, relatives and friends; Poles, Austrians,
Czechs, Indians; in short, every nation in the world but Germans, and the
few Germans there are can prove they have been in concentration camps or
have suffered by Nazi persecution of some kind. They all must have been
equally eager, six months ago, to prove themselves to be good Germans, and
they prove it now, by disgusting subservience, and by cringing, in the hope of
getting a fag, or some other minor favour. Berlin is in a frightful mess, and it
must have been considerably worse when it surrendered to the Russians two
months ago. Seeing the empty shells of houses, and the heaps of debris, one
wonders where all the people one sees in the streets do live, and how they
manage to keep fairly clean.

There is no water in most of the houses, no gas, no coal; the people burn
the wood of the broken trees of the Tiergarten for cooking their meals,
and I think there is not one tree that has remained undamaged. The main
thoroughfares have just been cleared, but minor roads and sidewalks are
still blocked in many places. There is no machinery to help clearing up;
chains of women are handing on the material, brick by brick, and pail by pail.

It is amazing how much has been done already, under these conditions. No effort has been made, yet, to remove the innumerable wrecks of tanks, guns and, most of all, motor vehicles of every description. Everybody who has no permanent job – very few have due to the destruction of factory, workshop and office buildings – is in the 'Ersatz', that means he or she is registered with the employment exchange, and obliged to do any work required. Thus one starts wondering how Berlin can live at all, seen as an economic body. One cannot support oneself by just clearing away one's own dirt. So, to my mind, there is a more important and sounder reason for the shortage of food, for the not-coming-in of supplies, than the normally quoted general shortage, and the lack of transport. The Russians are obviously bringing in as much as they can; but seen economically, the bulk of those supplies must be considered as charity, given less out of kindness, perhaps, than out of prudence and – fear. Fear of epidemics and disease, not of riots; the population seems rather exhausted and tired of fighting.

Do you remember the memorandum I wrote, about three years ago? It is now as I then expected it: the three groups of people – the active anti-Fascists who have taken control; the inert majority, now cursing Hitler, and prepared to do anything they are asked to and to say anything they think they are expected to; and those few stubborn Nazis who managed to survive the purge, who have gone into hiding, and whose objectionable presence you can only feel... Their presence also manifests itself, e.g. by a little girl chalking a swastika on a wall, and wiping it off quickly on my approach...

This, now, is the moment to act. The re-education must be started now; there must be no dawdling and hesitating. The iron is hot. Bring along the hammer of the new, the reasonable ideology, before the coolness of frustration and despair sets in, and forge a happier future for all mankind, here in the very heart of its former fiercest foe![96]

A large Nazi eagle and swastika towers above part of a damaged grandstand at the former Nazi Party rally site in Nuremburg.

THE ALLIED NON-FRATERNISATION POLICY

In order to strengthen the Allied occupation of Germany, while also assisting efforts to 'de-Nazify' the local populations, a strict non-fraternisation policy was imposed by the Allied authorities. Occupying troops from Britain, the United States and other nations were discouraged from speaking to or socialising with the local German people. Posters and leaflets, such as the British example whose text is shown here, were distributed in order to explain and justify this course of action.

Such a strict rule was found to be increasingly difficult to adhere to, however, and so the prohibitions were soon relaxed – first by allowing occupying troops to talk to German children, then, soon afterwards, to adults. By September 1945, the non-fraternisation policy was abandoned completely in Germany and Austria as the work to reconstruct Europe gathered pace.

Personal Message from the Commander-in-Chief

(to the population of the British Area in Germany)

You have wondered, no doubt, why our soldiers do not smile when you wave your hands, or say 'Good morning' in the streets, or play with the children. It is because our soldiers are obeying orders. You do not like it. Nor do our soldiers. We are naturally friendly and forgiving people. But the orders were necessary; and I will tell you why.

In the last war of 1914, which your rulers began, your Army was defeated; your Generals surrendered; and in the Peace Treaty of Versailles your rulers admitted that the guilt of beginning the war was Germany's. But the surrender was made in France. The war never came to your country; your cities were not damaged, like the cities of France and Belgium; and your Armies marched home in good order. Then your rulers began to spread the story (legend) that your Armies were never really defeated, and later they denied the war guilt clauses of the Peace Treaty. They told you that Germany was neither guilty

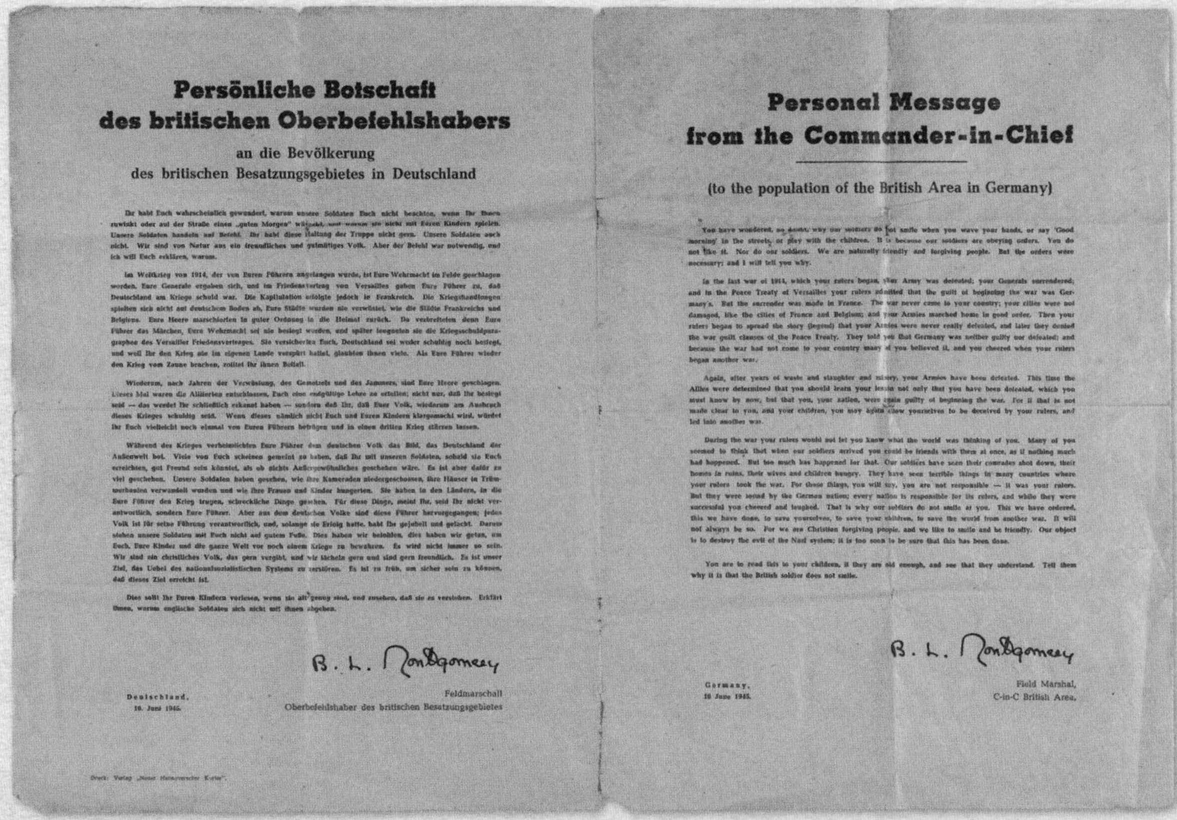

Persönliche Botschaft des britischen Oberbefehlshabers

an die Bevölkerung
des britischen Besatzungsgebietes in Deutschland

Ihr habt Euch wahrscheinlich gewundert, warum unsere Soldaten Euch nicht beachten, wenn Ihr ihnen zuwinkt oder auf der Straße einen „guten Morgen" wünscht, und warum sie nicht mit Euren Kindern spielen. Unsere Soldaten handeln auf Befehl. Ihr habt diese Haltung der Truppe nicht gern. Unsere Soldaten auch nicht. Wir sind von Natur aus ein freundliches und gutmütiges Volk. Aber der Befehl war notwendig, und ich will Euch erklären, warum.

Im Weltkrieg von 1914, der von Euren Führern angefangen wurde, ist Eure Wehrmacht im Felde geschlagen worden. Eure Generale ergaben sich, und im Friedensvertrag von Versailles gaben Eure Führer zu, daß Deutschland am Kriege schuld war. Die Kapitulation erfolgte jedoch in Frankreich. Die Kriegshandlungen spielten sich nicht auf deutschem Boden ab, Eure Städte wurden nie verwüstet, wie die Städte Frankreichs und Belgiens. Eure Heere marschierten in guter Ordnung in die Heimat zurück. Da verbreiteten denn Eure Führer das Märchen, Eure Wehrmacht sei nie besiegt worden, und später leugneten sie die Kriegsschuldparagraphen des Versailler Friedensvertrages. Sie versicherten Euch, Deutschland sei weder schuldig noch besiegt, und weil Ihr den Krieg nie im eigenen Lande verspürt hattet, glaubten ihnen viele. Als Eure Führer wieder den Krieg vom Zaune brachen, zolltet Ihr ihnen Beifall.

Wiederum, nach Jahren der Verwüstung, des Gemetzels und des Jammers, sind Eure Heere geschlagen. Dieses Mal waren die Alliierten entschlossen, Euch eine endgültige Lehre zu erteilen; nicht nur, daß Ihr besiegt seid — das werdet Ihr schließlich erkannt haben — sondern daß Ihr, daß Euer Volk, wiederum am Ausbruch dieses Krieges schuldig seid. Wenn dieses nämlich nicht Euch und Euren Kindern klargemacht wird, würdet Ihr Euch vielleicht noch einmal von Euren Führern betrügen und in einen dritten Krieg stürzen lassen.

Während des Krieges verheimlichten Eure Führer dem deutschen Volk das Bild, das Deutschland der Außenwelt bot. Viele von Euch scheinen gemeint zu haben, daß Ihr mit unseren Soldaten, sobald sie Euch erreichten, gut Freund sein könntet, als ob nichts Außergewöhnliches geschehen wäre. Es ist aber dafür zu viel geschehen. Unsere Soldaten haben gesehen, wie ihre Kameraden niedergeschossen, ihre Häuser in Trümmerhaufen verwandelt wurden und wie ihre Frauen und Kinder hungerten. Sie haben in den Ländern, in die Eure Führer den Krieg trugen, schreckliche Dinge gesehen. Für diese Dinge, meint Ihr, seid Ihr nicht verantwortlich, sondern Eure Führer. Aber aus dem deutschen Volke sind diese Führer hervorgegangen; jedes Volk ist für seine Führung verantwortlich, und, solange sie Erfolg hatte, habt Ihr gejubelt und gelacht. Darum stehen unsere Soldaten mit Euch nicht auf gutem Fuße. Dies haben wir befohlen, dies haben wir getan, um Euch, Eure Kinder und die ganze Welt vor noch einem Kriege zu bewahren. Es wird nicht immer so sein. Wir sind ein christliches Volk, das gern vergibt, und wir lächeln gern und sind gern freundlich. Es ist unser Ziel, das Uebel des nationalsozialistischen Systems zu zerstören. Es ist zu früh, um sicher sein zu können, daß dieses Ziel erreicht ist.

Dies sollt Ihr Euren Kindern vorlesen, wenn sie alt genug sind, und zusehen, daß sie es verstehen. Erklärt ihnen, warum englische Soldaten sich nicht mit ihnen abgeben.

B. L. Montgomery

Deutschland,
10. Juni 1945.

Feldmarschall
Oberbefehlshaber des britischen Besatzungsgebietes

Personal Message from the Commander-in-Chief

(to the population of the British Area in Germany)

You have wondered, no doubt, why our soldiers do not smile when you wave your hands, or say 'Good morning' in the streets, or play with the children. It is because our soldiers are obeying orders. You do not like it. Nor do our soldiers. We are naturally friendly and forgiving people. But the orders were necessary; and I will tell you why.

In the last war of 1914, which your rulers began, your Army was defeated; your Generals surrendered; and in the Peace Treaty of Versailles your rulers admitted that the guilt of beginning the war was Germany's. But the surrender was made in France. The war never came to your country; your cities were not damaged, like the cities of France and Belgium; and your Armies marched home in good order. Then your rulers began to spread the story (legend) that your Armies were never really defeated, and later they denied the war guilt clauses of the Peace Treaty. They told you that Germany was neither guilty nor defeated; and because the war had not come to your country many of you believed it, and you cheered when your rulers began another war.

Again, after years of waste and slaughter and misery, your Armies have been defeated. This time the Allies were determined that you should learn your lesson not only that you have been defeated, which you must know by now, but that you, your nation, were again guilty of beginning the war. For if that is not made clear to you, and your children, you may again allow yourselves to be deceived by your rulers, and led into another war.

During the war your rulers would not let you know what the world was thinking of you. Many of you seemed to think that when our soldiers arrived you could be friends with them at once, as if nothing much had happened. But too much has happened for that. Our soldiers have seen their comrades shot down, their homes in ruins, their wives and children hungry. They have seen terrible things in many countries where your rulers took the war. For these things, you will say, you are not responsible — it was your rulers. But they were found by the German nation; every nation is responsible for its rulers, and while they were successful you cheered and laughed. That is why our soldiers do not smile at you. This we have ordered, this we have done, to save yourselves, to save your children, to save the world from another war. It will not always be so. For we are Christian forgiving people, and we like to smile and be friendly. Our object is to destroy the evil of the Nazi system; it is too soon to be sure that this has been done.

You are to read this to your children, if they are old enough, and see that they understand. Tell them why it is that the British soldier does not smile.

B. L. Montgomery

Germany,
10 June 1945.

Field Marshal,
C-in-C British Area.

nor defeated; and because the war had not come to your country many of you believed it, and you cheered when your rulers began another war.

Again, after years of waste and slaughter and misery, your Armies have been defeated. This time the Allies were determined that you should learn your lesson not only that you have been defeated, which you must know by now, but that you, your nation, were again guilty of beginning the war. For if that is not made clear to you, and your children, you may again allow yourselves to be deceived by your rulers, and led into another war.

During the war your rulers would not let you know what the world was thinking of you. Many of you seemed to think that when our soldiers arrived you could be friends with them at once, as if nothing much had happened. But too much has happened for that. Our soldiers have seen their comrades shot down, their homes in ruins, their wives and children hungry. They have seen terrible things in many countries where your rulers took the war.

For those things, you will say, you are not responsible – it was your rulers. But they were sound by the German nation; every nation is responsible for its rulers, and while they were successful you cheered and laughed. That is why our soldiers do not smile at you. This we have ordered, this we have done, to save yourselves, to save your children, to save the world from another war. It will not always be so. For we are Christian, forgiving people, and we like to smile and be friendly. Our object is to destroy the evil of the Nazi system; it is too soon to be sure that this has been done.

You are to read this to your children, if they are old enough, and see that they understand. Tell them why it is that the British soldier does not smile.

B.L. Montgomery, Field Marshal, C-in-C British Area.

Germany, 10 June 1945.[97]

The remains of Neukolln, Hermannplatz, Berlin. The building was demolished by the SS as they attempted to halt the Russian advance into Berlin at the end of April 1945.

Defendants in the dock during the Nuremberg war crimes trials. (Front row, left to right):
Goering, Hess, von Ribbentrop, Keitel, Kaltenbrunner, Rosenberg, Frank, Frick, Streicher,
Funk, Schacht; (Back row, left to right): Doenitz, Raeder, von Schirach, Sauckel, Jodl, von
Papen, Seyss-Inquart, Speer, von Neurath and Hans Fritsche.

THE NUREMBERG TRIALS

Following the end of the war, the Allies brought the leading civilian and
military representatives of Nazi Germany and Imperial Japan to stand trial on
charges of war crimes, crimes against peace and crimes against humanity. The
process would prove particularly important in establishing the facts regarding
the Holocaust and those within the Nazi regime who were responsible for
planning or carrying out such acts of brutality.

The International Military Tribunal at Nuremberg lasted from November
1945 to 1 October 1946. Twenty-two leading Nazis were tried, including
Martin Bormann, in absentia, whose body had yet to be located. Of that

The Officer in Charge of the Document Room at Nuremberg, taking out a ledger from the safe where all the original documents to be used as evidence against the Nazi war criminals were kept.

number, twelve were sentenced to death by hanging, seven to terms of imprisonment and three were acquitted.

The International Military Tribunal at Tokyo would be held between May 1946 and November 1948 to investigate war crimes committed by Imperial Japan. Twenty-eight defendants were tried, of whom seven were sentenced to death by hanging and eighteen to terms of imprisonment. Two of the defendants died from natural causes during the trial, while one was declared mentally unfit to be sentenced.

Elizabeth Hodges served as WRNS Chief Officer for north-west Europe, and happened to visit Nuremberg at an opportune moment to observe the trials being conducted.

The following morning off I went to see something of the trials of the twelve chief German war criminals. This was most impressive. The trials were taking place in a building rather similar to a theatre with tiered seats for the on-lookers. These seats were all fitted with headphones enabling one to hear verbatim all that was being asked of the prisoners either in English, French, German or Russian. Right at the back of the so-called stage were four glass booths, similar to telephone kiosks. Each of these had a woman who was translating all the evidence with one of the four different lawyers whilst the questioning and answering was taking place. On the left of the stage there were two rows of seating for the prisoners rather similar to choir stalls in a church and facing at right angles to our seats like the choir sit in normal churches.

The prisoners were all in their grey prison uniforms. Behind the prisoners stood US Military Police, commonly known as Snowballs by virtue of the white helmets which they all wore. All had pistols in their white belts. Also several of the prisoners' lawyers sat nearby. Opposite them quite a few judges and other legal figures sat. In the middle of the stage, on a small raised dais, one of the prisoners, when called, would stand to reply to various questions, having taken the oath. In front of him would be a microphone in order for all to hear his replies on being cross-examined.

I am unable to remember the names of all the twelve. Some of them were quite well-known to me, anyway, as also were the faces. Those I do remember and could easily recognise were: Field Marshal Goering, Generals Keitel and Kesselring, Admiral Doenitz, Rudolf Hess, von Ribbentrop (Ambassador to Great Britain immediately prior to the outbreak of hostilities) and Schacht, the armaments 'king'. There were also two men called Frick and Funck (why do Germans have these rather odd names?).

... At 1100 proceedings stopped for a break. The criminals all took hunks of black bread out of their pockets to munch, stood up to stretch their legs, etc. like the rest of us. Members of the press made mad dashes to the exits in order to telephone to their papers the latest news. This was by no means easy for them as there were so few telephones. Therefore it seemed to be 'first come, first served'.

After a short while the trial continued. Even in those days Hess appeared pretty vacant looking, his sunken eyes just staring into space. Von Ribbentrop's face looked grey, just about the same colour as his prison uniform. Of course, as was to be expected, the sole one showing any 'sparkle' at all was Goering. He played with his headphones, sometimes deigning to place just one ear to it (all the others keeping theirs tight on their heads). At times he would smile broadly, or do a sort of noiseless laugh, raising his eyes and eyebrows to heaven. Also, he would snap his fingers to draw his lawyer's attention for a little talk, in fact, absolutely 'steal the show'! Two days later he had committed suicide, poisoning himself by crushing a phial of cyanide in his mouth. I am told that this is a most terribly agonising manner in which to die. However, at least he had defied the court who otherwise would have hanged him, together with a lot of the others. No one discovered how he had acquired the poison, either through his lawyer or by bribing his guard, but at least he felt he had had the last laugh.[98]

DEMOBILISATION

By the very end of the Second World War, there were approximately 5 million men and women in the British armed forces. A mass demobilisation programme went into operation some six weeks after the end of hostilities in order to return the vast majority of personnel home, to enter normal civilian life once again.

The general demobilisation rule was that military personnel would be released in order, based on their age and length of service. Some soldiers who were deemed to be skilled in particular trades might be released sooner, in order to benefit the reconstruction process back home. Such exceptions, however, led to anger and frustration, with many servicemen and women complaining about the slow pace of the demob process.

For many former service personnel, their eventual return to civilian life might bring with it a multitude of new problems to face. A lot of homes and businesses had been destroyed due to enemy bombing, and this in turn caused unemployment and disruption. Reunited couples may not have seen each other for several years, and the post-war divorce rate was correspondingly high, with over 60,000 such applications in 1947. Rationing remained in place, and there were still food shortages and long queues.

At the end of October 1945, Eric Morgan was still awaiting demobilisation from the RAF, and the following letter clearly displays his frustration at the delays he was experiencing.

A demobbed soldier, preparing to return to civilian life, selects a tie to go with his demob shirt.

31.10.45

Dear Mum

Just a few lines once again hoping this finds you and all at home in the very best of health as it leaves me in good health, but very fed up because I am still at this blue pencil transit camp, but one good thing is that we are going on the boat in the morning so at least something is happening.

We put the trucks on the boat a few days ago so we have been expecting something soon, and it couldn't come quick enough for me as I will be right in to see the adjutant when I get over there as I['m] about fed up with this messing around when I could be getting this going, oh it does annoy me. I expect you are getting fed up back there as well waiting for results but it just can't be helped as the C.O. of this unit won't do anything for me and our own officer can't, or he says he can't but I don't think he tried very hard as he could have seen our C.O. for me when he went over and told me what I had to do, but he didn't even do that and I am getting fed up with the business as the chance seems to be gradually slipping through my fingers. But I suppose it isn't.

Well I'm afraid I don't know what to write about as nothing has been happening here since we took the trucks down, as the day's work consists of loafing around reading and going for your meals, and of course writing if you can think of anything to write about and I get fed up with writing. I put it off as long as I can, but I suppose if I don't write I don't receive so it goes both ways. My feelings are almost boiling over out here now, as I haven't done anything of any real importance now for two months when I could be back in England doing more useful work and I only hope I am soon back there as well, as it gets one so mad I can tell you.

Cheerio and all my love,

Eric xxxxxx[99]

31. 10. 45.

1603468. L.A.C MORGAN.
M.T. SECTION
18 SQUADRON. R.A.F. C.M.F.

Dear Mum,

Just a few lines once again hoping this finds you and all at home in the very best of health as it leave me in good health, but very fed up because I am still at this this blue pencil transit camp, but one good thing is that we are going on the boat in the morning so at last something is happening, We put the trucks on the boat a few days ago so we have been expecting something soon, and it couldnt come quick enough for me as I will be right in to see the adjutant when I get over there as I about fed up with this messing around when I could be getting this going, oh it does annoy me. I expect you are getting fed up back there as well waiting for results but it just cant be helped as the C.O. of this unit wont do anything for me and our own officer cant, or he says he cant but I dont think he tried very hard as he could have seen our C.O. for me when he went over and told me what I had to do, but he didn't even do that and I am getting fed up with the business as the chance seems to be gradually slipping through my fingers, but I suppose it isnt. Well I'm afraid I dont know what to write about as nothing has been happening here since we took the trucks down, as the days work consists of loafing around reading and going for your meals, and of course writing if you can think of anything to write about and I get fed up with writing, I put it off as long as I can, but I suppose if I dont write I dont recieve so it goes both ways. My felings are almost boiling over out here now as I havent done anything of any real importance now for 2 months when I could be back in England doing some usefull work, and I only

THE FUTURE

Despite Winston Churchill's reputation as the wartime prime minister who
took his country to victory, he lost the subsequent general election in Britain
in July 1945. Clement Attlee's Labour Party pledged to nationalise industries,
create a National Health Service and enact a nationwide programme to
build new homes. Labour's election victory suggested that the British people
believed that the war had been fought not only to defeat the Axis powers, but
also to usher in a fairer society.

The post-war world would also see the beginning of decolonisation, a process
given impetus by the economic exhaustion of the main colonial powers. On
the second anniversary of VJ Day, Jawaharlal Nehru was appointed as the first
prime minister of an independent India. Between the end of the war and 1960,
some forty nations – containing more than a quarter of the world's population
– revolted against colonialism and won their independence. Yet despite the
lofty ideals held by those who celebrated the end of the Second World War,
the way in which the world began to reshape itself in the following decades
perhaps owed more to politics and national interests than anything else.

Les Reasey was a liaison officer attached to a USAAF bomber group based
in Hampshire. This letter, written to an American pen-friend, reveals his
thoughts on the war and hopes for the future.

*Mrs Scott and her father clear rubble from the front garden of their bomb-damaged home
in preparation for the arrival home of her husband, on leave from Holland.*

Friday, December 28, 1945

Dear Shirley

It was nice of you Shirley to express your hopes for my return to civilian status but alas! I am still in uniform and expect still another nine months or so further service. My release group is still high even though I have completed almost five years service... It is a terribly large chunk out of one's life and the time is irretrievably lost. However, one has to take a longer view and trust that the sacrifices every nation and person has made will in some way mean a better deal for those who follow.

We have conquered a terrible threat to Liberty and Freedom, those things which we prize so highly in our two countries. Let us hope and pray that it will never again be necessary to devote so much time and energy to the destruction of such a beastly enemy. I have often said this... and I repeat it to you, the moral leadership of the world has now passed to your great country and the Statue of Liberty is more than a piece of architecture. The torch of leadership has passed from us to you in a very large measure and I hope with every possible hope that the light it gives will shine all through the years.

I am proud to belong to this little island with so rich a history and contribution to the welfare of human life. I am proud of the men we have given to the world even though there are many periods in our national life of the past which make me ashamed to realise. But more than my pride in being English, I am prouder to belong to the whole race of... men and women who devoted their lives to the betterment of man's lot. My faith in human nature came very near to being lost just recently and indeed the morality of the world is in a very poor state right now, but one has to think again in a wider sense and immediately one's heart is gladdened with hope and courage and faith in man's ability to rise above himself and think and do immortal words and deeds.

Shirley, what with Atom Bombs and the like it leaves me breathless. The world moves much too quickly for my mind to realise what is happening. Perhaps this is better this way. I can only cling desperately to my belief in human nature and the over-riding protection of something stronger and wiser which I believe to be God. Without this double-conception, I should cease to feel the worth of life...

As ever sincerely,

Les[100]

El Alamein military cemetery, North Africa.

SOURCES

All location codes below relate to the Imperial War Museums archive.

1. Private Papers of Mrs C. A. P. Leahy (Documents.7800)
2. Special Miscellaneous UU (Documents.4998)
3. German Miscellaneous 337 (Documents.26164)
4. Miscellaneous (Documents.25371)
5. Chamberlain's announcement of war, 3 September 1939 (Sound 4321)
6. Private Papers of J. Coullie (Documents.10896)
7. Private Papers of Mrs M. Noble (Documents.19707)
8. Miscellaneous 3532 (Documents.13627)
9. Letter from Henry Moore (Art.IWM ARCH/01/001/002)
10. Private Papers of Miss B. Myatt (Documents.5973)
11. Special Miscellaneous J3 (Documents.8813)
12. Private Papers of J. E. Atkinson (Documents.22584)
13. Private Papers of L. D. Mallows (Documents.3315)
14. Private Papers of Mr and Mrs R. Foley (Documents.16858)
15. Private Papers of Mrs U. M. Streatfeild (Documents.2929)
16. Private Papers of G. Clarke (Documents.19803)
17. Private Papers of Flying Officer K. C. Gundry (Documents.6505)
18. Private Papers of Sir Michael Stoker (Documents.17651)
19. Private Papers of Major G. B. Matthews (Documents.12584)
20. Private Papers of T. F. Beel (Documents.6079)
21. Private Papers of Miss E. Churchill (Documents.17479)
22. Miscellaneous 84 (Documents.9127)
23. Private Papers of A. J. Ward (Documents.14896)
24. Private Papers of Squadron Leader T. G. Pace (Documents.11775)
25. Private Papers of P. C. Proops (Documents.14446)
26. Private Papers of J. L. S. Dunlop (Documents.8596)
27. Private Papers of Commander D. E. Barton (Documents.1939)
28. Private Papers of Squadron Leader H. E. Bodien DFC (Documents.17660)
29. Private Papers of D. Withers (Documents.13040)
30. Private Papers of A. A. Holt (Documents.8597)
31. Private Papers of Lieutenant Commander M. R. Todd RN (Documents.25901)
32. Private Papers of Miss S. Stiles (Documents.401)
33. Private Papers of Mrs W. C. Bowman (Documents.3769)

34. Private Papers of Brigadier R. B. T. Daniell (Documents.5771)
35. Private Papers of M. P. Troy (Documents.3257)
36. Private Papers of H. F. Lucas (Documents.397)
37. Private Papers of Colonel W. F. Page (Documents.9414)
38. Private Papers of Major J. D. H. Hedley (Documents.12713)
39. Private Papers of K. B. H. Stevens (Documents.2046)
40. Private Papers of Captain R. B. Ware (Documents.18990)
41. Private Papers of G. W. Scott (Documents.1810)
42. Private Papers of Captain A. G. Faber (Documents.26348)
43. Private Papers of Major C. A. Morris (Documents.7392)
44. Private Papers of Miss C. Horwitz (Documents.9756)
45. Private Papers of A. French (Documents.7833)
46. Private Papers of F. Blaichman (Documents.11889)
47. German Miscellaneous 232 (Documents.13687)
48. German Miscellaneous 199 (Documents.13238)
49. Private Papers of A. N. Midgley (Documents.4052)
50. Private Papers of Major S. D. H. D. Wallis (Documents.780)
51. Private Papers of V. Caressa (Documents.26543)
52. Private Papers of Squadron Leader R. J. Bushell (Documents.21101)
53. Private Papers of Mrs L. Allan (Documents.23729)
54. Special Miscellaneous E8 (Documents.24715)
55. Private Papers of F. Luederitz (Documents.12382)
56. Private Papers of H. J. Chart (Documents.24731)
57. Private Papers of Colonel J. A. Fraser (Documents.8513)
58. Miscellaneous 3757 (Documents.16094)
59. LI-2015-999-204-2-5
60. Private Papers of Miss W. E. Musson (Documents.19540)
61. Miscellaneous 3778 (Documents.16262)
62. Miscellaneous 516 (Documents.1957)
63. Special Miscellaneous N (Documents.1971)
64. Private Papers of D. K. Raikes (Documents.11316)
65. Private Papers of C. H. Smith (Documents.1091)
66. Private Papers of Miss M. Tetlow (Documents.3824)
67. Private Papers of J. S. Gurney (Documents.15658/C)

68. Private Papers of Miss E. M. Bolster (Documents.661)
69. Private Papers of Miss S. M. Batstone (Documents.219)
70. Private Papers of Mrs L. Rickman (Documents.12782)
71. Private Papers of Mrs N. Ridgway (Documents.19636)
72. Private Papers of Miss C. Willmot (Documents.13414)
73. Miscellaneous 3006 (Documents.8070)
74. Private Papers of A. Jones (Documents.1634)
75. Private Papers of Major G. Ritchie MC (Documents.11549)
76. Private Papers of Captain C. T. Cross (Documents.771)
77. Private Papers of Captain H. F. Collinson (Documents.17931)
78. Private Papers of Lieutenant Commander R. C. G. Macnab RN (Documents.11150)
79. Private Papers of T. W. Green (Documents.15754)
80. Miscellaneous 1724 (Documents.10321)
81. Private Papers of R. S. Gardiner (Documents.15488)
82. Private Papers of S. Irwin (Documents.7894)
83. Private Papers of M. Bock (Documents.10800)
84. Private Papers of Flight Lieutenant G. W. Attenborough (Documents.22282)
85. Private Papers of Miss F. E. Tate (Documents.3096)
86. Private Papers of Dr A. R. Horwell (Documents.1164)
87. Private Papers of Father P. Siemes (Documents.3146)
88. Private Papers of Captain V. Ramsden (Documents.18811)
89. Private Papers of Captain D. V. E. Howard (Documents.13232)
90. Private Papers of S. R. Pearson (Documents.8116)
91. Miscellaneous 4049 (Documents.25559)
92. Private Papers of S. W. Smith (Documents.618)
93. Private Papers of Lieutenant J. B. Harris (Documents.3157)
94. Private Papers of Flight Lieutenant G. P. Dawson (Documents.16764)
95. Private Papers of Dr R. Thompson (Documents.13176)
96. Private Papers of M. S. Singer (Documents.24256)
97. Miscellaneous 2458 (Documents.1861)
98. Private Papers of Mrs J. Hodges (Documents.8249)
99. Miscellaneous (Documents.27066)
100. Private Papers of L. F. Reasey (Documents.18820)

IMAGE REFERENCES

2 © IWM (D 9054); 4 (bottom left) © IWM (A 761); 4 (bottom right) © IWM (NA 12925); 4 (top left) © IWM (A 13323); 4 (top right) © IWM (B 5425); 12 (bottom left) © IWM (HU 36258); 12 (bottom right) © IWM (HU 36498); 12 (top left) © IWM (HU 48566); 12 (top right) © IWM (51010); 13 © IWM (COL 118); 14 © The rights holder; 16 © IWM (NYP 68065); 17 © IWM (HU 4255); 18 © Crown copyright: IWM (Documents.4998); 19 © the rights holder; 20 © The rights holder; 22 © IWM (Art.IWM PST 5873); 24 © IWM; 25 © IWM (HU 100438); 26 © IWM (HU 5538); 27 © IWM (HU 51008); 29 © IWM (Documents.10896); 31 © IWM (D 2742); 32 © The rights holder; 35 © IWM (Documents.13627); 36 © The rights holder; 38 © The Rights holder; 39 © IWM (Art.IWM PST 0076); 41 © IWM (Documents.5973); 43 © The Estate of the Late Lesley Milne Limited; 44 (bottom left) © IWM (HU 25980); 44 (bottom right) © IWM (F 4799); 44 (middle right) © IWM (HU 54418); 44 (top left) © IWM (HU 41240); 44 (top right) © IWM (HU 130331); 45 © IWM (HU 49148); 47 © IWM (Docuements.22584); 48 © IWM (HU 1520); 49 © The rights holder; 51 © IWM (HU 25966); 52 © IWM (Documents.16858); 54 (bottom) © IWM (HU 36872); 54 (top) © IWM (Art.IWM PST 5183); 56 © IWM; 57 © IWM (HU 73433); 59 © The rights holder; 60 (inset) © IWM (C 2418); 60 (main) © IWM (CH 734); 62 © The rights holder; 63 © IWM (HU 130320); 64 © IWM (Documents.17651); 66 (left) © The rights holder; 66 (right) © IWM (HU 9211); 68 © IWM (Documents.12584); 69 © IWM (A 4154); 70 © IWM (Documents.6079); 71 © IWM (HU 52264); 72 © IWM (HU 76027); 74 © IWM (Documents.17479); 75 (bottom) © IWM (N 375); 75 (top left) © IWM (CL 1811); 75 (top right) © IWM (CH4188); 76 © IWM (A 1); 77 © IWM (Docuements.9127); 78 © IWM (HU 52427); 79 © IWM (HU 3325); 81 © The rights holder; 83 © The rights holder; 84 © IWM (HU 374); 85 © The rights holder; 86 © IWM (ZZZ 3130C); 88 © The rights holder; 89 © IWM IWM (HU 112174); 90 (left) © IWM (HU 47560); 90 (right) © IWM (GM 1480); 91 © The Estate of A Kirby; 93 © IWM (C 4582); 95 © The rights holder; 96 © IWM (A 21179); 98 © The rights holder; 99 © IWM (A 20689); 100 © IWM (TR 1284); 101 © IWM (CHP 794); 103 © The rights holder; 104 © IWM (D 20889); 105 © IWM (TR 498); 105 © The rights holder; 106 (bottom left) © IWM (D 20134); 106 (bottom right) © IWM (Art.IWM PST 13857); 106 (top) © IWM (NA 8533); 107 © the rights holder; 109 © KP Gardner; 110 © IWM (CM 749); 111 © The rights holder; 112 © IWM (HU 39517); 113 © IWM (E 4792); 114 © IWM (Documents.5771); 115 © IWM (E 6135); 116 © IWM (HU 56120); 117 © IWM (Documents.3257); 118 Courtesy USA Government; 119 © Estate of Zina Oliver; 121 © The rights holder; 122 © IWM (HU 2787); 123 © The rights holder; 124 © IWM (HU 2781); 125 © IWM (HU2773); 126 © IWM (JAR 1240); 127 © IWM (Documents12713); 128 © the rights holder; 129 © The rights holder; 131 © The rights holder; 133 © IWM (49970); 134 © The rights holder; 135 © IWM (MH 28353); 136 © the rights holder; 138 © IWM (Documents.26348); 140–141 © IWM (Documents.7392); 142 (bottom) © IWM (EA 61283); 142 (top) © IWM (MH 13348); 143 © IWM (HU 88871); 145 © The rights holder; 147 © IWM (Documents.7833); 148 © the rights holder; 149 © IWM (IA 37578); 150 © The rights holder; 151 © IWM (NYP 68049); 153 © IWM (Documents.13687); 154 © IWM (86524); 155 © The rights holder; 156 © IWM (BU 3810); 159 © The rights holder; 160 (bottom) © IWM (TR 1522); 160 (middle) © IWM (E 18513); 160 (top left) © IWM (HU 21018); 160 (top right) © IWM (E 3753 E); 161 © IWM (E 3743 E); 163 © The rights holder; 164 © IWM (HU 111383); 166 © the rights holder; 168 © The rights holder; 170 (left) © the rights holder; 170 (right) © IWM (HU 49540); 171 © The rights holder; 172 © IWM (E 16406); 173–174 Reproduced with permission of Curtis Brown, London on behalf of The Estate of Winston S. Churchill © The Estate of Winston S. Churchill; 175 © IWM (HU 5131); 176 © IWM (Documents.12382); 178 © IWM (HU 90999); 179 © IWM (A 17961); 180 © IWM (Documents.24731); 181 © IWM (NYF 9892); 182 © IWM (TR 1802); 184 © IWM (Documents.8513); 185 © IWM (1984); 186 © IWM (Documents.16094); 187 © IWM (IA 15552); 188 (bottom) © IWM (98927); 188 (top left) © IWM (HU 16541); 189 © IWM (Documents.LI-2015-999-204-2-5); 190 (bottom left) © IWM (D 4355); 190 (bottom right) © IWM (HU 36259); 190 (top left) © IWM (H 9553); 190 (top right) ©IWM (Art.IWM PST 16606); 191 © IWM (Art.IWM PST 13894); 192 © The rights holder; 193 © IWM (HU 49833); 194 © IWM (ZZZ 6908 C); 195 © the rights holder; 197 © IWM (D 1677); 198 © IWM (HU 105014); 199 © the rights holder; 200 © IWM (HU 26596); 201 © IWM (Documents.1971); 202 © IWM (HU 50154); 204 © The rights holder; 205 © IWM (62359); 207 © The estate of EM Barritt; 208 © IWM (FRE 6539); 209 © the rights holder; 210 (left) © IWM (Art.IWM PST 14928); 210 (right) © IWM (Art.IWM PST 4773); 211 © The rights holder; 212 (left) © IWM (D 7274); 212 (right) © IWM (CH 2155); 213 © the rights holder; 214 © IWM (Art.IWM PST 8286); 215 © IWM (Documents.219); 216 © IWM (D 25034); 217 © The rights holder; 218 © IWM (Art.IWM PST 17009); 219 © IWM (D 11399); 220 © IWM (Art.IWM PST 14569); 220 © IWM (Documents.19636); 221 © IWM (D 2597); 221 (bottom) © IWM (EA 25644); 222 © the rights holder; 224 © IWM (EA 25491); 223 (middle) © IWM (A 23916); 223 (top) © IWM (H 39065); 225 Courtesy USA Government; 226 © IWM (TR 207); 228 Crown Copyright; 231 © the rights holder; 233 © IWM (CL 59); 234 © IWM (B 5050); 235 © the rights holder; 236 © IWM (B 5114); 237 © IWM (Documents.17931); 238 © IWM (FLM 2571); 239 © IWM (EA 26316); 241 © the rights holder; 242 © IWM (MH 1409); 243 © the rights holder; 244 © IWM (B 5144); 245 © IWM (BU 1121); 246 © IWM (B 10133); 247 © The rights holder; 249 © IWM (EA 29655); 251 © IWM (Documents.15488); 252 © IWM (B 5267); 254 © The estate of Stewart Irwin; 255 © IWM (HU 68178); 256 © The rights holder; 258 (bottom) © IWM (A 30548); 258 (top) © IWM (HU 140146); 259 © IWM (BU 5207); 261 © The rights holder; 262 © IWM (HU 36292); 264 © The estate of Francis Gaythorpe; 265 © IWM (BU 3794); 267 © The rights holder; 268 © IWM (MH 29427); 269 © the rights holder; 271 © IWM (MH 29447); 272 © IWM (Q HS 834 B); 273 © IWM (Documents.18811); 274 US Public Domain; 275 © IWM (EA 75893); 276 © The rights holder; 277 © IWM (A 19978); 277 © IWM (A 23720 A); 279 © IWM (Documents.8116); 280 © IWM (EA 75901); 281 © The rights holder; 282 © IWM (EA 75898); 283 © Estate of Zina Oliver; 285 © IWM (Documents.618); 286 © IWM (A 30522); 287 © The rights holder; 288 © IWM (CF 711); 289 (bottom) © IWM (BU 3822); 289 (top left) © IWM (BU 8054); 289 (top right) © IWM (HU 56732); 290 © IWM (FRE 12749); 291 © Andrew Burell; 292 © IWM (HU 81268); 293 © IWM (DEU 503403); 295 © The rights holder; 296 © IWM (BU 8635); 297 © IWM (Documents.24256); 299 © IWM (CL 3092); 301 Crown Copyright; 302 © IWM (HU 56713); 303 © IWM MH 24088); 304 © IWM (HU 87403); 305 © Mrs E Hodges; 307 © IWM (TR 1582); 309 © IWM (Documents.27066); 310 © IWM (D 24217); 311 © The rights holder; 312 © IWM (E 30352); Background textures; 1, 2, 3, 5, 14, 15, 16, 18, 37, 38, 40, 41, 42, 43, 46, 47, 137, 138, 228, 229, 230, 231, 232 (Annie Spratt on Unsplash); 3 (Nile from Pixabay); 21, 73, 74, 97, 98, 99, 139, 140, 141, 144, 145 (Annie Spratt on Unsplash); ; 23, 24, 85, 86, 101, 102, 103, 108, 109, 155, 157, 158, 159, 165, 166, 189, 208, 209, 250, 251, 281, 282 (mohamed Hassan from Pixabay); 26, 61, 62, 64, 65, 70, 71, 77, 78, 79, 80, 81, 105, 111, 112, 114, 115, 117, 118, 123, 124, 127, 130, 131, 132, 134, 135, 146, 147, 148, 150, 151, 168, 169, 183, 184, 186, 187, 195, 196, 201, 203, 204, 211, 212, 213, 214, 215, 217, 218, 220, 222, 235, 240, 241, 243, 244, 247, 248, 253, 254, 256, 257, 260, 261, 263, 264, 269, 270, 273, 274, 287, 288, 291, 292, 305, 306, 308, 309, 311, 312 (Free Creative Stuff from Pixabay); 28, 29, 30, 34, 35, 67, 68, 237, 238 (MrsMary from Pixabay); 32, 33, 58, 59, 91, 92, 94, 95, 128, 129, 152, 153, 171, 173, 174, 176, 177, 178, 180, 181, 192, 193, 266, 267 (louanapires from Pixabay); 49, 50, 278, 279, 284, 285, 297, 298 (Dan-Cristian Pădureț on Unsplash); 52, 53, 225, 226, 300, 301, 302 (ulotkidruk from Pixabay); 55, 56, 87, 88, 89, 120, 121, 162, 163, 206, 207, 275, 276, 293, 294, 295 (Free Creative Stuff from Pixabay); 82, 83, 198, 199 (Olga Thelavart on Unsplash)

Images have been artificially tinted from the original black and white.

ACKNOWLEDGEMENTS

For a book based upon the personal testimony of so many individuals, it is only right to thank them and their descendants for allowing us to publish their words. Few, if any, would ever have thought that their letter, diary entry or scribbled note might end up in published form, let alone preserved by a national museum! Heartfelt thanks are therefore due to those individuals who were so considerate as to share their experiences and memories in this way.

Books of this nature are very much a team effort, and thanks are therefore due to the personnel at Headline (Iain MacGregor, Tara O'Sullivan and Keith Williams) and IWM (David Fenton, Madeleine James and David Tibbs) for coordinating such a complicated project. In addition, I should like to offer my personal appreciation to Stephen Walton (for his historical advice and translation skills) and Lyn O'Kelly (for providing access to hundreds of original documents in the middle of a pandemic).

INDEX

Page numbers in **bold** refer to illustrations.

First published in 2021 by
HEADLINE PUBLISHING GROUP

1

Cataloguing in Publication Data is available from the British Library

Hardback ISBN: 9781472288110
eBook ISBN: 9781472288127
Audio ISBN: 9781472288141

Publisher: Iain MacGregor
Editorial and Project Management: Tara O'Sullivan
Design: Keith Williams, sprout.uk.com

Image credits listed on page 314

Printed and bound in Italy by L.E.G.O. SpA

MIX
Paper from
responsible sources
FSC® C104740
www.fsc.org

Headline's policy is to use papers that are natural, renewable and recyclable products and made from wood grown in well-managed forests and other controlled sources. The logging and manufacturing processes are expected to conform to the environmental regulations of the country of origin.

HEADLINE PUBLISHING GROUP
An Hachette UK Company
Carmelite House
50 Victoria Embankment
London EC4Y 0DZ

www.headline.co.uk
www.hachette.co.uk